THE NEW ESSENTIAL STEINER

THE NEW ESSENTIAL STEINER

An Introduction to Rudolf Steiner for the 21st Century

EDITED AND INTRODUCED WITH NOTES BY
Robert McDermott

Lindisfarne Books
2009

Lindisfarne Books
AN IMPRINT OF ANTHROPOSOPHIC PRESS, INC.
PO Box 749
Great Barrington, MA 01230
www.steinerbooks.org

Copyright © by Robert A. McDermott, 2009
All rights reserved. No part of this book may be reproduced in any form without the written permission of the publishers, except for brief quotations embodied in critical articles and reviews.

BOOK & COVER DESIGN: WILLIAM JENS JENSEN

LIBRARY OF CONGRESS CATALOGING-IN-PUBLICATION DATA

Steiner, Rudolf, 1861–1925.
[Selections. 2009]
The new essential Steiner : an introduction to Rudolf Steiner for the 21st century / edited and introduced with notes by Robert McDermott.
  p. cm.
Includes bibliographical references and index.
ISBN–13: 978-1-58420-056-7
ISBN–10: 1-58420-056-1
 1. Anthroposophy. 2. Steiner, Rudolf, 1861–1925.
I. McDermott, Robert A. II. Title.
BP595.S85112 2009
299'.935—dc22

2009022070

Contents

	Preface	vii
	Introduction:	
	Rudolf Steiner and Anthroposophy	1
	Significant Events in the Life of Rudolf Steiner	73
	Autobiographical Notes: "The Barr Document"	80
	"Introducing Rudolf Steiner," by Owen Barfield	91
	Works of Rudolf Steiner:	
1.	Philosophy: Self and World	96
2.	Evolution: Cosmic and Human	100
3.	Anthropos: Body, Soul, and Spirit	112
4.	Spiritual Intelligence	134
5.	Christ and Other Exalted Beings	159
6.	Reincarnation, Karma, and the Dead	179
7.	Arts	200
8.	Society	213
9.	Education	230
10.	Psychology	254
11.	Health and Healing	271
12.	Gaia and the Future	290
	A Guide to Further Reading	307
	Index	314

Preface

Initial encounters with Rudolf Steiner and Anthroposophy often lead discoverers to exclaim, "Why haven't I encountered this until now?" As I recounted in the preface to the first edition of *The Essential Steiner*,[1] "It was not until 1975, after I had taught comparative philosophy and religion for eleven years, had read widely and traveled around the world twice, that I came across the name Rudolf Steiner for the first time." The first sentence of the introduction to that same volume asked a question that was very difficult to answer: "If, as his followers insist, Rudolf Steiner is a genius in twelve fields, why do we so seldom come across his name in colleges, in scholarly writings, and in the popular press?" Relative to his genius, generosity, and ability to explain and solve some of the deepest problems of our culture, it has been difficult to understand why Steiner's influence has not been more evident during the more than eighty years since his death. Although Steiner's contributions are now far more widely acknowledged than when *The Essential Steiner* was published twenty-five years ago, the reasons for his limited influence invite continuing review.

Some who encounter Steiner's work for the first time question whether someone who displays virtual omniscience, offering so much new and at times seemingly implausible information on topics both central and obscure, should be engaged at all. In his essay on Steiner (in the introductory section of this volume), the distinguished literary and cultural critic Owen Barfield asks, "Why should anyone accept that one man was capable of all those revelations?" This volume attempts to answer that question by presenting and explaining the content of his esoteric research,

---

1. San Francisco: HarperSanFrancisco, 1984

with its profoundly positive applications, and by stating the case for the esoteric method that Steiner practiced and recommended to others.

Another reason for Steiner's limited influence seems to rest with those of his followers who regard all of Steiner's pronouncements, both exoteric and esoteric, with fundamentalist certitude. Further, contrary to his attitude and example, Steiner's followers typically expound his ideas in separation from, and over against, other great thinkers and movements. During his lifetime Steiner had many thousands of followers, as well as many thousands more whom he influenced indirectly by his writings, lectures, and practical recommendations, but he had no esoteric equals who challenged his ideas, their expression, or implementation. By contrast, both Thomas Merton, until his untimely death, and, more recently, the Dalai Lama have engaged scientists, artists, and other spiritual teachers who represent worldviews very different from their own.

Despite obstacles to the spread of Steiner's ideas and their influence, there is increasing evidence that they have become more familiar and have received more credit than they did a generation ago. It is no longer unusual to observe academics and spiritual seekers acknowledging that Steiner's innovations such as Waldorf education, biodynamic agriculture, anthroposophically extended medicine, and anthroposophic arts represent significant contributions to contemporary thought and culture.

Through his hundreds of volumes and his innumerable activities, Steiner might have blinded us to his significance, but he was surely right in his conviction that the darkness of the time requires that many lights be lit, many doors opened, many exhibitions mounted, and, especially in a culture of mendacity, many true words be spoken. Although Anthroposophy is rooted in meditative practice, it is also devoted to the word—both in its original singular meaning, *Logos*, Word, and in its plural meaning, the countless words employed, artfully to the extent possible, in service of spiritual ideas, ideals, and realities.

This volume on Steiner's work is similar to *The Essential Steiner,* in that it includes a representative range of Steiner's writings and lectures, accompanied by my introductory essay and guide to further reading. The differences between these two volumes are also worth noting. At seventy pages, the introduction is far more extensive, and the selections by Steiner cover twelve areas instead of five. All of the pages by Steiner have been newly translated and revised since 1990 and, consequently, all use gender-inclusive language and a contemporary style of expression. The eighty-five-page annotated guide to further reading in *The Essential Steiner* was important at the time but has been omitted in this volume, since descriptions of hundreds of volumes by and about Steiner and Anthroposophy are readily available on the SteinerBooks website (www.steinerbooks.org).

I am delighted that readers of *The Essential Steiner* have found my pages readable and helpful to their attempts to understand Steiner's ideas, but it would be contrary to my intent if the reader would allow the American style of my introductory essay to substitute for the relatively more challenging and rewarding work of engaging Steiner's thinking processes and mode of expression directly.

Steiner's teaching is a *dharma* (a detailed worldview and a specific set of spiritual practices) that requires the development of *upaya* (skillful means). Steiner's works and his recommendations run a wide range, from immediately accessible to complex and difficult to understand, remember, and implement in one's thinking and action. Despite the challenge of his teachings for those of us with only the slightest capacity for reliable imagination, the study and practice of his teachings constitute a truthful and efficacious path for spiritual transformation. To engage Steiner's worldview and practices requires one to eschew dogmatism and contention and, as with all genuine and efficacious spiritual work, to embrace humility and reverence.

Robert McDermott
San Francisco
November 2009

Rudolf Steiner, 1923

Introduction

Rudolf Steiner and Anthroposophy

1. Rudolf Steiner's Life and Mission

RUDOLF STEINER (1861–1925), a highly original and increasingly influential spiritual and esoteric teacher, is the founder, teacher, and exemplar of Anthroposophy. *Esoteric* refers to a worldview and to specific ideas that are very difficult to know without a special capacity such as clairvoyance or intuition. Anthroposophy combines *anthropos*, the ideal of the human being, and *Sophia,* divine feminine wisdom. The word *Anthroposophy* refers to spiritual knowledge gained by the conscious integration of three disciplines: thinking, feeling, and willing. Anthroposophy includes esoteric research and spiritual practice. Through extraordinary capacity and diligent effort, Steiner made significant theoretical and practical contributions to philosophy, sciences, social sciences, arts, education, and religion. He also wrote and lectured extensively on various esoteric subjects such as the early evolution of the Earth and humanity, karma and rebirth, and the collaborative interrelationships among Krishna, Buddha, and Christ, as well as the relationships between Christ and Sophia and Christ and the Archangel Michael. In addition to writing approximately forty books, beginning in 1891 with *Truth and Knowledge,* his philosophy doctoral dissertation, and ending in 1924, the year before his death, Steiner delivered more than six thousand lectures, most of which have been published in more than three hundred volumes. He is perhaps best known for the Waldorf school movement, which today consists of several thousand schools in more than one hundred countries. Waldorf teachers continue to draw guidance from Steiner's hundreds of lectures on child development, curriculum, and pedagogy.

We can treat Steiner's teaching under two headings: first, its content, the results of his esoteric research; and second, its practice, the path by which others can attempt to develop a capability comparable to Steiner's. As a path, or spiritual discipline, Anthroposophy includes a detailed method for schooling one's consciousness, leading to the attainment of spiritual knowledge and the gradual transformation of the individual practitioner.

Steiner's practical contributions—which include the Waldorf school movement, biodynamic farming, new art forms, the sciences, anthroposophically extended medicine, and social concepts—are the fruits of a clairvoyant capability that was both innate and further developed. Through his foundational books, *The Philosophy of Freedom* (1894), *How to Know Higher Worlds* (1904), *Theosophy* (1904), and *An Outline of Esoteric Science* (1909),[1] Steiner offers a spiritual worldview and a discipline through which others can develop higher capacities. All of these works serve the same essential task of Steiner's Anthroposophy, or spiritual science: an attempt to gain a loving and creative knowledge of the spiritual in the individual and the spiritual in the universe, and the relation between them.

Anthroposophists are understandably in awe of the fruits of Steiner's spiritual-scientific research and thus tend to emphasize the study of his writings and practical recommendations at the expense of cultivating their own spiritual cognition. Even in his own day, this mistaken emphasis caused Steiner considerable frustration and sadness, and it almost certainly has limited the effectiveness of Anthroposophy as a spiritual esoteric teaching and movement. He intended his research concerning spiritual realities to exemplify his method and to show the need for solutions on a higher level of insight than the level on which arguments ordinarily swirl.

---

1. See "A Guide to Further Reading" for bibliographic details on these works.

Rudolf Steiner's teachings are continuous with Rosicrucianism, Theosophy, and esoteric Christianity. He referred to his particular esoteric teaching as Rosicrucian to emphasize its close relationship to the tradition of deep esoteric knowledge of the human being and higher beings cultivated first in Egypt, then Greece, and then entwined somewhat with Christianity. *Esoteric Christianity* refers to the profound spiritual teachings and texts such as the Gospel of John or the writings of Dionysius the Areopagite that are difficult for most people to understand but have indirectly exercised a significant influence on the more accessible, exoteric teachings of Christianity. In the same way, and for the same reasons, that esoteric and mystical dimensions of Christianity tend to be held at a distance by the institutional church and advocates of its dogmatic teachings, Steiner's life work seems to have had very little influence on Christian traditions, whether Roman Catholic or Protestant. Steiner delineated a comprehensive and detailed account of the evolution of consciousness, both cosmological and human, as a background to his plea for the transformation of thinking, feeling, and willing and for the role of the Christ and other spiritual beings.

While they are continuous with past esoteric teachings, Steiner's research and method are characterized by a modern Western sensibility, in that they strive for scientific validity and verification by others. Hence, another name for anthroposophic research is *spiritual science.* Steiner confronts the fact that in recent centuries human beings, particularly in the modern West, find it increasingly difficult to know the spiritual world. One of his tasks was to show how modern Western humanity generally lost the direct knowledge of the spiritual world that had been possible, and typical, in earlier times—for example, that of shamanic guides of indigenous peoples worldwide, the pharaohs of Egypt, the prophets of Israel, and the teachers in the mystery centers in ancient Greece. Anthroposophy is a method for reforging such connections, though in a way that is appropriate for contemporary consciousness. Steiner offers a method through which each individual spiritual seeker can develop a warm and will-filled means to overcome the alienation that he shows to be characteristic of modern Western consciousness. Steiner considered the purpose of the evolution of human consciousness, for which he regarded the incarnation of the Christ as the central event, to be the attainment of human love and freedom.

Not only was Rudolf Steiner endowed with a capacity for imagination, inspiration, and intuition, he also carefully explained how such modes of knowing could be cultivated. He emphasized that the cultivation of these capacities by a Western individual is difficult because modern Western culture firmly rejects the very possibility of spiritual and esoteric knowledge. He tried to show that ordinary ways of knowing and knowledge by faith cannot lift Western humanity out of its present impasse. Rather, it requires a form of knowing that is individual and objective, spiritual and reliable.

Steiner's spiritual and esoteric teachings are positive about the evolution of the cosmos and of the natural world and optimistic about the future of humanity—though not without a great struggle. Steiner was profoundly aware of evil and, in various ways, suffered its effects, but he was nevertheless positive in his attitude toward people, challenges, and initiatives. He died at age sixty-five, probably as a result of desperate esoteric struggles with negative forces and unceasing labors in service of his spiritual mission. Steiner's life serves as a model of a spiritual-esoteric researcher, servant, and teacher.

Rudolf Steiner was born on February 27, 1861, in Kraljevec, Croatia, within the Austrian Empire. His parents, Johann Steiner (1829–1910), an employee of the Southern Austrian Railroad, and Franziska Blie Steiner (1834–1918), were both born in southern Hungary. Steiner spent his early childhood, from the age of two to age seven, in the Austrian countryside; his grade school years were spent in a rural town south of Vienna. He attended a scientific high school and then graduated from a polytechnic college in Vienna. As a college student, Steiner was employed as a tutor to a family of boys, the youngest being Otto Specht, who had Down syndrome. The boy's family had given up the idea that he would live a normal life. After two years of patient work, however, Steiner educated the boy to the level of those of his age and equipped him for productive life. Otto eventually became a physician and, later, lost his life in World War I.

At age twenty-two, through his professor Karl Julius Schroer, Steiner became the editor of Goethe's natural scientific writings. At age twenty-five, he wrote *Goethe's Theory of Knowledge: An Outline of the Epistemology of His Worldview*. In 1891, at the age of thirty, he received his doctorate in philosophy from the University of Rostock, and a year later, he published his dissertation under the title *Truth and Knowledge*. In 1894, he published his primary work in philosophy, *The Philosophy of Freedom* (published as *Intuitive Thinking as a Spiritual Path*), followed immediately by *Friedrich Nietzsche: A Fighter against His Time* and *Goethe's Worldview*.

If karma, or destiny, is to be taken at all seriously, clearly Steiner was born to be an initiate; that is, he was sent by the spiritual world to undertake an important work for humanity. Steiner was seven years of age when, in the railroad station where his father was stationmaster, his aunt who had committed suicide, and whom he had never met, appeared in ghostly form to the boy and sought his help. The woman must have seen some special capacity in this boy as she viewed the human world she had left behind.

When his elementary school teacher gave him a geometry book, Steiner found that the pure geometric forms were rather like the world of spiritual forms with which he was already familiar. This discovery of geometry was one of the great experiences in his early life, for it provided reassurance that knowledge of the spirit world could be shared and communicated.

At age fourteen, Steiner realized that he had to study Kant[2] and confront the limits to knowledge that Kant had established in his extremely influential work, *The Critique of Pure Reason* (1781). Subsequently, Steiner was also led to the early nineteenth-century idealist philosophies of Fichte, Schelling, and Hegel. He used Fichte's concept of the "I" as a basis for his doctoral dissertation. From his earliest philosophical writings, however, it was clear that Steiner would not rest exclusively in subjective idealist

---

2. In their early years, Martin Buber, C. G. Jung, and Hannah Arendt all began their study of Kant on their own.

philosophy, but would add to it the more objective natural philosophy of Goethe, as well as his own esoteric empiricism, his careful observation of the inner life of the natural world. This synthesis typifies Steiner's intellectual and spiritual work: he habitually sympathized with diverse and competing positions in such a way as to save and reconcile the positive contributions of each. We should also acknowledge, however, that throughout Steiner's life, he was severe in his opposition to Kant's *Critique* and the influence of the Kantian worldview. By his thought and action, Rudolf Steiner repeatedly brought together perspectives ordinarily kept separate. Together, his life and his thought can be seen as an attempt to embody the reconciliation of polarities: science and art, matter and spirit, individualism and community, and many other dichotomies that can be brought into a higher and truer synthesis.

In a brief autobiographical sketch (included in this volume) called "The Barr Document," written in 1906,[3] Steiner acknowledged meeting his master, but does not identify him:

> I did not at once meet the M. [master], but first someone sent by him who was completely initiated into the mysteries of the effects of all plants and their connection with the universe and with human nature. For him, converse with the spirits of nature was a matter of course, which he described without enthusiasm, thereby awakening enthusiasm all the more.

This intermediary was an herb gatherer named Felix Koguzski. He gave Steiner his first opportunity to share with another human being the reality of the spiritual world manifested in nature, which had been an integral part of Steiner's experience from his earliest years. After meeting the herb gatherer, Steiner's spiritual master, or initiator, reportedly gave him several tasks, including the seemingly impossible task of reversing the plunge of Western thought and culture into atheistic materialism, as well as the more specific task of restoring to the West an understanding of the dual concept of karma and rebirth.

---

3. Steiner wrote this document in Alsace, France, while visiting his friend, Edouard Schuré, author of *The Great Initiates* (Blauvelt, NY: Garber, 1976).

Prior to 1899, Steiner's intellectual and academic work was brilliant, but not yet publicly esoteric. He was not yet known for his ability to tell the secrets of the natural or spiritual world. It was not until age thirty-nine that he publicly manifested clairvoyant capacities, the ability to "see clearly."[4] At that time, as he later reported in his autobiography, Steiner entered a deep spiritual struggle, after which he experienced the mystery of Christ in the evolution of Earth and humanity. As a result of this life-transforming experience, his spiritual-scientific research and teachings were bathed in the light of Christ guiding the cosmos, the Earth, and human destiny.

Despite the increasingly significant role that he ascribed to Christ, Steiner continued to lecture to large audiences of theosophists, most of whom, it seems, focused more on Krishna and Buddha than on Christ.[5] From 1902 to 1909, he served as general secretary of the German branch of the Theosophical Society. In 1909, during the Theosophical Congress in Budapest, Steiner recognized that he would need to separate from the Theosophical Society, primarily because Annie Besant, its president, was not amenable to Steiner's increasingly Western perspective and emphasis on the importance of Christ. Besant also opposed Steiner's introduction of the arts into the annual meetings of the Theosophical Society. The break came in 1911, when C. W. Leadbeater and Annie Besant announced that sixteen-year-old J. Krishnamurti was the vehicle of a coming world teacher. Leadbeater believed that his student was the Master Jesus. Whether Besant held the same conviction or not, she agreed with Leadbeater and created the Order of the Star as a vehicle for Krishnamurti, who renounced this claim at age twenty-one.

---

4. When Jesus refers to those "with eyes to see" he is similarly referring to sight of the inner realities, of the mysteries of the spiritual life.
5. In the quarter century after Col. Olcott and H. P. Blavatsky founded the Theosophical Society in New York City, it developed branches and wide influence in Europe and India, where it established its international headquarters. Unfortunately for the possibility of Steiner's continuing collaboration with the Theosophical Society, H. P. Blavatsky, obviously a great clairvoyant teacher and author, died in 1891.

From 1904 until 1909, Steiner wrote three of his foundational books: *How to Know Higher Worlds* (1904), *Theosophy* (1904), and *An Outline of Esoteric Science* (1909). He also lectured on a wide variety of themes in the history of Western esotericism. Beginning in 1909, he delivered many lectures on events in the Christian Gospels, as well as on the interrelationships among Krishna, Buddha, and Christ.

In 1912 in Berlin, Steiner's followers, principally those who had worked with him in the Theosophical branches and had heard hundreds of his lectures throughout Europe, formed the Anthroposophical Society. Steiner neither founded nor joined the society that his followers formed at that time, but ten years later, during Christmas week of 1923, Steiner reestablished the General Anthroposophical Society and became its leader. In 1913, Steiner laid the foundation stone for the Goetheanum,[6] an enormous wooden structure that he designed, to be built on an imposing hill near Basel, in Dornach, Switzerland. Since then, the Goetheanum has served as the public and esoteric center for the worldwide work of the Anthroposophical Society.

Steiner chose the name *Goetheanum* to honor Goethe's aesthetics. Steiner's architecture, including the double-cupola structure, with various spiritually enlightened forms, was unprecedented and influential. The building was made of various types of wood from all over Europe and North America and was under construction from 1913 to 1922. During World War I, workers from seventeen nations, including Austria, Germany, France, and England, lived and worked together on a hill in Switzerland, within hearing of the guns and battles raging around them. Soon after the Goetheanum was completed, an arsonist burned it to the ground on New Year's Eve 1922.

In 1899, Steiner married Anna Eunike, the widowed mother of five children for whom Steiner had been a resident tutor. Steiner had his own section of Frau Eunike's house for his work and for meetings with colleagues. When asked about that relationship, clearly a marriage of convenience lasting approximately three years, he dismissed the inquiry, stating simply, "Private relations

---

6. Named in honor of Johann Wolfgang von Goethe.

are not something to be publicized." Anna Eunike died in 1911. In 1914, at the outbreak of World War I, Steiner married Marie von Sievers soon after she crossed the border from Germany into Switzerland. Throughout the previous decade, von Sievers had been his assistant in the German branch of the Theosophical Society. While we remain uninformed about their marriage, it is clear that Marie Steiner shared every detail of Steiner's work on behalf of Anthroposophy. She was particularly helpful to Steiner's many contributions to the spiritual and esoteric renewal of the arts.[7]

Steiner believed that his relationship with Dr. Ita Wegman, his personal physician, extended through previous lifetimes. For more than two decades they collaborated on medical research, some of the results of which are published in their book *Extending Practical Medicine: Fundamental Principles Based on the Science of the Spirit*.

With the exception of his teaching on karma and rebirth and his founding the General Anthroposophical Society in 1923, Rudolf Steiner's entire lifework was in response to people's requests for help. In 1924, he delivered a series of nineteen lectures to followers who had joined the School of Spiritual Science (an esoteric membership at the core of the Anthroposophical Society dedicated to spiritual-scientific research). Except for these lectures and those he delivered to priests of The Christian Community (see section 5 of this introduction), Steiner gave all of his innovative ideas and methodologies openly, and in a way intended to be shared by anyone interested in them.

Just a few months before his death, in a series of letters written to members of the Anthroposophical Society and published as *Anthroposophic Leading Thoughts*, Steiner wrote the following characterization of Anthroposophy:

> Anthroposophy is a path of [spiritual] knowledge, to guide the spiritual in the human being to the spiritual in the universe. It arises in the human being as a need of the heart, of the life of

---

7. Unfortunately, she was also influential after Steiner's death, when she played a major role in expelling the British and Dutch societies from the General Anthroposophical Society, as well as Ita Wegman, Steiner's personal physician and close colleague.

feeling, and it can be justified only inasmuch as it can satisfy this inner need. Only those who find in it what they themselves feel impelled in their inner lives to seek can acknowledge Anthroposophy. Only those who feel certain questions on the nature of the human being and the universe as an elemental need of life, just as one feels hunger and thirst, can be anthroposophists.

Anthroposophy communicates knowledge that is gained in a spiritual way. Yet it only does so because everyday life, and the science founded on sensation and intellectual activity, lead to a barrier along life's way—a limit where the life of the soul in the human being would die if it could go no further. Everyday life and science do not lead to this limit in such a way as to compel the human being to stop short at it. For at the very frontier where the knowledge derived from sensory perception ceases, the further outlook into the spiritual world is opened through the human soul itself.[8]

As this frequently quoted description indicates, Anthroposophy refers to human wisdom, or a way of knowing the essentially human, in contrast to knowledge gained by faith or by other traditional ways of understanding divine revelation. It was Steiner's aim to enable human beings to develop their spiritual faculties and, thereby, develop knowledge of the spiritual reality of the cosmos without the help of a religious tradition, though he was careful to emphasize that Anthroposophy is, in principle, compatible with all religious traditions. According to Steiner, this achievement is possible by a kind of thinking that he describes synonymously as active, loving, spiritual, and free. He tries to show that this new mode of spiritual thinking is at the core of great advances in science, art, and religion. He intends his ideal of spiritually active thinking as a work of the heart, of the affective, and artistic. He develops his concept and method of spiritual "living" thinking as a contrast to religious revelation, ordinary intellectuality, and passive, sensory-based awareness.

Perhaps Steiner's most significant contribution to contemporary humanity is the method he developed for acquiring spiritually

---

8. *Anthroposophical Leading Thoughts: Anthroposophy as a Path of Knowledge: The Michael Mystery* (London: Rudolf Steiner Press, 1998), p. 13.

clear knowledge. Through his contributions to thought and culture and the methods he bequeathed for others to test and advance his insights, Rudolf Steiner remains one of the most important exemplars of the transformative and practical effects of esoteric knowledge. Although there would seem to be many clairvoyants throughout the world, Steiner is distinctive, and perhaps unique, in the degree to which he understood his clairvoyance, disciplined it, applied it to numerous fields of knowledge and culture, and, most important, published instructions for those born with ordinary consciousness to develop a modicum of spiritual intuition.

The following introductory summary of these initiatives corresponds to the twelve chapters of selections from Steiner's writings and lectures reprinted in this volume.

II. RUDOLF STEINER'S WORKS

1. Philosophy: Self and World

The essential principles of Steiner's spiritual science, or Anthroposophy, are based primarily on three works that treat esoteric epistemology and methodology: *Intuitive Thinking as a Spiritual Path: A Philosophy of Freedom* (1894), *How to Know Higher Worlds* (1904), and *An Outline of Esoteric Science* (1909). Each work reveals, in different ways, Steiner's case for the possibility of, and approach to, spiritual and esoteric[9] knowledge. This section on philosophy discusses *Intuitive Thinking as a Spiritual Path*. Section 2, "Cosmic and Human Evolution," discusses *An Outline of Esoteric Science*. Section 4, "Meditation and Spiritual Cognition," discusses *How to Know Higher Worlds*.

To understand Steiner's teaching on free (or spiritual) thinking and the acquisition of spiritual knowledge, one must first bear in mind the power of the dominant secular worldview and the difficulty of overcoming its pervasive influence. Steiner's claim that it is possible for non-clairvoyant individuals to acquire some degree of esoteric insight is rather radical; everything in modern

---

9. *Spiritual* and *esoteric* clearly overlap, but spiritual does not necessarily suggest knowledge, whereas esoteric definitely does.

and postmodern (twentieth- and twenty-first-century thinking) militates against this possibility.

In 1894, having just defended his dissertation in philosophy (*Truth and Knowledge*), Steiner set out in his *Philosophy of Freedom* to demonstrate that thinking does not arise in, nor is it limited to, the brain. Rather, following Fichte and Hegel, Steiner wants to show that thinking precedes all thoughts, and precedes as well the evolution of human life and all human thought. Thinking is not only taking place all the time, but also has been active since before the evolution of Earth. Steiner is a thorough evolutionist. Earth, plants, animals, humans, and even spiritual beings such as angels and gods have all been evolving and will continue to do so. Moreover, in a reversal of Darwinism, Steiner argues that human evolution follows from thinking. He seldom mentions God (and never gives an argument for God's existence, as most Christian philosophers do), but his idea of thinking is rooted in something like a divine (or at least trans-human and trans-earthly) ground of being. Anyone who finds such a thought implausible might want to try to answer the fundamental question: Where does it all (cosmic, earthly, and human evolution) come from—and how? If thinking arises from the natural world, where does the natural world come from? Steiner argues that we can answer this question decisively through our individual experience by attending to our thinking. When we do this, we notice that thinking is already present, pointing to itself, uncaused; it is the only "given."

In *Intuitive Thinking as a Spiritual Path*, Steiner establishes the theoretical and experiential possibility of accessing spiritual ideas, those reached by sensory-free thinking. Many Christian thinkers, from Augustine in the fifth century to Descartes in the seventeenth century, have argued that ideas could be intuited clearly and distinctly. Then, in the eighteenth century, John Locke argued that no ideas come to the mind except through the senses, and, essentially, he established what has been the dominant theory of knowledge in the West to the present day. In his *Intuitive Thinking as a Spiritual Path*, Steiner argues against Locke's idea that all knowledge derives exclusively from sensory experience. He also argues against Kant's *Critique of Pure Reason,* which places knowledge of God, the immortal soul, and freedom of the will, all ideas not available to sensory experience, beyond the reach of human reason. Steiner argues that by concentrated effort the human mind can think independently of sense experience.

Because the book is not particularly rewarding to the typical intellectual method of reading, it is not unusual for readers to find it frustrating or disappointing. By this book, Steiner tried to show the causes of alienated thinking and the possibility of thinking in a new, more creative, more integrating way. The problem for most readers of *Intuitive Thinking as a Spiritual Path* is that they are limited by the very obstacle that Steiner is trying to expose and overcome, namely, conventional (non-intuitive) thinking. The book begs the reader to attempt a different way, or different level, of thinking. It is intended to be its own verification. Unfortunately, for some readers it proves the reverse: ordinary intellectual reading produces ordinary intellectual knowledge, if any, and provides negative evidence for the kinds of ideas that Steiner wants the reader to experience. The result of working conscientiously through Steiner's *Intuitive Thinking as a Spiritual Path* should be none other than what the title suggests—to think freely, to intuit ideas and ideals that live in the spiritual world of which the free thinker is a creative member.

Steiner emphasizes repeatedly that our faulty (nonspiritual, unfree) thinking is due to alienation, both innate and imposed, from other human beings and from cosmic rhythms. This same metaphysical isolation leads to an erroneous image of human beings, particularly of children, the aged, the ill, and the disabled. Concerning all of these special populations, Steiner offers analyses and methods of care. He argues that thinking characteristic of the past three centuries has led to a disregard for the life of feeling. Steiner's Anthroposophy offers a critique and a way of transcending both sense-based and scientific-rationalistic thinking, or any kind of thinking that excludes the intuitive, affective, and artistic dimensions of life. His method of spiritual science aims to restore the affective not merely to the rational-intellectual in general, but particularly to the sciences and the kinds of practical thinking, such as technology, that is characteristic of the modern West.

It is worth reflecting on the other two English translations of the work, *The Philosophy of Spiritual Activity* and *The Philosophy of Freedom* (the literal translation of *Die Philosophie der Freiheit*). They emphasize the spiritual and active character of philosophy itself, the subject matter of the book. As a title, *Intuitive Thinking as a Spiritual Path: A Philosophy of Freedom* gives greater emphasis to the book's use in a spiritual discipline that develops the reader's power of intuition—clearly not the usual meaning of philosophy. In general, Steiner tried to use standard vocabulary, whereas some philosophers, such as Alfred North Whitehead, introduce many neologisms. However, by doing so, Steiner fails to protect the reader from misunderstandings. Throughout his writings and lectures, the reader should modify the word *thinking*, for example, with words such as *free, spiritual, deep,* or *higher*. Such thinking should be understood to be interdependent with one's authentic feeling and one's independent volition. When reading or discussing Steiner's philosophy, it is important to keep in mind that he is trying to combine the best of Goethean natural philosophy with the best of German idealist epistemology. This results in a double affirmation, or foundation, consisting in the objective reality of the natural world, able to be known by affective attention, combined with a theory of knowledge rooted in the knowing "I."

Steiner's *Intuitive Thinking as a Spiritual Path*, then, offers an epistemology that argues for the possibility of each person being able to contact the source of one's individual thinking (and thoughts), *Thinking* itself. This thinking is the source of both true ideas (part I) and true moral principles (part II). It should be acknowledged more often that Steiner's epistemological project resembles Kant's *Critique of Practical Reason* (1788), in which Kant argues that, while it is not possible to know God, freedom, or immortality through pure theoretical (certain) knowledge, it is possible to know these and similar ideas through practical or moral reasoning. Steiner argues that, by thinking freely (which for him is the same as thinking morally, and consequently thinking not based on sensory impressions, physical impulses, or social convention), a person can know true ideas and moral ideals. The crucial difference between Kant's and Steiner's ideas would seem to be Kant's argument that we cannot have certitude concerning this realm, whereas Steiner argues that, through free spiritual thinking, it is possible to know the spiritual world, spiritual ideas and ideals, with certitude.

Steiner considers Kant's restriction to be arbitrary and contrary to some individuals' deep intuitive experience. It might also be the case, however, that the importance of Steiner's *Intuitive Thinking as a Spiritual Path* does not depend significantly on whether it is a way to certitude, but rather whether it is a way to deep, original, and spiritually efficacious thinking. Steiner's way is clearly on the side of freedom, individuality, and intuition and, in that respect, seems superior to Kant's practical moral philosophy, which considers individual human beings to be interchangeable. The difference between the ethics of Steiner and Kant, then, is simply that Kant intended a universal rational agent, whereas Steiner insists that each individual is entirely unique and, therefore, must reach unique moral principles consistent with one's own life circumstance and karmic destiny.

According to Steiner, the will itself is not free on its own, but it can be made to act freely through free thinking, which is the source of free action. By freely making the principle of one's action (rather like Kant's categorical imperative: "So act that the maxim of your act would deserve to serve as universal law"), one can act freely; one can start a new chain, the opposite of *reaction* to external influence.

As Gertrude Reif Hughes explains in her helpful introduction to *Intuitive Thinking as a Spiritual Path*, every chapter of that book "calls us to become free by recognizing and developing the spiritual nature of our human cognitive powers." She continues: "His book speaks to us if we seek the basis for human freedom in an understanding of human thinking and knowing so that our moral decisions can be based on knowledge, not just belief."[10] The most important idea in this book would seem to be that selfhood is not isolating but profoundly social. The entire book, particularly the second half, builds the case against restricting individuals to their type, whether by gender, age, class, ethnicity, or any other category that might blind us to the other person's individuality. Quoting Hughes again, "I can use my selfhood to recognize yours.... A free society requires of its members not less individualism but more" (ibid., xviii).

Admittedly, *Intuitive Thinking as a Spiritual Path* is a challenging book. However, those who persevere will almost certainly find that Steiner's philosophizing gives the meditative reader an artistically rendered inspiring worldview. It is a work of imagination that fosters imagination. As Steiner wrote in 1918, when the book was republished on its twenty-fifth anniversary, "Philosophy is an art. All real philosophers have been artists in the realm of concepts." One wonders whether, in writing this sentence, Steiner had in mind that he was paraphrasing Emerson: "Philosophers are artists in the medium of theory."

In his formulation of the concept of "self," Steiner was influenced by the German idealist philosophers Fichte, Schelling, and Hegel. In his formulation of nature, Steiner was influenced by Goethe. In his formulation of the individual and everything with which it is in relationship, Steiner seems to have drawn from, and sought to extend, the entire Western spiritual and esoteric tradition, particularly the esoteric Christian view of love. Michael Wilson notes that Steiner regarded his philosophy to be one of freedom, as "a Pauline epistemology,"[11] a theory of knowledge based on the central idea of the Epistles of Paul, that the individual self must transform itself so as to be conscious of its identity with Christ. Paul wrote, "I live, no, not I, Christ lives in me" (Galatians 2:20). Similarly, Steiner recommends that the

---

10. Gertrude Reif Hughes, introduction to Rudolf Steiner, *Intuitive Thinking as a Spiritual Path* (Great Barrington, MA: Anthroposophic Press, 1995), pp. xiv–xv.
11. Michael Wilson, introduction to Rudolf Steiner, *The Philosophy of Freedom: The Basis for a Modern World Conception* (London: Rudolf Steiner Press, 1999).

individual think and act from a deeper and wider reality, understood in the Christian tradition as *Christ,* in the Hindu tradition as *Krishna,* in Buddhist tradition as *Buddha,* in the Chinese tradition as *Tao,* and in the Western philosophical monist tradition as the Self, or the Absolute. Steiner's *Intuitive Thinking as a Spiritual Path* is especially rich because it includes the natural world as an essential component. Freedom of the self comes through, or rather is identical with, the ideal relationship of the individual and the world, the relationship between "the spiritual in the individual and the spiritual in the universe." Anything and everything to do with the individual human being and the universe is both relational and evolutionary; nothing exists in isolation and nothing is static.

2. Evolution: Cosmic and Human

Even a brief outline of Steiner's disclosures concerning the evolution of consciousness would include the course of cosmic history, from ages preceding the formation of the Earth to the present; the formation of the human body; the rise and fall of civilizations; and some previsions of the overall direction of cosmic and human evolution.

In broad outline, Steiner's account of the evolution of consciousness, particularly during the past three millennia of Western civilization, focuses on the steady decrease in spiritually intuitive thinking and a corresponding increase in the capacity for and reliance on intellect. Steiner paints this evolutionary drama on an enormous canvas—including the evolution of the planets, the evolution of plant and animal life, and the early evolution of humanity through ancient and medieval civilizations to the extraordinary cultural and material changes of the nineteenth and twentieth centuries. His account of ancient events, including the emergence and disappearance of civilizations, represents the results of his ability to "read" (which can also be understood as suprasensory *seeing*) the essential events recorded in, or through, what is known in esoteric traditions as an *astral,* or *akashic,* record, a comprehensive memory of all important events and ideas. As Steiner read this akashic record, he surmised that the civilization known as Atlantis,[12] a continent, he claimed, off the western coast of Europe, came to destruction, by sinking, in approximately the tenth millennium B.C.E.

Subsequent to the destruction of Atlantis, according to Steiner's reading of the akashic record, the wisdom achieved during the Atlantean civilization was transmitted through exceptional beings called the seven *rishis* (spiritual masters). Steiner refers to that civilization as "ancient India," the first epoch, which lasted from the eighth to the sixth millennia, more than seven thousand years earlier than the period of Indian civilization when the ritual and mystical texts of the Vedas and Upanishads were composed and recited by memory. These texts were preserved from approximately the third millennium B.C.E. to the present by mnemonic chanting. Steiner regards this five thousand year historical period of Indian civilization as a crystallization of the earlier, "Ancient Indian" consciousness.

The consciousness of the second epoch, from the sixth to the third millennium, was typified by "ancient Persia," by which Steiner means "the original source of the Persian civilization," which flourished from the fifth to the third millennia B.C.E. Steiner identifies the third epoch, from the third millennium to the eighth century B.C.E., with Babylonian, Chaldean, Hebraic, and Egyptian civilizations. Unlike the first and second epochs (eighth to third millennia B.C.E.), which refer to modes of consciousness to which contemporary scholarship has very limited access by ordinary historical research, the third epoch refers to historical civilizations for which extensive records exist.

---

12. For a meticulously researched and readable case for Plato's account of Atlantis, see Mary Settagast, *Plato Prehistorian: 10,000 to 5,000 B.C.: Myth, Religion, Archaeology* (Great Barrington, MA: Lindisfarne Press, 1990). Nevertheless, scholars regard the references to Atlantis in Plato's *Timaeus* (24e–25a) and *Critias* (113) to have been literary, or mythic, devices. It is virtually impossible to find a contemporary scholar who takes seriously the possibility of a civilization in the middle of the Atlantic any time approximate to the tenth millennium B.C.E. Consequently, this introduction does not continue the use of Steiner's reference to the seven 2,100-year historical epochs as "post-Atlantean," but simply as first, second, third, and so on.

The paucity of historical data makes it difficult to evaluate Steiner's rendering of the first two epochs, i.e., the six thousand years from the end of Atlantis to the late Egyptian and early Hebraic civilizations in the middle of the second millennium B.C.E. During Steiner's time, it seemed obvious that only someone with comparable capacity for historical intuition could properly corroborate or revise his account of those ancient times. Archeological research of the past half century, however, invites comparisons (and contrasts) between Steiner's spiritual-scientific research and conventional empirical archeological research. His accounts of the third, fourth, and fifth epochs are even more subject to exoteric historical assessment and revision.

Readers who are new to Steiner's vast and sometimes astonishing writings on the evolution of consciousness might find it difficult to know how to assess the implications and veracity of his accounts of events from millennia and centuries long past. We almost always find the key to such complexity in his overall effort to explain how and why modern Western consciousness lost the clairvoyance it possessed during early post-Atlantean epochs, and how we can turn such loss into a gain by developing clairvoyance that is simultaneously rational and spiritual. Unlike many New Age enthusiasts and others who long for a return to an ancient clairvoyance (variously called *primal, primordial, mythic,* and *archaic* consciousness), Steiner traces the loss of ancient clairvoyance without regret. It is precisely this loss that allowed the development of the rational intellect and scientific objectivity. The cause for regret, according to Steiner, lies in the failure of modern Western (rational or scientific) consciousness to develop a new thinking capability that can attain accurate spiritual knowledge.

Transition from direct spiritual intuition to reliance on intellect occurred most dramatically by the agency of the Greeks, at the beginning of the fourth post-Atlantean epoch. This epoch, for which Steiner considers the Greco-Roman-Christian consciousness to be paradigmatic, extends from approximately the eighth century B.C.E. to the fifteenth century C.E. It is during these two millennia, particularly because of innovations wrought by classical Greece, that human consciousness in the West can be seen to have developed a new paradigm, one that significantly replaced the mythic by the intellectual.

In Steiner's view, the last several centuries (particularly the twentieth century, which was Steiner's primary concern), are characterized by an intellectual paradigm that is deadening and desperately in need of spiritually grounded imagination,[13] but not the same that was prevalent in ancient consciousness. Such a return would be unproductive and, in any case, impossible. According to Steiner, primal consciousness was, and continues to be characterized in the few places where it remains, by a capacity for imagination through which it is possible for human beings to sustain an easy relationship to higher beings. By contrast, modern Western consciousness is characterized by individual human intelligence. The new consciousness that Steiner recommends and exemplifies is the result of individual effort to perform free, loving thinking, feeling, and willing. The epoch that began in the fifteenth century, which Steiner calls the fifth Post-Atlantean epoch, and which he expects to prevail for two millennia, has the task of developing a kind of spiritual thinking characterized by love and will. The sixth and seventh epochs in this seven-part cycle are, of course, far in the future, though Steiner also gives some notes on broad possibilities to be achieved in those two periods.

The present time is approximately the right distance from which to see the beginning, development, and end of the fourth cultural epoch, and therefore seems to offer the best opportunity for assessing Steiner's interpretation of these seven epochs. Potentially, the most important contribution of Steiner's account is simply that it might enable a better understanding of how and why human beings, particularly in the West, have come to think, feel, and will as they do, and how modern Western consciousness differs from other modes of consciousness, both ancient and non-modern contemporary consciousness. Most of the distinctive features of modern Western culture arose during the fourth cultural epoch, or the centuries of

---

13. Rudolf Steiner uses the terms *imagination, inspiration,* and *intuition* not in the ordinary sense but to indicate fundamental levels of esoteric initiation.

transition from Greek thought and culture to Roman and then to Christian. Greek thought represents a remarkable transition from the old clairvoyance represented by the gods of ancient Greek religion, to the possibility of rational, intellectual thinking represented by Socratic inquiry, Platonic dialectic, and Aristotelian logic.

According to Steiner, during the several centuries after ancient Greek civilization reached its peak and was only partly successful in transmitting its genius to the Alexandrian and then Roman empires, Western civilization was in a slow but certain decline. During the first century C.E., in a Jewish community governed by Rome, in an apparently insignificant corner of the Roman Empire, the *Logos,* or Christ being, incarnated and set in motion a profound spiritual process intended to rescue human evolution from ever-increasing control by the material world. Steiner frequently asserted that the Christ released a spiritual power, well summarized in the Gospel of St. John, which allowed a more creative and individualized thinking capacity. Steiner sees the incarnation of Christ as the instrument of a potentially universal transformation, one that aims to reunite the spiritual and physical. According to Steiner's esoteric research, the Christ, or Logos, was from the beginning and continues to be the source of cosmic and human evolution. By entering the body of Jesus of Nazareth, the Logos brought to the Earth a spiritual impulse that can help lead humanity to greater freedom and love.

Steiner's teachings are permeated by the Christ impulse but are not constrained by Christian dogma or the ideal of faith. Instead, he proposes that, in the present age, we can best realize the Christ through our own Logos nature, through thinking, loving, and acting from freedom. Steiner's writings and lectures include countless exercises aimed at developing true individuality. For such practices, Christ is the essential source, goal, and guarantor, but other high beings, including Krishna of the Bhagavad Gita, Brahman of the Hindu Vedanta tradition, Buddha, Sophia, and several archangels, particularly Michael, are also active on behalf of humanity.

During the early cultural epochs, it seems every human being had powers of imagination, the capacity to know or to see images or pictures of spiritual realities otherwise unavailable to the typical modern Western individual. Increasingly, modern Western societies, and particularly their educational systems, insist that spiritual or intuitive knowing of images is not possible by ordinary thinking—is not now and never was.

In direct opposition to this reductionist perspective, Steiner argues that, because Moses and Homer, for example, lived in the consciousness of their time (specifically, the third cultural epoch), Moses presumably did hear the voice of Yahweh saying to him "I Am Who Am." Similarly, Homer would have been able to hear the advice of the goddess Athena. Because they were exceptional individuals, they were able to express their respective hearing-seeing-knowing in a way that modern people can still appreciate, though only by working past the limitations on knowledge set by the currently dominant epistemological paradigm.

Rudolf Steiner is not recommending a return to the consciousness of Moses or Homer, but rather that humanity should develop the capacity for a kind of knowing that is more awake and more appropriate for a person who lives in and through modern Western consciousness. Steiner wants his readers to think lovingly of Moses or Homer, Plato or the Apostle Paul, but through a contemporary mode of consciousness, not as they thought. This discipline could enable practitioners to enter the consciousness of individuals and cultures entirely different from their own, but without loss of a contemporary perspective at once critical and appreciative. Steiner understands that the widespread inability to experience the thinking, feeling, and willing of others would seem to be at the root of ethnic, gender, and generational misunderstandings and violence, and he offered spiritual disciplines by which to overcome the alienation that afflicts modern Western individuals and groups.

Steiner's account of the evolution of consciousness presents certain problems for the reader. In particular, his cosmology appears to be Earth- and human-centered, and his view of human history appears to be a somewhat straight line from the ancient Near

East to early twentieth-century Europeans. This account could seem to be another "story by the winners," roughly equivalent to a North American history by white European males. Further, Steiner's account of Christ as the most significant transformative event in human history will be an obstacle for many readers.

Steiner attributes to the Earth a unique and very significant role in the evolution of the cosmos, including the formation of the actual bodies of such high beings as Zoroaster, Christian Rosenkreutz, Gautama Buddha, and above all, Jesus Christ. However, the Earth is not the goal of history. Rather, it is the center of a seven-planet evolution, preceded by Saturn, Sun, and Moon, and to be followed by Jupiter, Venus, and Vulcan. Steiner ascribes a very special role to humanity, but it is important to see humanity in relation to all nine hierarchies, as well as to the Earth and the entire cosmos of physical bodies and spiritual beings. Finally, Steiner presents Christ as the single most important being in the cosmos, but he also sees Christ in close collaboration with other beings such as Krishna and Buddha and with the Earth, which Steiner says Christ has embraced and surrounds at the present time.

Finally, some readers find Steiner's account too deterministic; it seems to claim knowledge of the future. Many of Steiner's statements about the future—for example his descriptions of the sixth consciousness age (beginning fifteen centuries from now)—might seem wildly speculative, perhaps bizarre, especially in light of the human destruction of the Earth currently in process. Steiner never claims certainty for such visions. Rather, he describes what he sees unfolding and consistently affirms that both the agency of human beings and spirit beings working against human evolution can plunge humanity, the Earth, and cosmos into retrograde developments.

No matter how Steiner's account of the evolution of consciousness might be justified, it seems necessary, nevertheless, to acknowledge that his perspective, even granting his amazing powers of intuition into the great thoughts and events of the near and ancient past, is limited by his time. The hundred years since Steiner's lectures on the evolution of consciousness have shown the limitations and the tendency toward exceptionalism of a

European (and American) worldview. While the level of insight and method of rendering would seem to be valuable, and perhaps unsurpassed in depth and detail, Steiner's account will have to be extended to include indigenous, Jewish, Islamic, Asian, and feminist modes of consciousness. Regrettably, and unacceptably, in Steiner's account, people of color are almost invisible. The quality of his work is profound and important but will not continue to be so unless it is extended to the past, present, and future of the entire human community.

We should not consider an extension of Steiner's account of the evolution of consciousness unfaithful to his mission, but rather its appropriate, even necessary, continuation. A full century after Steiner predicted and recommended certain powers of insight, including particularly a deeper and more universal humanity, those very powers have brought into focus a view of the evolution of consciousness that is beginning to include segments of the human community previously neglected, especially the experience of indigenous peoples, cultures of the southern hemisphere, Asia, Islam, and women throughout the world.

Such an expansion of consciousness can come about only through the activity that Steiner urged on his readers and listeners during the first quarter of the twentieth century—that is, a deliberate effort to warm thinking by will and love. This effort was made possible by many advances in human evolution in the past two and a half millennia, essentially since the first Axial Age around the sixth century B.C.E. In Steiner's view, the great task, and possible advance, is for humanity to recognize the effects of the incarnation of Christ throughout the cosmos and particularly in human heart-filled thinking—in human love wherever it is attained, irrespective of whether it is nurtured by Christ or identified with Christianity.

3. *Anthropos: Body, Soul, and Spirit*

Most of Steiner's later work, particularly his research and teachings concerning the arts, sciences, and education, is based on his theory of human nature. Although it is complex and perhaps confusing in places, Steiner's account of the components of the human being in *Theosophy* remains his fundamental statement on this topic. All of his writings and lectures need to be thought through and contemplated to realize their full effect, and the foundational books (*Theosophy, How to Know Higher Worlds,* and *An Outline of Esoteric Science*) present both an intellectual study and a spiritual challenge. Steiner urged readers to ponder meditatively each sentence in these foundational books. In addition to the inherent difficulty of the unusual ideas in these books, some readers may be confused by the sheer number of categories and their occasional intermingling:

Three capacities of the human being: thinking, feeling, and willing

Three parts of the individual corresponding to the threefold social order: economic aspect, the area of politics and rights, and the cultural and spiritual

Threefold, fourfold, sevenfold, and ninefold constituents of the human being: physical, etheric (subtle), soul (astral), and spirit ("I")

Before discussing the third of these organizational sets, we should focus briefly on the other two. Thinking (along with its lower counterpart, sensing), feeling, and willing are psychological activities of soul life. The threefold social division (economic, political rights, and cultural-spiritual) do not correspond directly to thinking, feeling, and willing, or to threefold (or fourfold) constituents of the human being. They do correspond to the threefold system of the physical organism: the economic sphere corresponds to the head and sensory system; the rights sphere corresponds to the rhythmic system; the cultural and spiritual sphere corresponds to the metabolic system. The remainder of this section will discuss the organization of the human being as presented in "The Essential Nature of the Human Being," the first chapter in *Theosophy,* at the start of which, Steiner quotes the following passage by Goethe:

As soon as we become aware of the objects around us, we start to consider them in relationship to ourselves, and rightly so, because our fate depends entirely on whether they please or displease, attract or repel, help or harm us. This very natural way of looking at and assessing things appears to be as easy as it is necessary, yet it exposes us to thousands of errors that often put us to shame and make our lives miserable.

We undertake a much harder task when, in our keen desire for knowledge, we strive to observe natural objects in and for themselves and in their relationship to one another, for we soon feel the lack of the standard of liking and disliking, attraction and repulsion, usefulness and harmfulness, that came to our aid when we were considering objects in relationship to our human selves. We are forced to renounce this standard totally and, as dispassionate and quasi-divine beings, to seek out and examine what is, and not what pleases us. This means that neither the beauty nor the usefulness of any plant should move true botanists, who rather should study its morphology and its relationships to the rest of the plant kingdom. Just as the sun shines equally on all plants and entices them forth, so too should botanists observe and survey them all impartially and take the data and standards for their assessment, not from the human domain, but from the domain of the things under observation. (pp. 21–23)

Steiner introduces his description of human nature by inviting the reader to make a simple observation. He uses a moving passage by Goethe to help the reader recognize the three ways in which each individual in connected to the world.

Readers who thoughtfully follow the words of Goethe with care will be led to the conclusion that they perceive the world, receive impressions from it, and gain knowledge about it. A person accepts, as fact, objects brought to the senses; impressions give the world meaning; knowledge is a goal toward which one must strive. These three experiences correspond to the three parts of human nature: body, soul, and spirit. It is through the body that one's environment is revealed; it is through the soul that the individual experiences pleasure and displeasure, attraction and aversion, as well as other emotions in relation to the world; it is through the spirit that the individual experiences the world, in Goethe's terms, as an objective "divine being."

In most contexts, this threefold conception stands as Steiner's fundamental theory of human nature. It is an affirmation of, or return to, the view of human nature as held by the Christian Church until it was condemned as heresy by the Ecumenical Council of Constantinople of 869.[14] It also stands in opposition to the dual principle, or body-soul, concept of human nature, which has been a general characteristic of both Christian and post-Christian thinking. To be accurate, however, and to gain the full benefit of Steiner's spiritual-scientific knowledge, we should recognize a fourth constituent of human nature, variously called life body, ether body, or formative-force body. In itself, the physical body is lifeless and incapable of supporting the other two components of human nature, the soul or astral body, and the spirit or "I." The etheric body provides life forces for the physical body and links it to soul and spirit. "We belong to the world of life through our ether body."[15] These four concepts, corresponding to the four constituent parts of the human being, will be more understandable when considered in two other contexts: first in relation to levels, or modes, of knowledge; and second, in relation to the experiences of sleep and death.

The following discussion of the correspondence between levels of knowledge and levels of the human being concern the path of higher knowledge described in the next section on meditation and simultaneously serve as necessary background for the sixth chapter, on karma and rebirth. Throughout his writings, and most systematically in *Theosophy* and *An Outline of Esoteric Science*, Steiner describes four levels of apprehension, corresponding to four levels of the individual human being. Steiner does not consider the first level, sensory perception; he reserves the term *knowledge* for the three remaining levels, which are progressively higher states of knowledge:

Sensory perception, made possible by the physical body;

---

14. See A. P. Shepherd, "The Battle for the Spirit: The Council of Constantinople, 869 A.D.," in *The Golden Blade* (London: Rudolf Steiner Book Shop, 1963).
15. Rudolf Steiner, *Theosophy*, p 37.

Imaginative knowledge, made possible by the etheric body;
Inspirational knowledge, made possible by the astral or soul body;
Intuitive knowledge, made possible by spirit, or "I."

According to Steiner's theory of imagination as presented in the next section, our relation to the external world must be more than the simple reception of sensory impressions. Rather, such impressions provide an opportunity for the formation of imaginative pictures, or images. These pictures arise through the knower in relation to the etheric forces of the object, signaling the development of a capacity for spiritual thinking. Steiner's case for a new science of biodynamic farming, for example, is the result of his ability to see, or grasp, an image of the etheric formative forces at work in the mineral and plant kingdoms. This ability to picture a spiritual form independent of the sensory level of perception is the first necessary step toward the kind of free, spiritual thinking that leads gradually to a clairvoyant sight into spiritual realities. Seeing the etheric formative forces in the world of nature both cultivates and reveals the etheric body in the individual knower.

In the section of *How to Know Higher Worlds* entitled "Preparation," immediately following the section reprinted in the fourth chapter in this volume, Steiner recommends that we practice the exercise of fixing our attention on objects and events in the natural world, paying attention particularly to the phenomena of growth and decay. He explains that, through such observations and spiritual penetration of plant metamorphosis, we can begin to develop the first stages of clairvoyance. He also explains that, from the ability to see images related to physical objects (such as the etheric body of a particular plant), it is a relatively short step to seeing etheric forces as independent realities. Steiner calls this latter seeing "inspirational knowledge."

At the level of imagination, images are tied closely to physical objects; at the level of inspirational knowledge, however, spiritual forces and beings can be perceived independently of physical realities. In *An Outline of Esoteric Science*, Steiner gives the following exercise in inspiration, a meditation on the process of a plant's becoming and decaying:

If we want to achieve the corresponding inspiration, we must do the exercise differently. We must reflect on the actual soul activity that derived the idea of becoming and decay from the image of the plant. We must allow the plant to disappear completely from our consciousness and meditate only on our own inner activity. Only exercises of this sort make it possible to rise to the level of inspiration.[16]

This "rise to the level of inspiration" is an ascent to knowledge of one's soul, or astral body. We can best understand this body, which is entirely spiritual and capable of existing independently of the physical and etheric bodies, as consciousness. It is the vehicle through which I consciously experience, remember, and gather to myself a personal identity that has enduring significance. The astral body, and the inspirational knowledge of which it is distinctively capable, relates the physical and etheric bodies to the spirit, or "I." As the physical and etheric worlds work on the astral body from below, forcing it to deal with the limits of these lower realms, the spiritual world works on the soul (astral body) from above downward into it. "It is the soul that cognizes. What food is to the body, feelings are to the soul."[17]

The third level of higher knowledge, intuition, corresponds to the fourth level or fourth constituent part of the human being. From our ordinary, commonsense vantage point, we might assume that the higher stages of knowledge are progressively more vague and obscure. Predictably, Steiner claims the reverse: sensory knowledge (or sensory perception, which technically is not knowledge at all) is clear only to the extent that we illumine the material world by the cognitive capacities of imagination, inspiration, and intuition. More to the point, we can truly understand our own self only by ascending to the level of intuition. In other words, we know our self only when we see the physical body as an expression of the etheric, the ether body as an expression of the astral, and the astral as an expression of the "I."

---

16. *An Outline of Esoteric Science* (Anthroposophic Press, 1997), p. 341.
17. *How to Know Higher Worlds* (Anthroposophic Press, 1994), p. 21.

But the soul, or astral body, is not a fixed or simple entity. It evolves with the other parts of the self. "Thus the soul, like the body, consists of three distinct members—the sentient soul, the mind soul, and the consciousness soul."[18]

Steiner notes that the word *I* is peculiar, in that it is the only term that no one outside myself can address to me:

> In ordinary life, we have only one "intuition"—namely, that of the "I" itself, for the "I" can in no way be perceived externally. It can be experienced only in the inner life.... There is one word that each of us can apply only to ourselves. This is the word *I*. No other person can call me "I." To anyone else, I am "you." Likewise, everyone else is "you" to me. Only I can say "I" to myself. This is because each person lives not outside but within the "I." Similarly, in intuitive cognition, one lives in all things. The perception of the "I" is the prototype of all intuitive cognition. Thus, to enter all things, one must first step outside the self. We must become "selfless" in order to blend with the "self," or "I," of another being.[19]

By developing the ability to know intuitively, I can know my self, the "I," on which my physical, etheric, and astral bodies depend. I can also know other beings who are independent of the three lower parts of the person. "The 'I' lives in the soul...[and] radiates outward from there, filling the entire soul and exerting its influence on the body through the soul."[20] Steiner does not prove the existence of the "I" or other spiritual beings he claims we can know through the practice of spiritual science; rather, he describes what he sees through his own intuition and insists that others can work similarly through imaginative and inspirational knowledge toward intuitive knowledge of higher beings. The most dramatic examples and details of Steiner's spiritual knowledge are his examples of sleep and death, as described in chapter 6. Steiner often presents a set of ideas in one form, and then another, and yet another.

---

18. *Theosophy*, p. 46.
19. *The Stages of Higher Knowledge* (Anthroposophic Press, 2009), pp. 7–8.
20. *Theosophy*, pp. 50–51.

With respect to the structure, or perhaps layers, of the human being, we can fix in our minds a summary such as the one outlined in the following chart.

CORRELATION OF HUMAN DEVELOPMENT
AND HISTORIC EPOCHS ACCORDING TO RUDOLF STEINER

CULTURAL PERIOD	FIRST	SECOND	THIRD	FOURTH	FIFTH	SIXTH
Dates	7000–5000 B.C.E.	5000–3000 B.C.E.	3000–750 B.C.E.	750 B.C.E.–1500 C.E.	1500–3600 C.E.	3600 C.E.–
Epoch	Ancient Indian	Ancient Persian	Egyptian-Hebrew	Greco-Roman-Christian	modern Western global	Slavic
Soul mood	will	feeling	sentient soul thinking	intellectual soul thinking	consciousness soul thinking	
Aspiration	goodness	beauty	truth	(history?)	individualism	individual and community

- The human body is composed of three members: physical, etheric, soul.
- The human soul is composed of three modes of consciousness, or soul life: sentient, intellectual, consciousness.
- Spirit lives in the "I," and the "I" lives in the soul and body. As a spiritual being, the "I" has three members: spirit body (*atman*); life spirit (*buddhi*); and spirit self (*manas*).

4. Spiritual Intelligence

The most important task in approaching Steiner's or any other spiritual practice is motivation. On this topic, as on so many concerning meditation and spiritual cognition, Steiner's counsel is perfectly clear: "Every insight that you seek only to enrich your own store of learning and to accumulate treasure for yourself alone leads you from your path, but every insight that you seek in order to become more mature on the path of the ennoblement of humanity and world evolution brings you one step forward."[21]

Anthroposophy represents a method of spiritual growth and transformation that creates an ideal harmony among thinking, feeling, and willing. This harmony in turn fosters a true and deep relationship between self and world. Steiner recommends rather simple exercises that cultivate thinking, feeling, and willing, forming a basis for the more advanced work of spiritual science. As virtually all spiritual teachers insist, spiritual or esoteric exercises can be harmful when practiced by those whose exoteric (ordinary, observable) personality and character are poorly formed. Students of yoga, for example, know that the first two of the eight steps in Patanjali's *Yoga Sutras* set out the moral preconditions for progress in physical and spiritual exercises.

Steiner offers a set of six exercises that prepare a healthy entry to spiritual and esoteric work. These six exercises also help to protect the spiritual practitioner from the negative influence of beings working against humanity. Ideally, the practitioner should add one exercise each month. The first three of these six preliminary practices refer to the three strands of spiritual discipline needed for modern Western consciousness, namely thinking, willing, and feeling. These exercises are more important and challenging than they might seem at first glance. When practiced faithfully, they serve as a definite foundation on which to build other exercises and disciplines.

1. *Thinking.* Practice concentrating: gain control of one's thoughts for a few minutes faithfully every day. Choose a simple object such as a pin or paper clip and think about it by generating a series of deliberate thoughts. Because it is difficult to protect this time every day, and because it is difficult to stay focused on an insignificant object for five minutes, this thought exercise is also a will exercise.
2. *Willing.* Practice controlling the will: perform one or more positive but relatively insignificant tasks the same time of day, say in the middle of the afternoon: turn your watch, or your ring, or

---

21. *How to Know Higher Worlds*, pp. 24–25.

rub your hands. Try to avoid the reminder of an external stimulus, such as your alarm or getting in the car in the morning, though at the beginning of this practice, such a reminder might be necessary.
3. *Feeling.* Practice equanimity: learn to stabilize fluctuations of pleasure and pain, joy and sorrow. This exercise should not lead to indifference, but rather toward a steady objective concern for all that happens. It works against self-indulgence, whether in sympathy or antipathy, and in favor of a selfless commitment to improving what can be improved and accepting what cannot.[22]
4. *Practice seeking the positive.* Without denying what is negative, this exercise requires that we practice finding something positive in every event.
5. *Practice openness to new experiences and ideas.* Without abandoning one's reasonable judgment and values, this exercise requires that we at least consider without bias new ideas, or previously opposed persons or groups, or a way of behavior that one finds distasteful or too unusual.
6. *At the start of the sixth month, practice repeating and harmonizing the first five exercises.*

These six exercises, which most practitioners find challenging, are only a start and students should supplement these with other exercises and practices that Steiner recommended in his books, lectures, and private instruction from 1904 to 1924.

How to Know Higher Worlds, the book in which Steiner first introduced these six basic exercises, is an esoterically profound handbook for the development of clairvoyance or suprasensory perception, the possible attainment of which Steiner affirms in the opening paragraph:

> The capacities by which we can gain insights into higher worlds lie dormant within each one of us. Mystics, gnostics, and theosophists have always spoken of a world of soul and spirit that

---

22. Compare the Serenity Prayer, "God, give us grace to accept with serenity the things that cannot be changed, courage to change the things that should be changed, and the wisdom to distinguish the one from the other," widely used in Alcoholic Anonymous circles and probably first written by the mid-twentieth century American Protestant theologian Reinhold Niebuhr.

is as real to them as the world we can see with our eyes and touch with our hands. Listening to them, we can say to ourselves at every moment: "I know that I, too, can experience what they talk about, if only I unfold certain forces within me that today still lie dormant there." All we need to know is how to begin to develop these faculties for ourselves.

Only those who have already developed such powers for themselves can help us to do this. From the beginning of the human race, a form of training has always existed in which persons possessing higher faculties guide those who seek to develop these faculties for themselves. Such training is called esoteric, or mystery training; and the instruction one receives there is called esoteric, or occult, teaching. (pp. 13–14)

In principle, secret, esoteric, or occult knowledge is available to anyone who seeks it by a method guaranteed by a genuine spiritual school and teachers genuinely disciplined in the methods of that school. In actuality, however, it is difficult to attain esoteric knowledge, more difficult, certainly, than Steiner's comparison to learning to write.

Steiner offers two principles that govern access to esoteric knowledge. First, anyone who is eager to receive such knowledge and willing to meet the requirements of the discipline ought to be accepted by a teacher or a school, irrespective of that person's social, economic, or cultural resources. Similarly, as a second corollary, teachers should avoid making this knowledge available to those who are ill prepared in aspiration or ability.

Steiner emphasizes the continuity and the differences among levels of knowledge, specifically the progression from perception to imagination to inspiration to intuition. Almost everyone has at least a modicum of imagination, but in the modern West, fewer individuals are capable of inspired feeling, and even fewer are capable of intuition. It seems that, in general, modern Western individuals lack even the imagination to recognize that they regard these three higher modes of human consciousness, both past and present, as unreliable or impossible. The modern Western way of alienated thinking has led to the individual's separation from nature and from the cosmos as living realities. This alienation between our inner self and the inner life of all else—God, gods, goddesses, spirits, Buddha, Krishna, light, living forms, true ideals—is so well established that the modern Western person cannot ordinarily experience this alienation for what it is. To develop the capacity for non-alienated (or love-filled) thinking requires a significant commitment to a demanding discipline.

The steps to esoteric knowledge follow a systematic progression, not unlike the six levels of knowledge in classical Yoga and Vedanta, the ladder of knowledge in Plato, and the levels of spiritual knowledge in Christian mysticism. As Steiner describes it, this progression leads from intellectual knowledge through imagination, inspiration, and intuition. In Steiner's epistemology, each of these levels of higher knowledge corresponds to a part of the human being (as described in the previous section). Imagination is a capacity developed by, and in the realm of, the life principle (the etheric, or formative, principle); inspiration corresponds to the astral (soul) principle; and intuition corresponds to the "I" (the spiritual self). In this respect, the knowledge peculiarly available to modern Western people is knowledge that is even less clairvoyant than ancient spiritual knowledge. However, since it is based on the "I," which, significantly, is made possible by the impulse of Christ, such knowledge holds out the possibility of the richest combination: accurate spiritual knowledge grasped by a genuinely individual, knowing "I."

As Steiner demonstrates in many ways, science and art are equally fruitful disciplines by which to develop this spiritual thinking capacity. Progress in developing this capacity will lead to esoteric insight, as well as to a heightened faculty or capability for spiritual-scientific thinking that one can apply to all areas of inquiry. Like other great figures of spiritual esotericism, Steiner was able to manifest his spiritual powers in the widest possible range of enterprises, from natural science to the arts, philosophy, and history. Meditative or imaginative thinking according to the method of Anthroposophy can enable one to acquire higher ways of knowing, as well as a more fruitful relationship to one's self, to the rest of humanity, and to the universe.

Steiner does not pit spiritual perception against science and intelligence; rather, he sees the cool thinking of science as a necessary and positive development in human evolution. These two competing, yet complementary, capabilities—the intellectual and the intuitive—are both needed for human progress and survival in the present age. The task of the modern age, then, is to bring a new kind of spiritual seeing and thinking capability to the physical world. Steiner urges the development of spiritual perception through the cultivation of cognitive powers appropriate for the present stage of cultural and psychic evolution, with intellect at the base, or the start, then three higher capacities: imagination, inspiration, and intuition. Compared to these three more spiritual and creative modes of thinking, our usual modes of thinking, at the level of intellect, tend to be determined by impersonal forces, such as culturally engendered habits or physical impulses. Steiner refers to ordinary thinking as dead; he could have used Plato's allegory, according to which ordinary thinking is cave-like. The modern thinking person is capable of rationality, but generally incapable of the clairvoyance characteristic of past epochs. By disciplined effort, however, the modern person can learn clairvoyant imaginative, inspirational, and intuitive thinking.

In important ways, it may be regrettable that humanity had to lose its capacity for clairvoyance and the intimate relation with the external world that seems to have been common in the ancient world. However, those losses allowed the development of scientific intelligence and a degree of individual freedom unimagined by primal consciousness. This loss of clairvoyance also led to the human estrangement and alienation that is characteristic of the modern Western experience. The separation of mind from nature, as formulated by Descartes in the seventeenth century, is the birthright and fundamental life problem of the modern Western individual. The solution to this inescapable problem lies in a new kind of clairvoyance based on an intensely active spiritual thinking. The nature and function of such thinking constitute the essence—the spiritual methodology, or discipline—of Anthroposophy.

Steiner never claimed certitude for his clairvoyant findings. Nor did he dismiss ordinary texts and interpretations that were inconsistent with his esoteric research. On some points, he revised and supplemented his earlier research. For example, in his 1925 preface to *An Outline of Esoteric Science* (originally written in 1909), he acknowledged that he was then able to include material that had been unavailable to him only five years earlier, when he wrote *Theosophy*. Steiner explained that, when he wrote *Theosophy*, facts of cosmic evolution were not present to him to the same extent: "In my imaginations, the spiritual being of the individual stood before my soul, and I was able to describe it, but this was not yet true of the cosmic relationships that were to be presented in *Esoteric Science*. Individual details were there, but not the total picture."[23]

Steiner's recommendations for meditative or contemplative practice focus primarily on capacities and, incidentally, on attainment, first on the ability to see and hear the spiritual realities and, second, on what one sees and hears. It is these capabilities that each person takes across the threshold on the great journey between death and the next rebirth. It is important to note that a full understanding of what Steiner presents as preconditions of spiritual practice—reverence and humility—shows them to be attainments. The kind of knowledge that Steiner bequeathed and recommended is closer to humility, reverence, and love than to the conception of knowledge and its fruits in contemporary Western culture. If Steiner were working today among anthroposophists, he might comment that, as a result of his research, his followers possess amazingly deep and useful knowledge, but that their knowledge could be deepened and rendered more efficacious by greater reverence, humility, and love.

Those who come to Steiner's writings on meditation and spiritual cognition understandably ask where to begin. The best answer seems to be the six exercises combined with reverence and humility. As Steiner states, "Every feeling of *true* devotion unfolded in the soul produces an inner strength of force that sooner or later leads to knowledge,"[24] and "reverence in us quickens all the feelings in our soul.... Disrespect, antipathy, and dis-

---

23. *An Outline of Esoteric Science*, p. 1.
24. *How to Know Higher Worlds*, p 18.

paraging admirable things, on the other hand, paralyze and slay our cognitive activities."[25] Similarly, humility is an indispensable basis for spiritual practice, and may well be its very core. "Only a person who has passed through the gate of humility can ascend to the heights of the spirit."[26]

Steiner offered numerous explanations, examples, and instructions for spiritual practice, including specific exercises that he introduced in 1904, when he served as the primary teacher for the Theosophical Society in German-language countries. His teaching then and throughout his years as a teacher of Anthroposophy remained simple (though certainly not easy): give birth to and thereafter attend to one's higher self and help it to develop. One must first think and discover the higher self through a higher mode of thinking. By so doing, one should experience profound humility. What else should one experience in the moment of realizing that it is the soul that cognizes the means of thinking that is ever ready to make itself available to the active soul? "We forget that it is the soul that knows. Feelings are to the soul as food is to the body."[27] It is easy to see the relationship between Steiner's spiritual epistemology and that of Emerson, who wrote: "The one thing in the world, of value, is the active soul."[28]

Anthroposophic spiritual practice is not a separate, special activity, but the substance of daily life. It resembles Sri Aurobindo's counsel: "All life is a secret yoga."[29] Two individuals may seem to be performing the exact same action, but one person might be acting from the ordinary ego, while the other might be doing "secret yoga," or joining "the spiritual in the individual

---

25. Ibid., pp. 21–22.
26. Ibid., p 17.
27. Ibid., p. 21.
28. "The American Scholar," in Ralph Waldo Emerson, *Essays and Lectures* (New York: Library of America, 1983), p. 57. This passage continues: "This every man is entitled to; this every man contains within him, although, in almost all men, obstructed, and as yet unborn. The soul active sees absolute truth; and utters truth, or creates. In this action, it is genius; not the privilege of here and there a favorite, but the sound estate of every man."
29. Sri Aurobindo, in Robert McDermott, ed., *The Essential Aurobindo* (Great Barrington, MA: Lindisfarne Press, 1987), p. 165.

to the spiritual in the universe." One's action or thought may be moved by ordinary thinking or by a free, spiritual, original, heart-filled thinking; the difference is in the awareness, consciousness, and motivation. "Secret yoga" thinking, or anthroposophic thinking, turns ordinary ideas into ideals, into spirit: "Every idea that does not become an ideal for us kills a force in our soul. However, every idea that becomes our ideal creates forces of life within us."[30]

Such a transformation of both thoughts and actions is the work of a special kind of thinking, the kind that issues from the spiritual world through the soul. The thinking involved in this stream of world events lifts me, and my soul with me, and I live in those events when I allow their essence to flow into me through my thinking. In any given situation, such thinking might look the same as ordinary thinking but inwardly, motivationally, at the soul level, it is entirely different. It is free precisely because it is rooted in thinking. The world thinks itself in the human soul: "It is not merely I who thinks, for it thinks in me—world-becoming expresses itself in me and my soul provides only the stage upon which the world lives as thought."[31] Again, "In thinking, I experience myself united with the stream of cosmic existence."[32] Compare Emerson: "I could not be but that the absolute life circulates in me."[33]

A second step on the anthroposophic path might be a daily meditative recitation of the "Foundation Stone Meditation" and, in particular, dwelling on its four parts: the Ground of Being, the Logos principle, the Spirit, and the very different mood of the fourth part in which Steiner describes the two missions of the Incarnation of Christ ("to simple shepherds' hearts, Light that

---

30. *How to Know Higher Worlds*, p. 25.
31. *A Way of Self-Knowledge: And the Threshold of the Spiritual World* (Great Barrington, MA: SteinerBooks, 2006), p. 69.
32. *Start Now! A Book of Soul and Spiritual Exercises* (Great Barrington, MA: SteinerBooks, 2004), p. 64.
33. William H. Gilman, et alia, eds., *The Journals and Miscelaneous Notebooks of Ralph Waldo Emerson* (Cambridge: Harvard University Press, 1960), vol. 5, p. 391; cited in Gertrude Reif Hughes, "Emerson's Epistemology with Glances at Rudolf Steiner," in Kate Farrell, ed., *Anthropsophy & Imagination: Classics from The Journal of Anthroposophy* (Ann Arbor, MI: Anthroposophical Society in America), no. 76, summer 2006. p. 35.

enlightens the wise heads of kings").[34] Steiner himself meditatively read the prologue to the Gospel of St. John and recited the Lord's Prayer aloud each day while standing.

5. Christ and Other Exalted Beings

The spiritual knowledge scattered throughout Steiner's hundreds of volumes includes disclosures—some quite startling—concerning such topics as evolution of the Sun, Moon, and planets, especially the Earth, as well as the etheric, formative forces working in the plant and animal worlds. He describes the role of great spiritual beings such as Krishna, Buddha, and Christ, the work of the tempters of humanity, Lucifer and Ahriman, as well as the mission of angels and archangels, especially, as noted, the Archangel Michael (whom Steiner regards as the regent of the current age). This vision also includes descriptions of the salient characteristics of Western civilization, which he places in a detailed evolutionary sequence, including historically significant and paradigmatic individuals such as the pharaohs of ancient Egypt, the patriarchs and prophets of Israel, Zoroaster, Plato, and Aristotle, as well as Christ and a series of influential Christian personalities. He particularly emphasizes the descent of the spiritual Sun being—the Christ—into history through the cooperative agency of Jesus of Nazareth and several predecessors. His phrase "the Mystery of Golgotha" refers to the redemptive, world-transforming presence of the Christ in Jesus. When discussing his experience of the Mystery of Golgotha (which he first disclosed in 1902 in *Christianity as Mystical Fact* and subsequently developed in writings and in several hundred subsequent lectures on the events depicted in the New Testament), Steiner explained that his understanding was based entirely on direct vision. He consulted standard scriptural sources and scholarly interpretations only as a way of relating his own spiritual insight to conventional scholarly interpretations. In the *Autobiography*, he writes:

---

34. *The Christmas Conference: For the Foundation of the General Anthroposophical Society, 1923/1924* (Hudson, NY: Anthroposophic Press, 1990), p. 74.

The Christianity that I had to find was not in any of the existing confessions. After the severe, inner struggles during that time of testing, I found it necessary to immerse myself in Christianity and, indeed, in the world where spirit itself speaks of it.... During the period when my statements about Christianity seemed to contradict my later comments, a conscious knowledge of real Christianity began to dawn within me. Around the turn of the century, this seed of knowledge continued to develop. The soul test described here occurred shortly before the beginning of the twentieth century. It was decisive for my soul's development that I stood spiritually before the Mystery of Golgotha in a deep and solemn celebration of knowledge.[35]

Following the prologue to the Gospel of John, Steiner considers Christ to be the Logos (the Word), who was "at the beginning,"[36] and who entered a darkened world that did not comprehend him. According to Steiner, however, his coming was not in vain, for it has been bringing about the gradual transformation of humanity and the Earth. Using the same words that Steiner used to characterize Anthroposophy: the incarnation, death, and resurrection of Christ lead the spiritual in the individual to the spiritual in the universe. More specifically, the life of Jesus Christ advanced and continues to hasten spiritual thinking, feeling, and willing, and harmonious relationships among them. According to Steiner, these three capacities, as well as the relationship between the spiritual in the individual and spiritual in the universe, have been strengthened because Christ strengthens the reality of the spiritual self, the "I," which is itself an expression of Christ. In Steiner's view, it is the aim of each human life and humanity as a whole to be able to say with St. Paul, "I live, no, not I but Christ lives in me" (Galatians 2:20).

In an act that is not strictly a part of Anthroposophy, Steiner responded to the requests from ministers and theology students

---

35. *Autobiography: Chapters in the Course of My Life, 1861–1907* (SteinerBooks, 2006), p. 188.
36. The English translation of *arche* as beginning expresses half of the meaning of the Greek original, the other half being source, foundation, structure as in *arche-type, archi-tecture.*

for help in renewing Christian life and liturgy. He inspired and helped fashion an institutional and ecclesiastical structure called the Christian Community (also called the Movement for Religious Renewal). For this community he disclosed seven sacraments, including a liturgy called the Act of Consecration of Man, a ritual similar to the Roman Catholic Mass. In contrast to Anthroposophy, whereby individuals strive mainly on their own to experience spiritual ascent, the Act of Consecration of Man allows participants to experience a descent of the divine into the assembled liturgical community.

A single lecture on Christ and other higher beings cannot provide an adequate sense of the profound mysteries that Steiner discusses in the hundreds of lectures that he delivered to audiences familiar with his detailed accounts of hierarchies. Such lectures discuss the nature and history of archangels (Michael, Raphael, Gabriel, Uriel) and very advanced human beings such Hermes, Moses, John the Baptist, John the Evangelist, the mother of Jesus, and many others. We can characterize Steiner's research concerning these higher beings by the Buddhist term *Mahayana,* the greater vehicle, the name of the Buddhist stream that considers Buddha not limited to the finite and temporal life of Gautama, but infinite and eternal. Steiner also introduced a new method of initiation continuous with the Greek mystery religions. He showed that initiation is a process of transformation from one nature to another, from a schooled but still somewhat ordinary, consciousness to a nature in direct relationship with spirit beings, including one's higher self. This was the experience of Lazarus who, according to Steiner, was initiated and became John the Beloved Disciple, the disciple to whom the crucified Christ commended his mother at the foot of the cross, and who, again according to Steiner, wrote the Fourth Gospel and the Book of Revelation.

The lecture included here as chapter 5 (the last of ten lectures that Steiner delivered to about ten people in a Hamburg living room in 1908) presents an entirely new and extremely profound description of the Virgin Sophia and the Holy Spirit. One of the results of meditation and spiritual practice is the purification of the human astral body. In this lecture on the

Virgin Sophia, Steiner states that, in esoteric Christianity, the cleansed and purified astral body is called the "pure, chaste, and wise Virgin Sophia":

> Through all that is received during catharsis, the student cleanses and purifies the astral body so that it becomes transformed into the Virgin Sophia. Moreover, when the Virgin Sophia encounters the cosmic, or universal, "I," which leads to illumination, the student is surrounded by spiritual light. Even today, in esoteric Christianity this second power that approaches the Virgin Sophia is called the "Holy Spirit." Therefore, according to esoteric Christianity, it is correct to say that, through his processes of initiation, Christian esotericists attain the purification and cleansing of the astral body; they make the astral body into the Virgin Sophia and are illumined from above. If you prefer, you may call it overshadowed by the "Holy Spirit," or cosmic, universal "I."[37]

In the conclusion of this lecture Steiner reminds his audience that in his view Christianity "is just at the beginning of its activity and that its true mission will be fulfilled once it has been understood in its true spiritual form."[38] Steiner was convinced that spiritual and esoteric knowledge of the cosmos, the Earth, humanity, and particularly the works of higher beings such as Christ and Sophia will enable Christianity to serve, as intended, as a true expression of the transformative power of Christ in the world and in each human being.

6. Reincarnation, Karma, and the Dead

A presentation of Steiner's spiritual-scientific research must include a summary of his thoroughly detailed account of karma and rebirth. At the core of this teaching is his claim that each human being has two closely related life histories: one while awake and one asleep. The beginning of sleep represents a kind of death to the daytime biography, just as the beginning of waking consciousness is a kind of death to the sleeping biography. In

---

37. Rudolf Steiner, *The Gospel of St. John*, Anthroposophic Press, 1962. p. 179 (revised).
38. Ibid., p. 192.

addition to being like a death, these transitions are also a kind of rebirth. The activity of the soul after its earthly life parallels the activity of the soul during sleep. In sleep, the astral, or soul life, as well as the spirit, leave the remainder of the sleeping individual (the physical and etheric bodies) and return to the spiritual world.

In *Theosophy,* Steiner explains that sleep is an apt image for death because, while one sleeps, events pursue their own course independently of one's conscious life. "Our personalities are reembodied anew each morning in the world of our actions" (pp. 87–88). The activity of the soul after its earthly life parallels the activity of the soul during sleep. During the middle hours of daily sleep, the "I" and the astral body leave the physical and etheric bodies, which remain asleep on the bed, and return to the spiritual world. Because waking consciousness consists of the interaction between our astral and etheric bodies, the departure of the astral body to a separate state of being allows the etheric body to repair damage to the physical body incurred during its daytime activities.

The biography of the sleeping self is important in another respect, as well. After death, the sleep biography is relived in an ingenious reversal of our earthly life. We can best understand Steiner's account of this phenomenon, which reads like a fascinating blend of Dante's *Purgatorio,* by recounting the sequence of events that constitute death. Death of the physical body is immediate and irremediable, but the etheric, astral, and spirit bodies survive physical death for various periods. The etheric body, which has recorded all of the experiences of one's lifetime, remains attached to the astral body for approximately three days in order to present, in a vast, instantaneous panorama, the entire life that has just ended. As recounted in books on near-death experience by Raymond Moody, Elisabeth Kübler-Ross, and Kenneth Ring, many individuals who have nearly died (as, for example, by drowning or from a heart attack), have described similar experiences after being restored to consciousness.

Having absorbed the panoramic report of the etheric body, the astral body remains in existence for approximately one-third the duration of a person's lifetime. This is where sleep plays its significant and intriguing role. In this phase of soul history, the

"I" passes through a period called *kamaloca*. There are two major kamaloca experiences: during the first, the astral body, in which one's desires and emotions are embedded, continues to seek the kinds of satisfaction it enjoyed on Earth, but to the extent that it clings to physical satisfaction without its body, it can only be frustrated. By living through this frustration, the astral body gradually becomes purified of its attachment to physical life and eventually dissolves. In the second kamaloca experience, the "I" relives its entire past life backward, from death to birth. All of our past actions are now experienced again, but with a painfully appropriate karmic twist; at this point, the "I" receives the consequences of its earthly actions as these same actions were experienced by their recipients. Steiner describes this purgatorial experience in *Theosophy* and in one of his last and most profound lecture courses, *Anthroposophy and the Inner Life*:

> We now see that, after a few days, we must begin to experience what we have left unexperienced; and this holds for every single deed we have done to other human beings in the world. The last deeds done before death are the first to come before us, and so backward through life. We first become aware of what our last evil or good deeds signify for the world. Our experience of them while on Earth is now eliminated; what we now experience is their significance for the world.
>
> Then we go farther back, experiencing our life again, but backward. We know that while doing this we are still connected with the Earth, for it is only the other side of our deeds that we experience now.
>
> We feel as if our life from now onward were being borne in the womb of the universe. What we now experience is a kind of embryonic stage for our further life between death and a new birth. However, it is not born by a mother, but by the world, by all that we did not experience in physical life. We live through our physical life again, backward and in its cosmic significance. We experience it now with a very divided consciousness. Living here in the physical world and observing the creatures around us, we feel that we are pretty much the lords of creation. Even though we call a lion the king of beasts, we still feel that we as human beings are superior. We feel that the creatures of the other kingdoms are inferior. We can judge them, but do not

ascribe to them the power to judge us. We are above the other kingdoms of nature.

We have a very different feeling after death, however, when we undergo the experience I just described. We no longer feel that we are confronting the inferior kingdoms of nature, but kingdoms of the spiritual world that are superior to us. We feel that we are of the lowest kingdom, while the others stand above us.

Thus, in undergoing all that was previously left unexperienced, we feel beings far higher than we are all around us. They unfold their sympathies and antipathies toward all we now live through as a consequence of our earthly life. In the experience immediately after death, we are within a kind of "spiritual rain." We live through the spiritual counterpart of our actions, and the lofty beings who stand above us rain down their sympathies and antipathies. We are flooded by these, and in our spiritual being we feel that what is illumined by the sympathies of these lofty beings of the higher hierarchies will be accepted by the universe as a good element for the future, whereas all that encounters their antipathies will be rejected, for we feel it would be an evil element in the universe if we did not keep it to ourselves. The antipathies of those lofty beings rain down on an evil act done to another human being, and we feel that the result would be something exceedingly bad for the universe if we released it, if we did not retain it in ourselves. Therefore, we gather up all that encounters the antipathies of these lofty beings. In this way we lay the foundation of our destiny, of all that works into our next earthly life, so that it may find compensation through other deeds.[39]

The content of the kamaloca experience is in fact the history of our sleep life, with the important difference that it is fully conscious. While asleep, we relive a summary of our waking life, and we relive such summaries on the astral plane after death. Sleep time is also the occasion for the higher beings (whether angels, buddhas, or avatars) to influence our unconscious life. The two phases of earthly life—waking and sleeping—interact

---

39. *Anthroposophy and the Inner Life: An Esoteric Introduction* (London: Rudolf Steiner Press, 1994), pp. 116–118 (revised).

with each other, as do the two phases of soul life, earthly and afterlife. According to Steiner, if we do not take into account all four of these factors and complex relations among them, our understanding of human nature and destiny, both individually and collectively, will necessarily be partial and even counterproductive.

Rebirth and karma are the proverbial chicken and egg of human destiny: with the assistance of the Lords of Karma, the "I" chooses the personal and environmental conditions of its next life on the basis of attainments and limitations summarized by the astral life just prior to its dissolution. By keeping in mind Steiner's account of the four-part human nature, as well as his account of kamaloca, we can follow his fascinating description of the transition from the end of one life to the beginning of another. In one sense, this transition is the work of "I," the spirit principle, but we could equally understand it as the dynamic activity of karmic law. The "I" receives the impression of the astral body's summary and in turn presents it to its own spirit self. It is largely the karmic condition of the "I" at this point that determines the components of the next life— for example, one's parents, body, disposition, and capacities, as well as important intellectual and cultural influences. Steiner refers to the precise moment of transition from the end of one karmic life to the beginning of the next as the "cosmic midnight hour." At that time, the full effect of one's life has been gathered and sorted, and the "I" then begins the slow process of translating those distinctive credits and debits of capacity into the next earthly life.

The most mysterious aspect of the transition to the next life is the way that karma uses the influence of higher beings and heavenly bodies. The various parts of our next body will be formed with the aid of planetary beings and forces. First, the astral body is formed as the soul travels past and absorbs the influence of the spheres of the Sun and stars. Next, the etheric body, too, is formed under the influence of the Sun and stars. Then astral and etheric bodies join with the physical seed in the womb, which has been chosen in advance with the aid of higher beings. In this threefold body, the human being begins a life in union with its soul and spirit. When that life comes to an end, the entire process will begin again, but in the course of this life, the "I" that reincarnates will have changed and, one hopes, improved its capacities and karmic destiny.

The "I" that reincarnates brings with it the essential core of its multi-lived past, following a journey in the spiritual world guided by its angel and other spiritual beings who have a profound understanding of human beings and the cosmos, and particularly an understanding of the striving of consciousness toward freedom and love. Because of this unique past and prospect, we can think of each "I" being as a unique, singular, spiritual species. The distinctive significant fact about the human individual, of course, is that it enters the physical world by way of human conception—which is then joined by the etheric and astral bodies of the reincarnating individual person. It is one of the tasks of each person to make a connection to one's pre-life. Steiner says, "Reincarnation of the spiritual human being is a process that does not belong to the domain of outer physical facts but takes place exclusively in the spiritual domain, and, of all our ordinary mental powers, only thinking has access to this realm."[40]

Typically, Steiner recommends many spiritual practices as aids to attaining insights that he communicated to his audiences in thirty books and more than six thousand lectures. By "spiritual practice" he means meditative thinking, but clearly he also means artistic activity. As he states in the lecture on the arts contained here, architecture and sculpture are "an embodiment of the unconscious recollections of our life between death and rebirth."[41] They reproduce the unconscious experiential memory of the spiritual world before birth, so they "conjure the physical sense world.... If we were not suprasensory beings who enter this life through conception and birth, we would surely not engage in either sculpture or architecture."[42]

---

40. *Theosophy*, p. 76.
41. *Art as Spiritual Activity: Rudolf Steiner's Contribution to the Visual Arts* (Anthroposophic Press, 1998), p. 241.
42. Ibid., p. 241.

Perhaps the most significant implication of Steiner's account of karma and rebirth is simply that each individual person would do well, in this life and after, to think of one's thoughts and actions as part of a vast drama, each person appearing and reappearing, working on the same set of problems, getting ready for the next challenge, the next set of relationships, each one met with one's spiritual capacities developed in a previous life, particularly the abilities to see and to hear spiritual realities. Steiner states, "We are not created anew each morning, nor is the human spirit created anew as it starts the journey of its earthly life.... I start my new life in an environment corresponding to my actions in the previous life."[43]

This view of rebirth and karma is hardly new. It is essentially similar to the dominant Hindu view and has been restated by Sri Aurobindo in terms scarcely distinguishable from Steiner's account.[44] Nevertheless, Steiner has an additional purpose: to bring karma and rebirth into the Christian West.

7. Arts

In response to a request by a young dancer for a new approach to dance, Steiner developed not a new way of dancing but a new art of etheric movement. Superficially resembling forms of dancing and gliding, with distinctive movements, we can think of this new art called *eurythmy* as a way of making the inner qualities of speech and music visible. Like all true art forms, eurythmy is spiritually restorative by forming and strengthening the performer's subtle, etheric body, which surrounds and pervades the physical body. Steiner developed eurythmy for three distinct purposes: as a performance art, for therapeutic use, and for pedagogical use in schools. In addition to eurythmy, Rudolf Steiner also offered new methods and creative innovations in a variety of traditional art forms, including sculpture, architecture, painting, and music.

Between 1910 and 1913, Steiner wrote four mystery dramas so that modern Western audiences could experience, in the form

---

43. Rudolf Steiner, *Theosophy*, pp. 83, 88.
44. See Robert McDermott, ed., introduction and afterword, *The Essential Aurobindo* (Lindisfarne Books, 1987), pp. 92–119 and 257–268.

of drama, the karma of paradigmatic individual lives over several incarnations. First performed in 1907 at a meeting of the Theosophical Society in Munich, Steiner's dramas continue to be performed at the Goetheanum in Switzerland, with its enormous auditorium and stage that Steiner designed especially for performances of eurythmy and mystery dramas. He hoped that the Goetheanum, where virtually all of the arts continue to develop, would give future generations of spiritually searching visitors clues about the health-giving capacity of spiritually based artistry. Steiner's own health suffered a devastating blow when fire completely destroyed the first Goetheanum.

To the dismay of Annie Besant (the leader of the Theosophical Society), Steiner brought a serious commitment to the arts, including his mystery dramas and accompanying arts, to the international meeting of the Theosophical Society in Munich in 1907. In later years, he collaborated with many artists, particularly with Marie von Sievers Steiner, a speech artist. Rudolf Steiner approached each art in response to a request for help by an artist in that field, with an eye for its capacity to transform one of the four aspects of the human makeup: physical, etheric, astral, or "I." In working with sculptors, for example, he emphasized the importance of breathing in a sculpture. In this way, he helped the sculptor bring the etheric into play in the physical substance of the sculpture. Architecture and eurythmy are also art forms that activate the etheric through the physical, whereas music and painting activate the astral body, and poetry is an expression of the "I." Steiner explains that the human astral body "contains the actual element of music":

> After death, when we reach the point of laying aside the astral body, we also lay aside everything of a musical nature that reminds us of this life on Earth. But at this cosmic moment music is transformed into the music of the spheres. We become independent of what we formerly experienced as music through the medium of the air; we lift ourselves up and live our way into the music of the spheres. What we experience as music in the air here is the music of the spheres up there. The reflection of this higher music makes its way

into the element of air; it condenses into what we experience as earthly music.[45]

At the end of Rudolf Steiner's life, when asked if there were anything he would have done differently, he said that he would have spent more time working with the arts and that, for the West, the arts are the most effective way to spirit.

For Steiner, aspiring to spirit never means working only on the interior. It is equally a conscious and loving relationship with the exterior, and most of all it means working in both directions so as to unite the interior with exterior. "Anthroposophy is a path of knowledge to lead the spiritual in the individual to the spiritual in the universe."[46] It is important, then, to work in sculpture and architecture as well as in music and poetry. Whereas architecture and sculpture are an experience of working from the outside, music and poetry work from the inside outward.

8. Society

The economic and social ills of the years before, during, and after World War I led Steiner to develop an elaborate social, political, and economic philosophy that he referred to as the threefold social order. "A healthy social organism must be divided into three branches."[47] It was clear to him, lecturing in 1914, that the failure to develop and sustain healthy relationships between these branches had led to the virtual destruction of Europe: "We are now living in the midst of something that must be called a cancer of our human social life, a carcinoma of the social order. This carcinoma has now burst, becoming what people call the World War."[48]

He based his ideal of a harmonious commonwealth—the exact reverse of the condition that led to World War I and, it seems, to World War II and to the Cold War—on the threefold nature of

---

45. *Art as Spiritual Activity*, p. 244.
46. *Anthroposophical Leading Thoughts: Anthroposophy as a Path of Knowledge* (London: Rudolf Steiner Press, 1998), p 13.
47. *The Esoteric Aspect of the Social Question: The Individual and Society,* (Rudolf Steiner Press, 2001), p. 79.
48. Ibid.

the individual and society, according to which rights and responsibilities are defined according to a proper relationship among the economy, the law and rights, and culture. Among the many significant implications of this three-way division is the ideal of sustaining the integrity of the cultural sphere (which includes religion, education, and the arts, along with all other expressions of individual freedom and creativity), free from domination by the economic sphere.

Because he was critical of the power of the modern European state, which he saw as an opponent of individual freedom, Steiner was neither a socialist nor communist. The state should establish just laws but should not control economic activity. His criticism of capitalism centered on its tendency to allow for the employer to be rewarded at the expense of workers. "The trouble is not capitalism itself, but the misuse of intellectual, or spiritual, capacities."[49] In the tradition of Marx, Steiner considered the major economic problem to be the commodification of labor. He argued that labor must be a relationship between employee and employer, not based on goods or services produced.

Steiner lamented that the modern Western individual has become increasingly lonely: "Most lonely of all are those who have been torn from life and become connected with nothing but barren machines, with the factory on the one hand and soulless capitalism on the other."[50] Steiner provides an analysis concerning loneliness similar to his analysis of scientific materialism, namely that a materialist worldview isolates the individual from the sources of freedom and creativity but it also provides a stimulus for the individual and groups to will a reunion with the inner realities of the social and natural worlds. "Humanity needs to go through this historic moment of loneliness in world evolution, so that, out of their loneliness of soul, people can develop spiritual life."[51]

In the early 1920s, at the request of Ralph Courtney, who was organizing a group of anthroposophists in New York City to implement Steiner's social philosophy, Rudolf Steiner wrote what

---

49. Ibid., p. 85.
50. Ibid., p. 80.
51. Ibid., p. 81.

has come to be called "The America Verse," an expression of the distinctive spiritual striving of the peoples of the United States.

> May our feeling penetrate
> into the center of our heart,
> and seek, in love, to unite itself
> with the human beings seeking the same goal,
> with the spirit beings who—bearing grace,
> strengthening us from realms of light,
> and illuminating our love—
> are gazing down upon
> our earnest, heartfelt striving.

9. *Education*

> A child's reverence for others develops into a reverence for truth and knowledge.[52]

In 1919, Emil Molt, owner of the Waldorf-Astoria Cigarette Factory in Stuttgart, pleaded with Rudolf Steiner for help in educating the children of his employees. In response, Steiner developed a novel educational experiment based on anthroposophic research into the inner life and development of children. That model school became the template for the Waldorf school movement, which today counts more than a thousand schools around the world, including more than two hundred in North America. Waldorf schools, which constitute the largest nonsectarian private-school movement in the world, attempt to integrate the work of the head, heart, and hands (a disciplined cultivation of thinking, feeling, and willing). Waldorf schools are especially significant for a commitment to reconciling the sciences and arts based on a single source and methodology: active, heartfelt thinking. The aim is to educate the total child toward freedom and responsibility for nature, the individual, and the global human community.

Steiner's suggestions for education tend to be very specific on child development, curriculum, and pedagogy. One of the best known and least understood features of Waldorf education is its reluctance to teach reading to children until they are seven

---

52. *How to Know Higher Worlds*, p. 17.

years old or, more accurately, until their teeth begin to change (though many children enter Waldorf kindergartens already able to read). Clearly, this is a topic that lends itself to ridicule; critics and skeptics have no doubt noted that children do not read with their teeth. What now seems to be dogma was first presented by Steiner as his suprasensory observation of what happens in the inner life of the child, which is reflected in the child's physical life, especially in the teeth. The change of teeth is not significant in itself, but it signals important changes that occur in the child around that time. Steiner's *Roots of Education* summarizes this process well:

> We have been speaking of ways to teach reading and writing according to the needs of the soul and spirit of children. If you can inwardly understand the relationship of soul and spirit to the physical body at the change of teeth, you not only see the truth of what has been said, but you will also be able to work it out in practical details. Until the change of teeth, a child lives entirely in the senses. A child surrenders entirely to the environment and is thus by nature a religious being.
>
> At the change of teeth, however, the senses, which permeate a small child's whole being, now come to the surface; they disengage from the rest of the organism and go their separate ways, so to speak. This means that the soul and spirit are freed from the physical body and the child can inwardly develop as an individual. Soul and spirit become independent, but you must bear in mind that the soul and spirit do not really become intellectual until puberty, because the intellect does not assume its natural place in a child's development before then.
>
> Before that time, a child lacks the forces to meet an appeal to the intellect. Between the change of teeth and puberty, the forces of comprehension and the whole activity of soul have a pictorial quality. It is a kind of aesthetic comprehension that may be characterized in this way: until the change of teeth children want to imitate what happens around them, what is done in front of them. Their motor systems are exerted in such a way—both in general and individually—that they enter an inner, loving relationship with all that surrounds them.

This alters at the change of teeth, when the child no longer goes by what is seen, but by what is revealed in the feelings and soul mood of the educator or teacher.[53]

Steiner's discussion of the significance of the change of teeth at age seven is but one of many examples of his attempt to explain an inner spiritual development by reference to physical change. Puberty is another important example on which he lectured at length. Steiner also offered many important observations concerning the transformation that takes place between ages twenty and twenty-one, specifically, the emergence of the "I" in the young person and the consequent ability to chart a free spiritual life. From a spiritual perspective, Steiner discussed all of the stages of transition, beginning with birth and proceeding every seven years through the change of teeth at age seven, puberty at age fourteen, emergence of the "I" at twenty-one, and through each seven-year phase until death. All of these phases, and the appropriate educational processes that ought to accompany them, occur in a social context that Steiner also reads from the vantage point of spiritual perception.

Clearly, we do immeasurable damage to children in elementary schools as a result of testing and electronic learning, among other mistaken and misused forms of pedagogy. Even greater damage seems to be in store for children and adolescents as a result of a failure to grasp, or at least consider, Steiner's understanding of the inner human life.

While reading Steiner's works on early childhood, it seems reassuring that he does not lose sight of his image of the adult human being, toward which children move unconsciously and mysteriously toward their destiny. The teacher, along with the child's parents and family, exercises a decisive influence in this great evolution. The key ingredient in the teacher's influence must be love. Steiner repeatedly stated as a kind of mantra for Waldorf teachers, and it applies equally for parents: receive the child in reverence; educate the child in love; send the child forth in freedom.

---

53. *The Roots of Education* (Anthroposophic Press, 1997), pp. 54–55.

The concept of love in the Waldorf approach to education is not a vague ideal or sentiment, but a deep truth. Love of the child must motivate all aspects of a child's education, including the curriculum, pedagogy, recreation, artistic expression, conversation, and especially the inner life and silent thoughts of the teacher. In a Waldorf school, all teaching should arise from inner, living experience. The teacher must either automatically or by the necessary effort come to love the child's appearance, temperament (whether sanguine, choleric, phlegmatic, melancholic), and development. As Steiner states:

> As teachers, we must aim at turning our young human beings into social beings by the time of puberty. We must also try to cultivate in them religious feelings, not in a bigoted or sectarian way, but in the sense that they acquire the seriousness necessary to recognize that the physical world is everywhere permeated by spirit. They should not feel inwardly satisfied with merely observing the outer sense world but should be able to perceive the spiritual foundations of the world everywhere....
>
> Only teachers whose natural authority awakens the belief that what they say and do is the right thing, and who in the eyes of the child become representatives of the world, will prepare their pupils to grow into really living human beings when, later on, they enter life. Such teachers prepare their pupils not by controlling their intellect or their capacity to form judgments but by setting the right example as living human beings.[54]

Teachers of children under the age of seven have the difficult, and rewarding, task of helping children remain in the world of healthy images as long as possible. Waldorf teachers and the parents of Waldorf students should cooperate in protecting children from images created to sell products or instill fear, while exposing them to attitudes and actions worthy of imitation. "During the first seven years, then, a child's activities mirror and imitate its surroundings—above all through gestures, including the subtle inner gestures that live in speech."[55] Class teachers, who ordinar-

---

54. *Waldorf Education and Anthroposophy 1* (Anthroposophic Press, 1995), pp. 120–121.
55. Ibid., p. 111.

ily (and ideally) advance with their classes from the first to eighth grades, must be worthy of children's trust, so that those children will naturally invest in the teacher's authority. Then, increasingly during the years following the onset of puberty, "children enter the time of life when they can form their own judgments on matters concerning the world at large."[56]

10. *Psychology*

In *What Is Anthroposophy?*,[57] Steiner offers three lectures on Anthroposophy from three perspectives: physical, psychological, and spiritual. The lecture on the psychological, reprinted in this volume, reveals Steiner's concept of the soul, and particularly its placement midway between the body and spirit (the human "I").

Steiner was a careful observer and a learned researcher of the natural world, including the Earth and the human body. He not only affirmed but actively researched the world from the perspective of the physical, the world of "minerals, plants, animals, and a ground to stand on—a world out of which the human being arose as the latest thing in the course of evolution."[58] But he also researched three realms that, by his account, live above the physical and give to the physical its nature and value. Knowledge of these three higher realms is available by three levels of initiation: by the cosmos, by sages, and by self-knowledge:

> When spiritual science speaks of the soul, it must speak out of the spirit of these three levels of initiation: by the cosmos, by the sages, by self-knowledge. In doing so, it traverses the different boundaries of soul life. But it is impossible to begin to take even the first steps on this path without love.[59]

Initiation by, or into, the cosmos is possible by participating[60] the cosmos cognitively. Steiner lectured often and wrote very

---
56. Ibid., p. 120.
57. *What Is Anthroposophy? Three Perspectives on Self-Knowledge* (Anthroposophic Press, 2002).
58. Ibid., p. 61.
59. Ibid., p. 63.
60. In contemporary participatory epistemology, "to participate" is increasingly

precisely on the origin, evolution, and myriad creative powers of the cosmos. This capacity is made possible by a relationship between the etheric world and the individual's etheric body:

> It is the etheric body that constantly stimulates us. Whenever we have a good intuition, it is the etheric body that is inwardly connected with the cosmos, that stimulates this intuition. We receive all the intuitions, all the genius we develop when we are awake, from the etheric body by way of the universe.[61]

In 1900, in lectures he delivered after his experience of Christ the previous year, Steiner introduced initiation by sages. He spoke first of Nietzsche, the person he recognized as the paradigmatic summation of nineteenth-century European consciousness. Steiner then spoke on the "secret revelation" in Goethe's fairy tale, *The Green Snake and the Beautiful Lily*.[62] Later that year, he lectured on Renaissance sages, including Meister Eckhart, Nicholas of Cusa, Paracelsus, Jakob Böhme, and Giordano Bruno.[63] More significantly, in 1901 Steiner delivered a series of lectures on the sages responsible for the change of consciousness prior to and following the incarnation of Christ, most notably Heraclitus, Pythagoras, Plato; the Christian Testament writers Paul and John; and Augustine.[64]

> Looking into the souls of those who came before us in the human soul life leads to the second level of the soul's being. To enter this sphere, we can begin with outer history. We can seek to grasp and understand in an inwardly living way what

---

    used as an active, transitive verb with a direct object in order to emphasize a person's active engagement with its object. See Jorge Ferrer and Jacob Sherman, eds., *The Participatory Turn* (Albany: SUNY Press, 2008).
61. *What Is Anthroposophy?*, p. 60.
62. See Johann Wolfgang von Goethe, *The Green Snake and the Beautiful Lily: A Fairy Tale* (SteinerBooks, 2006). See also, Paul Allen and Joan deRis Allen, *The Time Is at Hand! The Rosicrucian Nature of Goethe's Fairy Tale of the Green Snake and the Beautiful Lily and the Mystery Dramas of Rudolf Steiner* (Anthroposophic Press, 1995).
63. Rudolf Steiner, *Mystics after Modernism: Mystics after Modernism* (Steinerbooks, 2000).
64. Rudolf Steiner, *Christianity as Mystical Fact* (SteinerBooks, 2006).

still shines down to us from ancient times—for instance, the contents of the remarkable wisdom of the Vedanta[65] or other ancient wisdom teachings. Doing so, we actually begin to grasp *our own inner life* and, thereby, begin to approach cosmic initiation. Moreover, if we become truly and lovingly absorbed in such things (as I did in *Christianity as Mystical Fact*, in which I explained the relationship between the contents of the old Mysteries and the Mystery of Golgotha), then we begin to approach the sages' initiation.[66]

Keeping in mind the evolutionary framework in and through which Steiner interprets all temporal events, particularly the possible relevance of past revelations for the present, it is important to note that the contexts of evolving historical consciousness render specific ideas of past sages of questionable relevance for the present. Sages of the past had an easier, more direct relationship to the inner world. That immediacy can and must be recaptured, but the contemporary sage must transform a disenchanted world. The contrast between the task of a contemporary sage and that of the great sages of the past help reveal the origin and distinctive character of contemporary consciousness. The present age invites a sage to look impartially into the unprecedented challenge of contemporary interiority, into the spirit that illumines the soul of the individual and the culture. This is the third level of initiation required in our time: the initiation of self-knowledge.

11. Health and Healing

Scientists, artists, and those in social and political professions frequently asked Rudolf Steiner for advice. He was also asked for advice by physicians:

> The medical movement within the general anthroposophic movement came about when physicians in Germany and other countries realized that modern science and medicine raise questions that conventional methods cannot answer, at

---
65. The dominant school of the Indian Hindu spiritual philosophy based primarily on the Vedas and Upanishads.
66. *What Is Anthroposophy?*, pp. 62–63.

least not to the extent of providing a direct and rational connection between diagnosis and treatment. Those physicians approached me and asked whether Anthroposophy might contribute to the field of medicine by providing more penetrating insights into the human constitution than are possible using conventional methods.[67]

In perhaps fifty lectures to physicians, Steiner classified numerous herbs and other natural substances according to their various healing powers. He often explained that he was working with and recommending an approach to healing based on the fourfold constitution of the human being: the physical, etheric (subtle), astral (soul), and "I" (spiritual). In the process, Steiner showed that he neither rejected nor opposed conventional medicine. For the physical body, which it treats almost exclusively, conventional, or mainstream, medicine was clearly very powerful in Steiner's time and is surely more so now. It would be foolish for anyone to deny that conventional medicine is one of the most amazing and precious results of the modern Western scientific worldview.

All anthroposophic physicians practice mainstream medicine, including, of course allopathic medication and surgery. There are now more than two thousand physicians who enjoy the advantage of a double training and methodology: standard medical diagnostic and prescriptive treatment, accompanied by a capacity for insight that takes advantage of the image of the human being that Rudolf Steiner presented. Neither Steiner nor physicians who practice "anthroposophically extended medicine" regard their approach, or their practice, as a replacement for their own mainstream medical training and knowledge. Steiner explains:

> My purpose in presenting the medical consequences of anthroposophic research is not to introduce new ideas that will contradict the very thorough discipline of modern medicine, which is based on centuries of scientific precedent. The method of research I will describe here is not intended to overthrow modern medicine. On the contrary, it simply explores

---

67. *The Healing Process: Spirit, Nature, and Our Bodies* (Anthroposophic Press, 2000), p. 59.

some of the recent results of the rigorous, sense-based empirical methods that medicine inherited from the natural sciences and the great scope of the questions that arise. It concludes that modern medicine is heading in a direction that it will find difficult to maintain, simply because its well-known sensory-based, empirical research methods are so very conscientious and precise. The same factors that made science great and provided such significant foundations for medicine have also made it impossible to pursue certain ways of understanding the human being and human medicine.[68]

Speaking to physicians during the 1920s, Steiner offered an understanding of the human being that he had presented in his foundational books, particularly *Theosophy*. He offered a view of the human body, health and illness, and an approach to medicine that both complements and offers an alternative to (not a replacement for) "the very thorough discipline of modern medicine." He led his audiences of physicians to consider the reality of the human etheric, astral, and "I" in addition to the physical body, as well as the relationships among these four components of the human being. He also emphasized that, in order to take advantage of every patient's multi-layered understanding of the human being, the physician must be able to imagine the real but subtle dynamics behind the symptoms in evidence. To treat a patient holistically, the physician must think—intuit—holistically. In anthroposophically extended medicine, the physician must intuit the subtle functions of the major organs, particularly the liver, and must come to an understanding of the patient's health and illness in relation to the Earth and to many cosmic rhythmic forces affecting the body.

The prominence of cosmic and Earth rhythms and their effect on the human body, as well as the effectiveness of specific diluted substances in treating illness (as in homeopathy), are among the most prominent components of anthroposophically extended medicine. Concerning rhythm, Steiner claimed, "Some of the many processes that contribute to the functioning of the human body promote rhythm. These processes include not

---

68. Ibid., pp. 58–59.

only respiration and blood circulation, but also those that take place over more extended periods of time, such as the rhythm of digestion."[69] His claim concerning diluted quantities, or potentization, is as follows:

> We were able to prove that diluted quantities of a substance develop astonishing rhythm-based effects. We tested the effect of these minute quantities on the growth of very carefully selected grain seeds. The seeds were allowed to sprout in solutions of metallic compounds in different dilutions. We proved that solutions of metallic compounds in dilutions of 1:10, 1:20, 1:50, 1:100, 1:500, and so on really do influence the growth forces of plants. We graphed interesting and very regular curves, demonstrating that when the enlivening force is influenced in a specific way at a particular dilution, the effect is reduced if the compound is diluted further and enhanced again at a still higher dilution. The result is a curve that alternately rises and falls as an exact expression and confirmation of the effects of minute quantities of matter.[70]

Rhythm and potentization are two of many contributions that Steiner was able to bring to his audience of physicians, owing to his ability to utilize his power of intuition concerning the human constitution and the profound effects on the body of cosmic and earthly rhythms and substances. Steiner emphasizes that mainstream methods of medical research and treatment

> cannot grasp the essence of the human body's structure and functioning.... Although very great advances have been made in understanding the organization of the physical human being, the otherwise fruitful precision of these methods has excluded an entire aspect of the human being that is just as real as the physical. The success of scientific research is directly proportional to the tremendous amount of energy it has spent on excluding the human soul and spirit, which even in a medical context must be considered no less real than the physical human being.[71]

---

69. Ibid., p. 61.
70. Ibid., p. 62.
71. Ibid., p. 63.

Introduction: *Rudolf Steiner and Anthroposophy* • 63

In the conclusion of the lecture in this volume, Steiner commends the work, and particularly the attitude toward healing, of his collaborator Dr. Ita Wegman, MD. At the founding of the General Anthroposophical Society during the Christmas Foundation Meeting of 1923, Steiner appointed Dr. Wegman, one of his deepest and closest colleagues, to head the Medical Section of the School of Spiritual Science. It is very clear from their collaboration during the last few years of Steiner's life that he regarded Ita Wegman to be a physician capable of seeing holistically the inner life of the patient:

> This attitude bans all skepticism, a major obstacle to progress in medicine. The quality that Dr. Wegman possesses above all else is the all-important courage to heal.... When we have the courage to heal in each single case, when our only assumption and intention is that healing will take place, we possess the strongest possible incentive, namely, a truly scientific foundation for medicine. Rational treatments are not worked out as mere consequences of exact diagnosis but are discovered in the diagnostic process itself. Treatment is available as soon as the diagnosis is made.[72]

12. *Gaia and the Future*

Steiner's cosmology, and particularly his account of the living Earth, now appropriately called Gaia, provides the living context for what he refers to as *Anthropos*, the full extent and profound capacities of the human being. It also shows some of the implications of the evolution of consciousness. The concept *Anthropos* should connote the development of humanity, specifically the Cosmic "I," spread throughout the cosmos. The individual who develops higher capacities of thinking can know such realities. Steiner's epistemology, anthropology, cosmology, and account of the evolution of consciousness perfectly cohere. Humanity should learn to activate higher levels of knowing the cosmos, Earth, and humanity. Such knowledge will reveal the true nature and destiny of humanity and the individual human

---

[72]. Ibid., p. 75.

being; all existence, the cosmos, Earth, and every individual can and should evolve unceasingly with every new challenge and opportunity.

At the present time, while in the midst of the rapid evolution of human individuality, it is essential that humanity, every individual human being, reconnect with the Earth, not as an external object but as one's living body. As Steiner states: "The world around us is filled everywhere with the glory of God, but we have to experience the divine in our own souls before we can find it in our surroundings."[73] To reach this true and necessary realization to what appears to be entirely external, the individual must develop sufficient interiority to see the interiority of the cosmos and Earth. "Inner experience is the only key to the beauties of the outer world."[74] The great and urgent task at present is for individuals to activate their spiritual self to be able to see the cosmos and Earth as a spiritual self—exactly what Steiner intends by Anthroposophy: a path of knowledge to lead the spiritual in the individual to the spiritual in the universe.

In his series of lectures called *The Esoteric Significance of the Bhagavad Gita,* Rudolf Steiner lists three steps in spiritual development: instruction in the ordinary concepts of our thinking; the path of yoga (essentially the transformation of thinking, feeling, and willing); and the expansion of one's vision of the cosmos. Concerning the last of these, Steiner describes the profound spiritual relationship between the human being and the Earth.

> When we return to everyday consciousness, we feel how this plant-like life shrinks again and becomes the instrument for thinking, feeling, and willing in waking consciousness. One feels oneself going out of the body and returning into it as analogous to the alternation of summer and winter on Earth. In effect, we feel something summer-like in going to sleep and something winter-like in waking up, not the opposite way around, as one might imagine. From this moment on, we come to understand what the spirit of the Earth is and how

---

73. *How to Know Higher Worlds,* p. 23.
74. Ibid., p. 22.

it sleeps in summer and awakes in winter, not vice versa. We realize the wonderful experience of identifying ourselves with the spirit of the Earth. From this moment on, one may say, "I live not only inside my skin, but just as a cell lives within my bodily organism, I live within the Earth's organism. The Earth is asleep during summer and awake during winter, just as I sleep and awake with the alternation of night and day. Moreover, a cell is to my consciousness as I am to the Earth's consciousness."

The path of Yoga, especially in its modern sense, leads to this expansion of consciousness, the identification of one's own being with a more comprehensive being. We feel interwoven with the whole Earth. Then we no longer feel bound as humans to a particular time and place, but feel our humanity as it has developed from the very beginning of the Earth. We feel the age-old succession of our evolutions through the course of earthly evolution. Thus, Yoga leads us to feel unified with what goes from one incarnation to another in the Earth's evolution. That is the third stage.[75]

Since the ecology movement did not emerge as a force for sustainability and pressure against ecological devastation until Rachel Carson's *Silent Spring* in 1962, Steiner's writings and lectures are not explicitly ecological. Nonetheless, they do provide a solid, perhaps necessary, foundation for what we might call *esoteric ecology*. Steiner's entire worldview, after all, emphasizes the Earth as a living being, as Gaia. For Steiner, the Earth is alive and teeming with physical substances and etheric forces, and humanity is made of a combination, at one level, of soul and spirit and, at another, of these physical and etheric realities. As Steiner affirms the deep interdependence of every organism and a vast array of cosmic forces and cosmic beings, it seems right to regard Steiner's natural philosophy as a model of ecological insight and a corrective worldview for recovery from ecological destruction.

In many lectures dating from 1913, Steiner insisted that throughout the twentieth century and thereafter, the etheric body

---

75. Rudolf Steiner, *The Bhagavad Gita and the West*, Robert McDermott, ed. (SteinerBooks, 2009), pp. 124–125.

of the Sun being, the Cosmic Christ, would increasingly envelop the Earth. In a way similar to the great French Jesuit mystical scientist Pierre Teilhard de Chardin,[76] Steiner offers a vision of the Earth suffused with Christ. This union of Christ and the Earth seems to be so thorough that we should consider actions against the Earth, which is the dominant character of human behavior at present, to be deicide as well as biocide.

Steiner's colleague Ita Wegman, with whom he stated that he had collaborated in previous lives, explains Steiner's intent:

> The Christianization of the teaching consists in recognizing that the destiny of the Earth is included in the destiny of a human being. Whereas Buddhist teaching must be directed away from the Earth,[77] Christian teaching must be directed toward it. Humankind now living will feel itself increasingly responsible for the destiny of the planet Earth itself."[78]

Steiner's devotion to the Earth, and to the cosmos, is clear in many series of lectures, each given in response to a request for help. Answering the plea of farmers, for example, Steiner lectured extensively on a method of agriculture based on his suprasensory knowledge of the etheric forces operating in the Earth, plant, and animal worlds. This method of farming, called *biodynamics*, is an increasingly important agricultural alternative to chemically dominated farming.

Surely, the deepest component of Steiner's ecological worldview is his Goetheanism—his use of the natural philosophy of Johann Wolfgang von Goethe. Spiritual, or meditative, thinking applied to nature finds its fullest expression, prior to Steiner, in the writings of Goethe, who developed what he called "gentle empiricism," especially as applied to his pioneering observation

---

76. See Pierre Teilhard de Chardin, "The Mass of the Earth," in *The Heart of Matter* (New York : Harcourt Brace Jovanovich, 1980).
77. This negative view of the Buddhist teaching concerning the Earth was typical in the West at the time of this statement, but certainly contrary to fact at present. For essays by ecologically committed Buddhists, see Allan Hunt Badiner, ed., *Dharma Gaia: A Harvest of Essays in Buddhism and Ecology* (Berkeley: Paralax Press, 1990).
78. Ita Wegman, "The Mystery of the Earth," in *The Mysteries* (London: Temple Lodge, 1995), p. 97.

of the metamorphosis of plant forms. Goethe conducted thousands of investigations into the world of the plants and thereby began to develop living or imaginative thinking. He entered so deeply and sympathetically into the life of the plants that he realized he was able to "see-think" the plant's essential or formative idea. Goethe's highly conscious receptivity to the inner reality of what he termed the *Urpflanze* (the fundamental creative principle of the plant) is an example of what Steiner means by a path of knowing "to guide the spiritual in the individual to the spiritual in the universe."

While Steiner shared Goethe's interest in plants, and in fact shared virtually all of Goethe's interests, it was not in relation to plants that he sought to give imaginative thinking its most important role. Rather, Steiner claims to show that this kind of inner penetration of the natural world would reveal to the observer a capacity for thinking that is self-referential and self-confirming. Steiner contends that individuals conducting exercises such as Goethe conducted on plants (though it need not be on plants and would be equally effective on any organism or on the process of thinking itself) would eventually begin to notice their own new or more highly developed capacity for the intuitive/seeing/knowing of the interior.

For Steiner, the human development of intuition will lead to an intimate knowing of the world, including the Earth as Gaia, and such inner knowing will lead the knower to recognize his or her capacity for higher knowing through a higher dimension of self. Not only is there no conflict between spiritual development and a cognitive relation to the Earth, they are both positive and reinforcing. In chapter 12 of this book, he states:

> We would have good reason to avoid spiritual study if it took away the meaning of all the beauty that flows into our souls when we observe the wonderful world of flowering plants and fruiting trees or any other aspect of the natural realm, such as the starry heavens and so on, and if, as a result, we were advised to abandon all this in favor of spiritual contemplation. But this is not at all how it is.[79]

---

79. *At Home in the Universe: Exploring Our Suprasensory Nature* (Hudson,

For a large segment of humanity, particularly in the West, this separation of spirituality and love of the natural world is precisely how it is, and has been for centuries. For Steiner, spirituality is cosmic and Gaian:

> We can penetrate to the depths of our planet Earth, to its veins of metal ores of lead, silver, and copper, to everything that lives as the metallic elements of the rocky Earth.... As you perceive inwardly the metallic veins in their wonderful speech, you feel united with the innermost soul and heartbeat of the Earth itself, and you become aware of the memories that are not your own. Memories echo inwardly; they are the Earth's own memories of its earlier states, before it was the Earth.... Thus the metallic veins in the Earth lead us to the Earth's memories. When we have this inner experience, we can understand very clearly why we are sent to the Earth by the divine spiritual beings who guide the universal order.[80] Living in the Earth's memories like this causes us to gain a real sense of

---

NY: 2000), p. 89.

80. This is a reference to the nine spiritual hierarchies mentioned throughout Hebrew and Christian scriptures, as well as the Western esoteric tradition. The hierarchies were first systematically delineated by Dionysius the Areopagite in the sixth century C.E. In his *Outline of Esoteric Science* and in many subsequent lectures, Steiner introduces his own terms for these nine levels of spiritual beings. In his book *The Burning Bush* (Anthroposophic Press, 1997), Edward Raugh Smith provides a helpful chart:

Biblical Greek (Hebrew)	Christian Esotericism	Names given by Steiner
1. Seraphime	Seraphim	Spirits of Love
2. Cherubime	Cherubim	Spirits of Harmony
3. Thronos	Thrones	Spirits of Will
4. Kyriotetes	Dominions	Spirits of Wisdom
5. Dynamis	Mights	Spirits of Motion
6. Exusiai (Elohim)	Powers (Authorities)	Spirits of Form
7. Archai	Principalities (Primal Beginnings)	Spirits of Personality
8. Archangeloi	Archangels	Spirits of Fire (Folk)
9. Angeloi	Angels (Messengers)	Sons of Life (or of Twilight)

our own thinking for the first time. Because we have comprehended Earth's memories, we feel how our thinking is connected with the Earth itself. And the moment we make the Earth's memories our own, we are surrounded by the beings of the second hierarchy (kyriotetes, dynamis, and exusiai). This is how, even in earthly life, we may be surrounded by the beings who surround us at a certain time between death and a new birth.... We fully realize that we contact beings of the second hierarchy while we are incarnated on Earth between birth and death. But these beings do more than work with us between death and rebirth to transform our being; they also play a role in forming the cosmos as a whole. Here we see how the higher cosmic order gives these beings the responsibility for everything in the Earth related to the influences of those veins of metal.[81]

Steiner noted frequently that ancient texts such as the Bhagavad Gita retain some sense of the ways in which these beings built up the Earth and guide the human being between death and rebirth. From contemporary scientific cosmology, as well as through esoteric research, Steiner was aware of the ways in which the human being, as well as humanity and the Earth, can be overcome by feelings of insignificance in relation to the unfathomable vastness of the universe. He also frequently emphasized, however, that the human being is not adrift in a meaningless cosmos, but is a carefully attended resident of the universe guided by beings of infinite wisdom. The "starry worlds" are alive in human beings during their lives on Earth, and active on human beings between death and rebirth. Steiner once again emphasizes the advantage of spiritual or esoteric knowledge, in this case with respect to the living Earth:

> When observed with the ordinary senses, the metallic substances initially do little more than suggest the various kinds of earth in which they occur. But when we penetrate the Earth with the spiritually honed perception that tells us about the human spirit, something special happens to the metallic elements within the Earth. All the copper, silver, and gold in the Earth begin to speak in a rich and mysterious

---
81. Ibid., pp. 93–95.

language. As we live on Earth, we are confronted by something that gives us a more intimate relationship with the living soul being of the Earth itself. Metal ores tell us something—they become cosmic memories for us.... Along with the Earth, one remembers those ancient days when the Earth was united with the other planets in our solar system. One recalls ages when the Earth had not yet separated, because it had not yet condensed and become firm within as it is today. One recalls a time when the whole solar system was an ensouled, living organism, and human beings lived within it in a very different form.[82]

Steiner describes the role of the hierarchies in the formation and guidance of the Earth and humanity. Spoken in 1923, these words, if taken seriously, could deepen every book, essay, and lecture about the current threat of ecological devastation. Note that Steiner does not state that the predicted natural catastrophes toward which humanity is headed owing to global warming and species extinction will, or will not, happen. Rather, his lectures on this theme serve notice that humanity must restore its relation to the inner life of the Earth—in particular, to the Earth as a living expression of the inner life of the cosmos, the nine spiritual hierarchies. This is what it means for humanity to be "at home in the universe."

Steiner recounts that, in a sense, the angels, archangels, and archai whisper to human beings who are listening ("those who have ears to hear") that those beings participate in cosmic creation: we are the creative beings of the cosmos, and we look down on Earth existence upon the earthly forms shaped by the quartz rock and its relatives. Steiner explains that, as a result of this revelation by the angels, archangels, and archai, human beings in the spiritual world, after their death, recognize that they must return to Earth, because that is the only way for humanity to perceive the activities of the hierarchies on Earth. Steiner concludes, "To understand the human being, we must reach into all the mysteries involved in the being of nature as well as in the spirit of the cosmos. Ultimately, human beings are intimately connected with

---

82. Ibid., pp. 93–94.

all the mysteries of nature and universal spirit. The human being is in fact a universe in miniature."[83]

The Anthroposophical Society

In response to the needs of individuals who felt called to practice suprasensory, heart-filled thinking, Steiner founded the Anthroposophical Society, with the School of Spiritual Science as its core, as well as the anthroposophic movement. These are means of providing increased opportunities for collaboration and mutual support. By the time of the Christmas Foundation Meeting in 1923, Steiner's followers had spent ten years implementing his insights and, to a lesser extent, their own. The results, however, had proved uneven at best. In some respects, Steiner's life work was nearly in ruins: both the Goetheanum (destroyed by arson) and the anthroposophists themselves (given to dissension and dependency on Rudolf Steiner) seemed to suggest that the task of bringing Anthroposophy into the world was going to be more difficult than its founder had anticipated.

At the Christmas Foundation Meeting, Rudolf Steiner founded a public society, the members of which had (and have) simply to affirm the value of the kind of spiritual-scientific research conducted at or sponsored by the Goetheanum—that is, the spiritual-scientific research that Rudolf Steiner recommended. Soon afterward, he also founded an esoteric School of Spiritual Science. The General Anthroposophical Society is both an esoteric and exoteric community continuous with the Christian esoteric tradition, but is distinctively modern in its emphasis on individuality and freedom. Steiner intended the School of Spiritual Science to be a source and guide of esoteric teaching. As an esoteric community, it has its source and inspiration from the spiritual world. Members of this esoteric school are expected to be in the process of transforming spiritual-scientific content into a living soul mood, one that expresses warm and loving truths concerning the full range of human concerns.

Steiner created six sections of the School of Spiritual Science intended for individuals who were prepared to work out

---

83. Ibid., p. 104.

of the esoteric core of Anthroposophy: general Anthroposophy and pedagogy, speech and music, visual arts, letters, mathematics and astronomy, and natural science. In recent years, sections have been added for work in pedagogy, social sciences, nutrition and agriculture, and the spiritual striving of youth. More than eighty years after the founding of the General Anthroposophical Society and the School of Spiritual Science, spiritual research continues in a host of disciplines and on a wide range of critical issues, including cancer, soil research, early childhood and aging, new forms of banking, and others.

One of the most pressing problems facing the Anthroposophical Society and anthroposophists is the nearly overwhelming impact of Steiner's vast knowledge. It remains to be seen whether anthroposophists will pay sufficient attention to Steiner's recommendations concerning spiritual practice, particularly meditation, without which his research will become a resting place rather than, as he intended, a base for future research. The obvious significance of the Waldorf school movement, as well as spiritual-scientific research in sciences, social sciences, and arts, however, seem to suggest that Anthroposophy will eventually make an important, and perhaps even widely transformative, contribution to cultural renewal.

Membership in the Anthroposophical Society is open to all who wish to affirm the kind of esoteric research conducted by the Goetheanum. To become a member of the inner core of the Anthroposophical Society, the School of Spiritual Science, one should be a practitioner of Anthroposophy and be willing to represent it positively in the world.

Significant Events in the Life of Rudolf Steiner

A Chronological Survey (1861–1925)

Compiled by Paul M. Allen (abridged)

1861: Born February 27, 1861, in Kraljevec, Hungary, near the northern tip of Croatia. His father, Johann Steiner (1829–1910), is employed by the Southern Austrian Railway; his mother is Franziska Steiner (born Blie, 1834–1918). Both parents are from lower Austria.

1863–1868: Childhood in Pottschach, a stop along the Semmering line of the Southern Austrian Railway.

1868–1878: Youth in Neudörfl, on the River Leitha in the Burgenland. High school, Neustadt, 1872–1879.

1879: Enters technical college, Vienna at 18. Subjects: natural history, mathematics, and chemistry. Extensive philosophical reading, attended philosophy lectures at the University of Vienna. Karl Julius Schröer: German literature, especially Goethe. Met Felix Koguzki, the herb gatherer.

1883: Through Schröer, begins at 22 to edit Goethe's *Natural Scientific Writings* for Josef Kürschner's edition.

1886: Writes *Goethe's Theory of Knowledge: An Outline of the Epistemology of His Worldview.* Friendship with Marie Eugenie delle Grazie, Tutor and friend of the Specht family. Foundations in relations to education and psychology.

1888: Lectures before the Goethe Society of Vienna: *Goethe as the Father of a New Aesthetics.*

1889: First visit to Germany. Visits the Goethe-Schiller Archives at Weimar to discuss work he is to undertaking on the Weimar edition. Talks with Eduard von Hartmann. In Vienna enters friendship with Rosa and Karl Mayreder and with Marie Lang and theosophists.

1890: Moves to Weimar; end of his Vienna life. Enters the Goethe-Schiller Archives as a collaborator to edit the *Natural Scientific Writings of Goethe* for the Sophia Weimar edition of Goethe's works. Friendship with Hermann Grimm, Helmholtz, and Haeckel.
1891: Receives Ph.D. at University of Rostock. Thesis: *Truth and Knowledge,* published 1892. Lectured in Weimar and Vienna.
1892: Rudolf Steiner's *Truth and Knowledge* published.
1894: *Intuitive Thinking as a Spiritual Path: A Philosophy of Freedom* published. Visit to Friedrich Nietzsche's home.
1895: *Friedrich Nietzsche: Fighter for Freedom* is published.
1897: *Goethe's World View* published in Weimar. Begins work as editor of the *Review of Literature.* Moves to Berlin. Activities as editor, critic, and writer.
1898: Inner life passes through a "severe test." Articles in the *Review* show seed of future work in the art of speech. Experience of the darkness of the time.
1899: August 1899: articles on Goethe's fairy tale, *The Green Snake and the Beautiful Lily.* Marriage to Anna Eunike, October 31. Begins work as lecturer in the Workers' School, Berlin. Courses in public speaking, literature, and history. End of the struggle, in which he finds himself "standing in the spiritual presence of the Mystery of Golgotha in a most profound and solemn festival of knowledge."
1900: *The Riddles of Philosophy* published. *Haeckel and His Opponents* published. On June 17, gives the address at the 500th anniversary of Guttenberg. September 13, gives a memorial address for Friedrich Nietzsche for *Die Kommenden.* September 22, gives first lecture in Brockdorff's Theosophical Library, Berlin on Nietzsche; September 29, speaks on the secret revelation in Goethe's fairy tale. October 6, begins the cycle of lectures in the theosophical library (published in English as *Mystics after Modernism*).
1901: Cycle of lectures in the theosophical library: *From Buddha to Christ.* October 5, begins cycle of 25 lectures: *Christianity as Mystical Fact* (published 1902) .
1902: Founding of German Section of the theosophical Society, Berlin, October 19–20, with Steiner as general secretary and Marie von Sivers as secretary, in presence of Annie

Besant. October 20, gives first lecture on Anthroposophy. With Marie von Sivers, he makes his first visit to London in July to attend the annual meeting of the European sections of the Theosophical Society. *Goethe's Standard of the Soul* published.

1903: Development of theosophical work in Berlin and other cities of Germany. Establishes Theosophical Society headquarters. Attends the General Assembly of the Federation of the European Sections of the Theosophical Society, London, July 3 and 4. *Reincarnation and Karma* and *How Karma Works* published. *Luzifer* periodical begun.

1904: June, *Theosophy: An Introduction to the Spiritual Processes in Human Life and in the Cosmos* published. Also in June, attends Theosophical Congress in Amsterdam; lectures on mathematics and esotericism. First large lecture tours through Germany. Name of periodical changed to *Lucifer-Gnosis*, in which *Cosmic Memory* is serialized.

1905: *Schiller and Our Times* appears as first publication of the Philosophisch-Anthroposophischer Verlag, Berlin. Lectures on Richard Wagner. Extension of lecturing activities through Germany and Switzerland.

1906: *The Gates of Knowledge* published as a series of articles in *Lucifer-Gnosis*, May and June. Lecture course, *Founding a Science of the Spirit* (*At the Gates of Theosophy*), in Stuttgart. Meeting with Edouard Schuré.

1907: May 19, the Munich Congress of the Theosophical Society opens. *Occult Seals and Columns*. Lecture cycle in Munich, *The Theosophy of Rosicrucians*. Publication of the lecture, "The Education of the Child in the Light of Spiritual Science," which contains the fundamentals of Steiner education. Lecture tours continue in Germany, Czechoslovakia, and Switzerland.

1908: *Philosophy and Anthroposophy* published. First two lecture tours to Norway and Sweden: lectures in Germany, Netherlands, Denmark, Switzerland, Hungary, Austria, and Czechoslovakia. Lecture cycles *The Gospel of John* (Hamburg): *The Apocalypse of John* (Nuremberg): *Universe, Earth and Man* (Stuttgart): *Egyptian Myths and Mysteries* (Leipzig); single lectures on Kasper Hauser, Jakob Böhme, and the meaning of fairy tales.

1909: *An Outline of Esoteric Science* published. Lecture cycles *The Spiritual Hierarchies* (Düsseldorf); *The Gospel of John in Relation to Other Gospels* (Kassel); *The East in the Light of the West* (Munich); *The Gospel of St. Luke* (Basel); *Metamorphoses of the Soul* (Berlin); *Paths of Experience* (Berlin); *The Christ Impulse and the Development of "I"-Consciousness* (Berlin). Theosophical Congress in Budapest in May; last meeting between Rudolf Steiner and Annie Besant.

1910: August, the first mystery drama, *The Portal of Initiation*, performed in Munich. Lecture tours in Scandinavia, Austria, Italy, Denmark, and Switzerland. *Macrocosm and Microcosm* (Vienna); *The Manifestations of Karma* (Hamburg); *The Mission of the Folk Souls* (Oslo); *Genesis, Secrets of the Biblical Story of Creation* (Munich); *Gospel of Matthew* (Bern); *Background to the Gospel of St. Mark* (Berlin); Announcement of the lecture course *The Reappearance of Christ in the Etheric Realm* (Stockholm, Kassel, Stuttgart) Lectures *Occult History* (Stuttgart).

1911: The second mystery drama, *The Soul's Probation*. First lectures on *Faust*. Lecture cycles in various cities. *Occult Physiology* (Prague); *Wonders of the World* (Munich); *From Jesus to Christ* (Karlsruhe); *The Inner Realities of Evolution* (Berlin); *The World of the Senses and the World of the Spirit* (Hanover). At the International Philosophical Congress in Bologna. April 8, lectures: *The Psychological Foundations of Anthroposophy*; in June, *The Spiritual Guidance of Man and Humanity* (Copenhagen).

1912: The third mystery drama, *The Guardian of the Threshold*. Publication of *The Calendar of the Soul* and *A Way of Self-Knowledge*. *The Mission of Christian Rosenkreutz* (Vienna); *Spiritual Beings in the Heavenly Bodies and in the Kingdoms of Nature* (Helsinki); *Earthly and Cosmic Man* (Berlin); *The Spiritual Foundations of Morality* (Norrköping, Sweden); *Man in the Light of Occultism, Theosophy, Philosophy* (Oslo); *The Gospel of St. Mark* (Basel); *Life between Death and Rebirth* (Berlin); *The Bhagavad Gita and the Epistles of St. Paul* (Cologne). The beginning of the art of eurythmy. First preparations for establishing the Anthroposophical Society.

1913: The fourth mystery drama, *The Soul's Awakening*. Publishes *The Threshold of the Spiritual World*. Foundation of the Anthroposophical Society in Berlin February 2–3. Lecture tours. *The Mysteries of the East and of Christianity* (Berlin); *The Effects of Occult Development* (The Hague); *The Secrets of the Threshold* (Munich); *The Fifth Gospel* (Oslo); *Christ and the Spiritual World* (Leipzig). September 20, Steiner lays the cornerstone of the Goetheanum in Dornach, Switzerland, which becomes the center for the General Anthroposophical Society and Anthroposophy.

1914: January, Steiner leads the second general meeting of the Anthroposophical Society in Berlin, followed by the lecture course *Human and Cosmic Thought*. Speaks in many places about plans for a new building to be constructed in Dornach, initially called *Johannesbau*, later the *Goetheanum*. Lecture courses: *Life between Death and Rebirth* (Vienna); *Ways to a New Style of Architecture* (Dornach); *Christ and the Human Soul* (Norrköping). Visits Paris and Chartres with Edouard Schuré. Marries Marie von Sivers, December 24.

1915: The events of World War I curtail Steiner's lecture tours, and he spends much time in Dornach with the work on the Goetheanum. Lectures in Austria, Germany, and Switzerland. September lecture course: *Eurythmy as Visible Speech*.

1916: Lectures on the war; the spiritual activity behind history; Goethe's *Faust*; and reincarnation and karma. Begins the great series of lectures, *The History of Art*. His book *The Riddle of Humanity* published in September.

1917: Steiner's book, *The Riddles of the Soul*, appears. Lecture courses include *Cosmic and Human Metamorphoses* (Berlin); *Building Stones to a New Understanding of the Mystery of Golgotha* (Berlin); *The Karma of Materialism* (Berlin); *The Fall of the Spirits of Darkness* (Dornach).

1918: With the end of World War I, a European social crisis is approaching. Steiner tries to help people comprehend their current tasks by understanding the past. He presents a new view of the future in the light of present needs. Steiner's many lecture courses include *Earthly Death and Cosmic Life* (Berlin); *Anthroposophic Life Gifts* (Berlin); *Occult*

Psychology (Dornach); *Historical Symptomatology* (Dornach); *The Social Needs of Our Time* (Dornach); *How Can Mankind Find the Christ Again?* (Dornach). The Movement for the Threefold Social Order begins.

1919: Steiner's *Towards Social Renewal* is published. The first Waldorf school opens in Stuttgart. Steiner gives courses on education to the school's faculty and becomes active in the school's operation. He gives lecture courses on social matters. The first comprehensive science course for scientists at Dornach. Further developments of speech, drama, and eurythmy. Steiner speaks to workers at several large factories in Germany about his ideas on a threefold commonwealth. Goethe's *Faust* is performed at the Goetheanum.

1920: The Goetheanum opens. Second course for scientists. First course for physicians. Lectures on Thomas Aquinas, threefold commonwealth, education, speech, and color.

1921: The course on astronomy and on lecturing (Stuttgart). Courses on color, medicine and therapy, therapeutic eurythmy, and education. First courses to theologians (June and September). The Scientific Research Laboratory is established in Dornach. Courses given for the workers at the Goetheanum.

1922: Lecture tour through Germany: *The Nature of Anthroposophy* with eurythmy. Lectures in Holland and England, *New Ideals in Education*. The East/West Congress in Vienna, June 1–12. The *World Economy* course in Dornach. Oxford University in August, *The Spiritual Foundations of Education*; in September, *Cosmology, Religion and Philosophy* and a course for theologians, which leads to the establishment of the Christian Community. Lectures to the youth, *Becoming the Archangel Michael's Companions*. The beginning of biodynamic agriculture and gardening (Dornach). In December, the course *Man and the World of Stars* and a course on natural science. On the night of December 31, 1922, the Goetheanum is destroyed by an arsonist's fire.

1923: Throughout the year, preparation for reorganizing the Anthroposophical Society in Germany, Switzerland, Austria, Norway, England, and The Netherlands. The lecture course *Eurythmy as Visible Song* and courses on education, the arts, history of the anthroposophic movement, the four archangels, human nature, and mystery centers. In England, *Education and Modern Spiritual Life*. The Christmas Conference for establishing the General Anthroposophical Society from Christmas to January 1, accompanied by the lecture course *World History in the Light of Anthroposophy*.

1924: Continuing into 1925, Steiner's *Autobiography* published in seventy installments in the Anthroposophical Society newsletter. Steiner writes *Anthroposophical Leading Thoughts* (including *The Michael Mystery*) and letters to the members (*The Life, Nature, and Cultivation of Anthroposophy*). Courses on medicine for physicians; *Curative Education*; *Anthroposophy and the Inner Life*; education; eurythmy; and Anthroposophy. An extensive series of lectures on *Karmic Relationships: Esoteric Studies*; also *Eurythmy as Visible Speech*; biodynamic agriculture; *Speech and Drama* for actors; and *The Apocalypse* for theologians. Steiner lectures in Germany, Czechoslovakia, France, The Netherlands, and England. His final lecture was on Michaelmas, September 28, 1924.

1925: Steiner dies in his studio in Dornach on March 30.

Autobiographical Notes

"The Barr Document"

Rudolf Steiner

I

My attention was drawn to Kant at an early stage. At fifteen and sixteen I studied Kant intensively, and before going to college in Vienna I had an intense interest in Kant's early nineteenth century orthodox followers, who have been completely forgotten by official historians of thought in Germany and are rarely mentioned. In addition, I immersed myself in Fichte and Schelling. During this period—and this is already because of external spiritual influences—I gained complete understanding of the concept of time. This knowledge was in no way connected with my studies and was guided totally by the spiritual life. I understood that there is a regressing evolution, the occult astral, which interferes with the one progressing. This knowledge is the precondition of spiritual clairvoyance.

Then came acquaintance with the emissary of M (the Master). Then intensive study of Hegel.

Then the study of modern philosophy as it developed from the 1850s onward in Germany, particularly the so-called theory of knowledge with all its various branches.

My boyhood passed in such a way that, although no one consciously planned it, I never met anyone who was superstitious. If I did hear anyone speak of superstitious things, the emphasis was always strongly on their rejection. Although I became familiar with church worship, in that I took part in it as an altar boy, nowhere did I meet true piety and religion, not even among the priests whom I knew. On the contrary, I continuously saw certain negative traits of the Catholic clergy.

I did not meet the M. [the Master] immediately, but first an emissary who was completely initiated into the secrets of the plants and their effects, and into their connection with the cosmos and human nature. Contact with the spirits of nature was something self-evident for him, and he spoke of them without enthusiasm; thus he aroused enthusiasm all the more.

Officially, I studied mathematics, chemistry, physics, zoology, botany, mineralogy, and geology. These subjects offered a much firmer foundation for a spiritual view of the world than, for example, history or literature, subjects which German academic life at that time provided neither with a specific methodology nor with significant perspectives.

In my first years at college in Vienna I became acquainted with Karl Julius Schröer. Initially I attended his lectures on the history of German literature since Goethe's time, as well as his lectures on Goethe and Schiller, the history of German literature in the nineteenth century and Goethe's *Faust*. I also took part in his "Practicals in the Spoken and the Written Word." This was a proper college course, following the pattern of Uhland's course at the college in Tübingen. Schröer's background was German language studies and he had undertaken important research into German dialects in Austria; he was a researcher in the spirit of the Grimm brothers[1] and in the field of literary studies he was an admirer of Gervinus.[2] Previously he had been the director of the Viennese evangelical schools. He is the son of the writer and outstanding educator Christian Oeser.[3] While I knew him he was devoting himself entirely to Goethe. He has written a widely read commentary on Goethe's *Faust* and also on Goethe's other dramas. He studied at the German universities of Leipzig, Halle, and Berlin while German Idealism was still a strong force. He was the living embodiment of German education at its best. It was his human qualities that made him attractive. I soon became friendly

---

1. Jacob Grimm (1785–1863) and Wilhelm Grinm (1786–1859), German philologists and editors of *Grimms' Fairy Tales*.
2. Georg Gottfried Gervinus (1805–1871), German and literary historian.
3. Christian Oeser, pseudonym of Tobias Gottfried Schröer (1791–1850).

with him and thereafter spent much time at his house. He was like an oasis of Idealism in the dry, materialistic desert of German education. External events in this period centered on the nationality struggles in Austria. Schröer himself had no connection with the natural sciences.

But from early 1880 onward I started to work on Goethe's scientific studies. Then Joseph Kurschner founded the comprehensive *German National Literature*,[4] for which Schröer acted as editor of Goethe's dramas, also providing an introduction and commentary. On Schröer's recommendation, Kurschner commissioned me to edit Goethe's scientific writings.[5]

Schröer wrote a preface to them, in which he introduced me to the literary public. In this compendium I wrote introductions to Goethe's botany, zoology, geology, and theory of color. Theosophical ideas can already be found in these introductions, clothed in philosophical Idealism. They also deal with Haeckel.[6]

My *Theory of Knowledge* (1886) is like a philosophical continuation of these introductions.[7] Then I was introduced to the theological professors' circles in Vienna through my acquaintance with the Austrian writer M. E. delle Grazie, who had a fatherly friend in Professor Laurenz Müllner. Marie Eugenie delle Grazie wrote a grand epic, *Robespierre,* and a drama, *Shadows*.

In the late 1880s I became editor of the *German Weekly Review* for a short while.[8] This gave me the opportunity for intensive study of the folk souls of the various Austrian nationalities. The guidelines for a spiritual cultural policy had to be found.

In all this, the public display of esoteric ideas was out of the question. And the spiritual forces standing behind me gave me only one piece of advice: "Everything in the guise of Idealistic philosophy."

---

4. *Deutsche Nationalliteratur*, a large project to publish the works of German classical writers, begun in 1882 by Joseph Kürschner.
5. Steiner's introductions to these are in *Nature's Open Secret: Introductions to Goethe's Scientific Writing*, Great Barrington: Anthroposophic Press, 2000.
6. Ernst Haeckel (1834–1919), zoologist and popular philosopher.
7. *Theory of Knowledge Implicit in Goethe's World Conception*, New York: Anthroposophic Press, 1978.
8. Steiner edited that weekly journal for about six months in 1888.

Running concurrently with all this were my activities as an educator and private tutor of more than fifteen years.[9] The first contact with theosophical circles in Vienna at the end of the 1880s had no outward consequences. During my final months in Vienna, I wrote the little publication, "Goethe as Founder of a New Science of Aesthetics."[10] Then I was called to the Goethe and Schiller Archive in Weimar, which was founded at that time, to edit Goethe's scientific writings. I did not hold an official post at the Archive; I was merely employed to work on the large "Sophien" edition of Goethe's works.

My next aim was to present the foundations of my world conception in purely philosophical terms. This I did in the two books *Truth and Knowledge* and *The Philosophy of Freedom*.

A large number of prominent German and foreign academic, literary and other figures visited the Goethe and Schiller Archive. I became more closely acquainted with some of these people because of the friendship which I soon developed with the director of the Goethe and Schiller Archive, Prof. Bernhard Suphan, whose house I visited often. Suphan included me in many private visits paid to him by visitors to the Archive. On one such occasion the meeting with Treitschke took place.

At that time I entered into a more intimate friendship with the German mythologist Ludwig Laistner, who died not long afterward, and who wrote *The Riddle of the Sphinx*.

I had several conversations with Herman Grimm, who told me much about a project that he failed to carry out, a "History of German Imagination." Then the Nietzsche episode occurred. A short time previously I had written adversely about Nietzsche.

With my esoteric knowledge I recognized the necessity of introducing unobtrusively into contemporary thought a movement toward the truly spiritual. Knowledge is not gained by asserting only one's own point of view, but by immersion in streams of thought foreign to one's own.

---

9. See Rudolf Steiner, *Autobiography: Chapters in the Course of My Life, 1861–1907* (Great Barrington, Anthroposophic Press, 1999), chapter 16.
10. Contained in Rudolf Steiner, *Art: An Introductory Reader*, London: Rudolf Steiner Press, 2003.

Thus I wrote my book about Nietzsche by putting myself completely in Nietzsche's place.[11] Perhaps precisely for this reason it is the most objective book about Nietzsche in Germany. Complete justice is also done to Nietzsche as anti-Wagnerian and anti-Christian.

For a time I was considered to be the most uncompromising Nietzschean. At that time the Society for Ethical Culture was founded in Germany. This Society sought morality that was completely indifferent to any metaphysics. It was completely without substance and a danger to culture. I wrote a sharp article against its foundation in the weekly *The Future*. The result was some sharp replies. And my previous work in connection with Nietzsche led to the appearance of a pamphlet against me: "Nietzschean Fool."

The esoteric perspective calls for "avoiding unnecessary polemics" and "not defending yourself if at all possible." Calmly I wrote my book *Goethe's Worldview,* which formed the conclusion to my Weimar period.[12]

Immediately after my *Future* article, Haeckel approached me. Two weeks later, he wrote an article in *The Future*,[13] in which he publicly supported my view that ethics must be based on a specific metaphysical foundation.

Not long afterward, Haeckel's sixtieth birthday took place, celebrated with great festivity in Jena. Haeckel's friends invited me. I saw Haeckel for the first time on that occasion. His personality is enchanting, and stands in complete contrast to the tone of his writings. If, at any time, Haeckel had studied even just a small amount of philosophy, in which he is not merely a dilettante but a child, he would quite surely have drawn the highest spiritual conclusions from his epoch-making phylogenetic studies.

Now, in spite of all German philosophy, in spite of all the rest of German culture, Haeckel's phylogenetic idea is the most significant event in German intellectual life in the latter half of the nineteenth century. And there is no better scientific foundation

---

11. *Friedrich Nietzsche: Fighter for Freedom*, Blauvelt, NY: Garber, 1985.
12. *Goethe's World View*, Spring Valley, NY: Mercury Press, 1985.
13. "Ethics and Worldview."

to esotericism than Haeckel's teaching. Haeckel's teaching is exemplary, but Haeckel is the worst commentator on it. Culture is not served by exposing Haeckel's weaknesses to his contemporaries, but by explaining to them the greatness of his phylogenetic concept. I did this in my two volumes, *Thinking in the Nineteenth Century,* which is dedicated to Haeckel, and the little publication, *Haeckel and His Opponents* (1900).

At present, German spiritual life really exists only in the phylogeny of Haeckel. Philosophy is in a state of a hopeless inability to produce; theology is a web of hypocrisy, completely unaware of its dishonesty; and the sciences have fallen into the most barren philosophical ignorance, despite its great empirical progress.

From 1890 until 1897, I was in Weimar. In 1897, I went to Berlin to edit the *Magazine for Literature* (1897–1900). The publications *Thinking in the Nineteenth Century* and *Haeckel and His Opponents* belong to the Berlin period.

My next task was to bring a spiritual current to bear on literature. I put the *Magizine* at the service of this task. It was a well-respected title, which had been in existence since 1832 and had passed through various phases.

Gently and slowly I carefully but clearly guided it into esoteric paths by writing an essay for the one hundred and fiftieth anniversary of Goethe's birth: "Goethe's Secret Revelation," which merely repeated what I had already indicated in a public lecture in Vienna[14] about Goethe's fairy tale, "The Green Snake and the Beautiful Lily." A natural consequence was that the direction inaugurated in the *Magizine* gradually found a public. Although it began to grow, it was not fast enough for the publisher to see much financial future in the matter. My aim was to provide a spiritual foundation for this developing tendency in literature, and I was also in lively contact with the most promising representatives of this direction. But on one hand I was left dangling, and on the other this direction soon sank into superficiality or naturalism.

In the meantime a connection with the working classes had been established. I became a teacher at the Berlin Workers'

---

14. The lecture took place November 27, 1891, at the Vienna Goethe Society.

Educational Institute (1899–1904). I taught history and natural sciences. The thoroughly Idealistic historical methodology and my teaching method soon proved popular among the workers and comprehensible to them as well. The numbers attending rose. I was called to lecture almost every evening.

Eventually, in harmony with the spiritual forces which stood behind me, I was able to say to myself: you have provided the philosophical foundation for a world conception; you have shown your comprehension of current directions of thought by treating them as only someone who fully supports them would treat them; no one will be able to say: this esotericist speaks of the spiritual world because he is ignorant of the philosophical and scientific developments of our time.

By this time I had also reached my fortieth year. Before this no one must present themselves publicly as a teacher of esotericism in the sense of the Masters.[15] (Every instance of someone teaching earlier has been an error). Now I was able to devote myself publicly to theosophy. The most immediate result was that under pressure from certain leading Socialist figures in Germany a general meeting of the Workers' Educational Institute was called, to present a choice between Marxism and my teaching. But the decision did not go against me. At the general meeting everyone voted to keep me on as a teacher, with the exception of four votes.

But intimidation by these leaders resulted in my resignation after three months. In order not to compromise themselves, the matter was shrouded in the excuse that I was too occupied with the theosophical movement to have sufficient time for the Workers' Educational Institute.

Almost from the start of my theosophical work Ms. von Sivers was at my side. She also saw personally to the final stages of my relationship with the Berlin working classes.

---

15. Elsewhere, Steiner said of the Masters: "These elevated beings have already passed along the path that the rest of humankind has yet to travel. They act as the great 'teachers of wisdom and the harmony of human feelings'" (from a letter, January 20, 1905).

2

In the early part of the fifteenth century Christian Rosenkreutz[16] went to the East to find a balance between the initiations of the East and West. One consequence of this, following his return, was the *definitive* establishment of the Rosicrucian stream in the West. In this form Rosicrucianism was intended to be a strictly secret school for the preparation of those things that would become the public task of esotericism at the turn of the nineteenth century, when material science would have found a provisional solution to certain problems.

Christian Rosenkreutz described these problems as: 1) the discovery of spectral analysis, which revealed the material constitution of the cosmos; 2) the introduction of material evolution into organic science; 3) the recognition of a differing state of consciousness from our normal one through the acceptance of hypnotism and suggestion.

Only when *this* material knowledge had reached scientific fruition were certain Rosicrucian principles from esoteric science to be made public property. Until that time Christian-mystical initiation was given to the West in the form in which it passed through its founder, the "Unknown One from the Oberland," to St. Victor, Meister Eckhart, Tauler,[17] and so on.

Within this whole stream, the initiation of Mani, who initiated Christian Rosenkreutz in 1459, is considered to be of a "higher degree"; it consists of truly understanding the nature of evil. This initiation and all that it entails will have to remain completely hidden from the majority for a long time to come. For where even only a tiny ray of its light has flowed into literature it has caused harm, as happened with the irreproachable Guyau,[18] of whom Nietzsche became a student.

---

16. See, for example, Rudolf Steiner, *The Secret Stream: Christian Rosenkreutz and Rosicrucianism*, Great Barrington, MA: Anthroposophic Press, 2000.
17. See *Mystics after Modernism: Discovering the Seeds of a New Science in the Renaissance*, Great Barrington, MA: Anthroposophic Press, 2000.
18. Jean-Marie Guyau (1854–1888), a French philosopher, was inspired by Immanuel Kant, Herbert Spencer, and Alfred Fouillée, as well as the literature of Pierre Corneille, Victor Hugo, and Alfred de Musset.

3

The Theosophical Society was established in 1875 in New York by H. P. Blavatsky and H. S. Olcott, and had a decidedly Western nature.[19] In *Isis Unveiled,* which has such a Western character, Blavatsky revealed many esoteric truths. However, it must be said of this publication that it frequently presents the great truths it discusses in a distorted or even caricatured way. It is similar to a sight of harmonious proportions appearing distorted in a convex mirror. The things said in *Isis* are true, but *how* they are said is a lopsided reflection of the truth. This is because the great *initiates of the West*—who also inspired the Rosicrucian wisdom—*inspired* those truths. The distortion arises because of the inappropriate way H. P. Blavatsky's *soul* has received those truths. The educated world should have seen in *this* fact alone the evidence for a higher source of inspiration of these truths. For no one who rendered them in such a distorted manner could have created these truths.

Because the Western initiators saw how little opportunity they had to allow the stream of spiritual wisdom to flow into humankind by this means, they decided to drop the matter *in this form* for the time being. But the door had been opened: Blavatsky's soul had been prepared in such a manner that spiritual wisdom was able to flow into it. *Eastern* initiators were able to take hold of her. At first, these Eastern initiators had the best of intentions. They saw how Anglo-American influences were steering humankind toward the terrible danger of a completely materialistic impregnation of thinking. These Eastern initiators wanted to imprint their form of spiritual knowledge, which had been preserved through the ages, on the Western world. Under the influence of this stream the Theosophical Society took on its Eastern character, and the same influence was the inspiration for Sinnett's *Esoteric Buddhism* and Blavatsky's *Secret Doctrine.* But both of these again became distortions of the truth. Sinnett's work distorts the high teaching of the initiators through an extraneous and inadequate

---

19. See Rudolf Steiner, *Spiritualism, Madame Blavatsky, and Theosophy: An Eyewitness View of Occult History,* Great Barrington, MA: Anthroposophic Press, 2001.

philosophical intellectualism and Blavatsky's *Secret Doctrine* does the same because of her chaotic soul.

The result was that the Eastern initiators, too, withdrew their influence in increasing measure from the official Theosophical Society, and the latter became the arena for all sorts of occult forces that distorted the great cause. There was a short phase when Annie Besant[20] entered the stream of the initiators through her pure and elevated mentality. But this phase came to an end when she gave herself up to the influence of certain Indians who developed a grotesque intellectualism derived from certain philosophical teachings, German ones in particular, which they misinterpreted. This was the situation when I was faced with the necessity of joining the Theosophical Society.[21] True initiators stood at its cradle and *that is why* it is *presently* an instrument of current spiritual life, even if subsequent events have resulted in certain imperfections. Its continued fruitful development in Western countries is dependent completely on the extent to which it shows itself capable of assimilating the principle of Western initiation among its influences. Eastern initiations necessarily avoid the *Christ* as the central *cosmic* factor of evolution. However, without this principle the theosophical movement will have no decisive influence on Western cultures, which trace their beginnings back to Christ's life on Earth. If taken on their own, the revelations of oriental initiation would have to stand aside from the living culture in the West in a sectarian manner. They could only hope for success within evolution if the principle of Christianity were to be eradicated from Western culture. But this would be the same as eradicating the essential *meaning of the Earth,* which lies in the recognition and realization of the intentions of the *living Christ.*

To reveal these intentions in the form of complete wisdom, beauty, and activity is, however, the deepest aim of Rosicrucianism. Regarding the value of Eastern wisdom as the subject of study, one can only say that this study is of the highest value, because

---

20. Annie Besant (1847–1933) was president of the Theosophical Society from 1907 until her death.
21. Steiner became a member of the Theosophical Society in 1902 and worked independently within the society's German section until 1913, when he left to form the Anthroposophical Society.

Western cultures have lost their sense of esotericism, while the Eastern ones have preserved theirs. But equally it should be understood that the introduction of a correct esotericism in the West can only be of the Rosicrucian-Christian type, because this *latter* gave birth to Western life and because by its loss humankind would deny the meaning and destiny of the Earth.

The harmonious relationship between science and religion can flower only in this esotericism, while every amalgamation of Western knowledge with Eastern esotericism can only produce such unproductive mongrels as Sinnett's *Esoteric Buddhism*. The correct way can be represented schematically as:

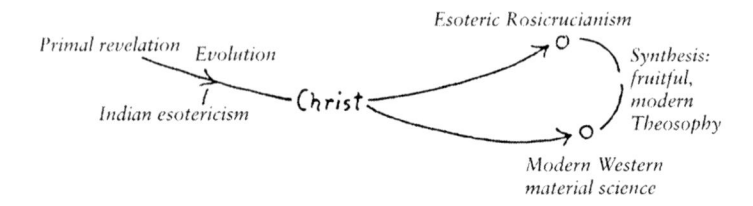

Primal revelation → *Evolution* → *Indian esotericism* — Christ — → *Esoteric Rosicrucianism* ○ / ○ → *Modern Western material science* ⟶ Synthesis: fruitful, modern Theosophy

The incorrect way, of which Sinnett's *Esoteric Buddhism* and Blavatsky's *Secret Doctrine* are examples, would be represented as:

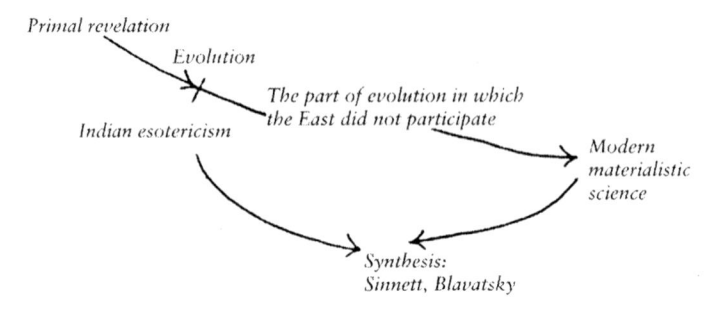

Primal revelation → *Evolution* ✗ *Indian esotericism* — *The part of evolution in which the East did not participate* → *Modern materialistic science* → *Synthesis: Sinnett, Blavatsky*

From "The Barr Document," in Correspondence and Documents, 1901–1925 *(Anthroposophic Press, 1988), pp. 9–19. Steiner wrote these notes for the French writer Edouard Schuré, who was planning a lengthy introduction for the French translation of Steiner's book* Christianity as Mystical Fact.

Introducing Rudolf Steiner

Owen Barfield

Rudolf Steiner was born on February 27, 1861, in Kraljevec (now in Yugoslavia) the son of a minor railway official. At the age of eighteen he entered the Technische Hochschule in Vienna, where he studied mathematics, science, literature, philosophy, and history, developing a special interest in Goethe. Three years later, still in Vienna, he was employed to edit Goethe's scientific writings for Kurschner's *German National Literature;* from 1890 to 1897, at the Goethe and Schiller Archives in Weimar, he was engaged editing, for another edition of the *Collected Works*, virtually the whole of Goethe's scientific writings published and unpublished. His autobiography tells how at this time he enjoyed the friendship of a number of eminent men, such as Ernst Haeckel, the dogmatic exponent of Darwinian evolution, and Hermann Grimm, the historian. It was during this period also that he took his Ph.D. at Rostock University with a dissertation later to be revised and published under the title *Truth and Science*. During the next four years, Steiner became deeply involved in the intellectual life—literary and dramatic societies and periodicals and so forth—of Berlin, while at the same time he began his lifelong lecturing activity by giving courses of lectures under the auspices of the Workers Education Movement.

It was not till the turn of the century that his true genius, unable to find expression through any of these outlets, but which had been steadily maturing within him, first came forth into the light. The historical moment was that one in which the Western mind had reached the lowest depths of materialism, and there were few who would even listen to what he had to say. Outstanding among those few were the members of the Theosophical Society, who were in the act of founding a German Section. Steiner joined it, became its president (making the condition that he would be free to propound the results of his own spiritual research whether or not they accorded with the tenets of the Society) and remained with it for some years, until the sensationalism and triviality which he felt was corroding the sound impulse that had led to the Society's foundation obliged him to separate himself from it altogether.

The next ten years of his life are best seen as the first phase of the anthroposophic movement, and in 1913 the society bearing that name was founded by his followers in Munich, where his four mystery plays were later to be written and produced. There is not space here to deal with the distinction between that and the General Anthroposophical Society, which he himself founded in December 1923, a little more than two years before his death on the March 30, 1925. Suffice it to say that, from 1902 to the end of his life, he devoted all his energies (writing some forty books and delivering not less than six thousand lectures) to the cultivation and dissemination of Anthroposophy—to which he also gave the name of *spiritual science*—and at last, to the affairs of the Anthroposophical Society, which he hoped would become the germ of a worldwide community of human souls.

So much for externals. As to the substance of his teachings and his life, I cannot see him otherwise than as a key figure—perhaps on the human level, *the* key figure—in the painful transition of humanity from what I have ventured to call original participation to final participation. The crucial phase in that transition was, and indeed is, modern man's inveterate habit of experiencing matter devoid of spirit, and consequently of conceiving spirit as less real, and finally as altogether unreal. That experience, for good and ill, lies at the foundation of contemporary science and technology, and is daily confirmed and ingrained by their predominance in all walks of life and areas of thought. Consequently, the redemption of science is a sine qua non for the transition. Goethe's scientific work, properly understood, went far toward achieving that redemption, and Steiner welcomed it for that reason and then went on to develop it further. We see Goethe achieving and applying what he called *objective thinking*, an activity and an experience that transcends the gulf between subject and object and thus overcomes that diremption[22] of matter from spirit to which I have referred. The redemption of science presupposes the redemption of thinking itself. But Goethe refused to think about the "objective thinking" he applied so effectively.

Steiner on the other hand did precisely that and in his earliest writings, for example *Truth and Science* and *The Philosophy of Freedom*, succeeded in transcending the crucial dichotomy epistemologically, too. The thinking of others, such as Hegel and the Nature Philosophers in Germany and Coleridge in England, had taken the same direction, but none of them had achieved their aim so authoritatively or so completely. Coleridge could write of "organs of spirit," with a latent function analogous to that of our more readily available organs of sense, and Goethe could apply his objective thinking to supplement causality with metamorphosis. But neither of them could carry cognition of spirit beyond spirit as phenomenally apparent in external nature; it was in Steiner that Western mind and Western method first achieved cognition of pure spirit. The others were all apostles of Imagination in its best sense, Steiner alone of those deeper levels he himself termed *inspiration* and *intuition,* but which may together be conceived of as Revelation—as Revelation in the form appropriate to this age—as a mode of cognition, to which the noumenal ground of existence is accessible directly, and not only through its phenomenal manifestation, to which therefore even the remote past can become an open book.

It seems that at any point of time when human consciousness is called on to take an entirely new direction, to effect a real transition, a seed surviving from the past is needed to shelter the tender germ of the future. Aristotle, the father of modern science, carried within him his twenty years under Plato in order to turn effectively away from them. In the early years of Christianity it was those in whom something of the old spiritual perception still lingered, who were best adapted to understand the cosmic significance of the life

---

22. *Diremption* (noun) = having been torn apart; a violent separation.

and death of Christ. Gnosticism had done its work before it was rejected by the Church. Steiner himself as a child brought with him into the world a vestigial relic of the old clairvoyance, the old "original" participation. Biographies and his own autobiography bear witness to it. And it is credibly reported of him that he took deliberate steps to eliminate it, not even rejecting the help of alcohol, in order to clear the decks for the new clairvoyance it was his destiny both to predict and to develop.

Rudolf Steiner was in fact not merely a phenomenally educated and articulate philosopher but also a Man of Destiny; and I believe it is this fact that is so grievously delaying his recognition. By comparison, not only with his contemporaries but with the general history of the Western mind, his stature is almost too excessive to be borne.

Why should we accept that one man was capable of all these revelations, however meaningful they may be? But there is also the other side of the coin. If those revelations are accepted, they entail a burden of responsibility on humanity which is itself almost beyond description. It is easy to talk of macrocosm and microcosm, but for man the microcosm not only to believe but to realize himself as such, implies a greatness of spirit, a capacity of mind and heart, which we can only think of as superhuman rather than merely human. The mental capacities which Steiner's lifework reveals even to those who reject his findings, and the qualities of heart and will to which all those testify who had personally to deal with him may reassure us, by exemplifying, that the stature of microcosm is not, or may at least not be in the future, out of reach of man as we know him. In him we observe, actually beginning to occur, the transition from *homo sapiens* to *homo imaginans et amans* [from human wisdom to human imagining and loving].

This biographical sketch first appeared in Towards, *fall/winter 1983.*

The Works of
Rudolf Steiner

I.

Philosophy:
Self and World

Individuality and Genus

THE VIEW THAT HUMAN beings are capable of self-enclosed, free individuality seems to be contradicted by the fact that, as human beings, we both appear as parts within a natural whole (race, tribe, people, family, male or female gender) and act within that whole (state, church, and so forth). We bear the general characteristics of the community to which we belong and we give to our actions a content that is determined by the place that we occupy within a larger group.

Given all this, is individuality possible at all? If human beings grow out of one totality and integrate themselves within another, can we consider separate human beings as wholes unto themselves? The qualities and the functions of a part are determined by the whole. An ethnic group is a whole, and all who belong to it bear the characteristics determined by the nature of the group. How the individual is constituted and how the individual behaves are determined by the character of the group. Thus, the physiognomy and the activity of the individual have a generic quality. If we ask why this or that about a person is this or that way, we must refer back from the individual to the genus. This explains to us why something about the individual appears in the form we observe.

But human beings free themselves from what is generic. If we experience it properly, what is humanly generic does not limit our freedom, nor should it be made to do so artificially. As human beings, we develop qualities and functions of our own, whose source can only be sought within ourselves. What is generic about us serves only as a medium through which we can express our own distinct being. We use the characteristics nature gives us as a basis, and we give these the form that corresponds to our own being. We look in vain to the laws of the genus for an explanation of that being's actions. We are dealing with an individual, and individuals can be explained only individually. If a human being has achieved such emancipation from the generic, and we still want to explain everything about that person in generic terms, then we have no sense for what is individual.

It is impossible to understand a human being fully if one bases one's judgment on a generic concept. We are most obstinate in judging according to type when it is a question of a person's sex. Men almost always see in women, and women in men, too much of the general character of the other sex and too little of what is individual. In practical life, this does less harm to men than it does to women. The social position of women is of little worth because, in many ways, it is usually not determined by the individual characteristics of a woman as an individual, as it should be, but by the general preconceptions that others form of the natural duties and needs of females. The activity of a man in life is determined by his individual capacities and inclinations; that of a woman is supposed to be determined exclusively by the fact that she is, precisely, a woman.

Women are supposed to be slaves of the generic, of what is universally woman-like. As long as men debate the suitability of women to this or that profession "according to their natural disposition," the so-called woman question cannot evolve beyond its most elementary stage. The capability of women according to their nature should be for women to determine. If it is true that women are suited only to the professions currently allotted to them, then they will hardly be able to attain any other on their own. But they must be allowed to decide for themselves what is appropriate to their nature. Anyone who fears a social crisis if women are accepted not as generic entities but as individuals should be told that social conditions in which one-half of humanity leads an existence as unworthy human beings are conditions that stand in great need of improvement.[1]

Those who judge human beings according to generic characteristics stop before the boundary beyond which people begin to be beings whose activity is based on free self-determination. What lies short of that boundary can, of course, be an object of scientific investigation. Racial, tribal, national, and sexual characteristics form the content of specific sciences. Only persons who want to live merely as examples of a genus can fit themselves into a generic picture derived from such scientific investigation. But all these sciences together cannot penetrate to the specific content of single individuals. Where the region of freedom (in thinking and action) begins, determination of individuals by the laws of the genus comes to an end. The conceptual content that, in order to have full reality, human beings must connect with a percept through thinking cannot be fixed once and for all and bequeathed in finished form to humanity. Individuals must gain their concepts through their own individual intuitions. How an individual should think cannot be derived from some generic concept. Each individual must set the standard all alone. Nor is it possible to tell, from general human traits, which concrete goals an individual chooses to seek.

Anyone who wishes to understand a particular individual must penetrate to that individual's particular being, not remain at the level of typical characteristics. In this sense, every single human being is a separate problem. All science concerned with abstract thoughts and generic concepts is only a preparation for the kind of cognition imparted to us when a human individuality communicates to us its way of viewing the world. And all such science is only preparatory for the kind of cognition we attain

---

1. As soon as this book appeared (1894), some argued that, within what is appropriate to their sex, women can already live as individually as they like and much more freely than men, who become de-individualized through school, war, and profession. Perhaps this point will be raised today (1918) more strongly then ever. Still, I must let these sentences stand and hope that there are readers who understand how completely such an argument is counter to the concept of freedom developed in this book, judging my sentences by standards other than the de-individualization of men through school and profession. —R. Steiner

from the content of a human individuality's willing. When we have the sense that we are dealing with the aspect of a person that is free from typical styles of thought and generic desires, then we must make use of no concept from our own mind if we want to understand that person's essence. Cognition consists in linking a concept with a percept through thinking. For all other objects, the observer must penetrate to the concept by means of his or her own intuition. Understanding a free individuality is exclusively a question of bringing over into our own spirit in a pure form (unmixed with our own conceptual content) those concepts by which the individuality determines itself. People who immediately mix their own concepts into any judgment of others can never attain understanding of an individuality. Just as a free individuality frees itself from the characteristics of the genus, cognition must free itself from the approach appropriate to understanding what is generic.

People can be considered free spirits within the human community only to the degree that they free themselves from the generic in this way. No human is all genus; none is all individuality. But all human beings gradually free a greater or lesser sphere of their being both from what is generic to animal life and from the controlling decrees of human authorities.

Our remaining part, where we have yet to win such freedom, still constitutes an element within the total organism of nature and mind. In this regard, we live as we see others live or as they command. Only the part of our action that springs from our intuitions has moral value in the true sense. And what we have in the way of moral instincts through inheritance of social instincts becomes something ethical through our taking it up into our intuitions. All the moral activity of humanity arises from individual ethical intuitions and their acceptance in human communities. We could also say that the ethical life of humanity is the sum of what free human individuals have produced through their moral imagination. This is the conclusion reached by Monism.

From Intuitive Thinking as a Spiritual Path: A Philosophy of Freedom *(Anthroposophic Press, 1995), pp. 225–230.*

2.

Evolution: Cosmic and Human

Egypto-Chaldean Civilization

THE THIRD POST-ATLANTEAN CULTURAL epoch first developed among the peoples who eventually migrated to the Middle East and North Africa: the Chaldeans, Babylonians, and Assyrians on the one hand, and the Egyptians on the other. They developed an understanding of the physical, sense-perceptible world that was different from that of the ancient Persians. Compared to other peoples, they had acquired a greater spiritual predisposition for intellectual endowment, the ability to think that had been developing since the later part of the Atlantean age. As we know, it was the purpose of post-Atlantean humanity to develop soul faculties that could be acquired through awakened powers of thinking and feeling and not stimulated directly by the spiritual world. These arise when people observe the sensory world, find their way into it, and adapt it. Conquering the physical world with these human faculties must be seen as the mission of post-Atlantean humanity.

This conquest proceeded gradually. In ancient India, although the constitution of the human soul directed people toward the physical world, they still viewed it as an illusion, and their spirits turned toward the suprasensory world. The people of ancient Persia, on the other hand, began an attempt to conquer the physical world of the senses. However, to a large extent they still did this through soul forces held over from a time when human beings could reach directly into the suprasensory world. The souls of those of the third cultural epoch had lost much of their suprasensory faculties. They had to investigate the spirit's manifestations within the sense-perceptible environment; their progress came from discovering and inventing the cultural means of advancement yielded by that environment. Human sciences arose by deriving the laws of the spiritual world from the physical sensory world that concealed it; technology and the arts, as well as their tools and methods, arose when they recognized and applied the forces of the sensory world. The Chaldeans and Babylonians no longer saw the sensory world as an illusion. Rather, they saw the natural kingdoms—the mountains and seas, the air and water—as manifestations of the spiritual activities of the powers behind that world, and they attempted to discover the laws governing those powers. To the Egyptians, the Earth was the stage for their work. The condition in which it was given to them necessitated transformation through their human intellectual forces, so that it would reflect the impact of human power.

The oracles that had been transplanted from Atlantis to Egypt originated primarily in the Atlantean Mercury oracle, but there were also others—the Venus oracles, for example. What these oracles cultivated in the Egyptian people became the seed of a new civilization. That seed originated with a great leader who had been trained in the Persian mysteries of Zoroaster and was a reincarnation of one of the disciples of the great Zoroaster himself. If we want to cite a historical name, we can call him Hermes. By absorbing the Zoroastrian mysteries, he was able to find the right way to guide the Egyptian people. In earthly life between birth and death, the Egyptians approached the physical world of the senses with their understanding in a way that allowed them to perceive the spiritual world behind the world of the senses to only a very limited extent. Nonetheless, they were able to recognize spiritual laws in the sense-perceptible world. Thus, Egyptians could not be taught about this spiritual world as one they would be able to enter during life on Earth, whereas it was possible to show them how human beings in the body-free state after death would commune with the world of spirits that left impressions in the sense-perceptible, physical domain during an earthly human lifetime. Hermes taught that, to the extent earthly human beings apply their forces to working in accordance with the intentions of spiritual powers, it becomes possible for them to unite with those powers after death. In particular, those who had worked most diligently in this way between birth and death would be united with Osiris, the exalted Sun being.

The Chaldean–Babylonian aspect of this cultural stream was more emphatic than the Egyptian in directing the human mind toward the physical world of the senses. The laws of this world were investigated, and spiritual archetypes were perceived in their sense-perceptible images. However, in many respects that people remained caught in the sense-perceptible element. The star was pushed into the foreground in place of the star's spirit; the same was true of other spiritual beings and their earthly manifestations. Only their leaders acquired truly deep knowledge of the laws of the suprasensory world and of how those laws worked together with the sensory world. The contrast between initiate knowledge and the mistaken beliefs of the people was stronger here than anywhere else.

Greco-Roman Civilization

Conditions were quite different in the areas of southern Europe and Asia Minor, where the fourth post-Atlantean cultural epoch blossomed. We can call this the Greco-Roman epoch. The migrants to these countries were the descendants of people from many different parts of the ancient world, and their oracles followed the traditions of many different Atlantean oracles. Some individuals possessed the legacy of ancient clairvoyance as a natural faculty; for others, it was relatively easy to acquire it through training. Particular centers not only preserved what had come down from the ancient initiates, but also developed worthy successors, who in turn trained disciples capable of rising to high levels of spiritual perception. This meant that they possessed an inner urge to create a place in the sense-perceptible world that would express the spiritual element in its perfect form within the physical element. That urge resulted in Greek art, among many other things.

If we can understand the Greek temple through spiritual sight, we can see that, in this marvelous work of art, people have transformed the sense-perceptible, material element so that every part expressed the spiritual. The Greek temple is the "house of the spirit." In observing its forms, we perceive what is otherwise observed only by seers. A temple of Zeus (or Jupiter) is fashioned in a way that presents our physical sense of sight with a worthy vessel for what the guardian of the Zeus or Jupiter initiation saw with spiritual sight. This is true of all Greek art.

In mysterious ways, the wisdom of the initiates flowed into poets, artists, and thinkers. In the constructs of ancient Greek philosophy, the mysteries of the initiates took the form of concepts and ideas. The influence of the spiritual life, the mysteries of the Asian and African initiation centers, flowed into the people and their leaders. The great Indian teachers, those associated with Zoroaster and the followers of Hermes, all trained disciples, as well as those disciples or their successors, then began initiation centers in which the ancient wisdom came to life in a new form. These were the ancient mysteries, whose disciples were prepared to attain states of consciousness whereby they could perceive the spiritual world.[2] Wisdom flowed from these initiation centers to those who cultivated the mysteries of the spirit in Asia Minor, Greece, and Italy.[3]

THE COMING OF THE CHRISTIAN ERA

During the post-Atlantean period, human life between birth and death also affected the after-death, body-free condition. As people focused increasingly on the physical sensory world, the possibility increased for Ahriman to work his way into human souls during earthly life and to retain that power beyond death. There had

---

2. More will be said about these ancient mysteries of antiquity in the final chapters of this book [*An Outline of Esoteric Science*]; other details are available in my book *Christianity as Mystical Fact*. —R. STEINER
3. In the Greek-speaking world, the Orphic and Eleusinian mysteries developed into important initiation centers. The great teachings and methods of wisdom from earlier times worked on in the Pythagorean school of wisdom because Pythagoras had been initiated into the secrets of a variety of mysteries during his extensive travels. —R. STEINER

been little danger of this among the peoples of ancient India, since they experienced the sensory world during earthly life as an illusion, which removed them from Ahriman's power after death. The danger was greater for the ancient Persians, who took an active interest in the physical world between birth and death. They would have succumbed more to Ahriman's enticements if Zoroaster's teachings about the Light God had not shown them that a world of the Spirits of Light exists behind the physical world of the senses. To the degree that the souls of that culture absorbed the ideas stimulated by Zoroaster, they were able to escape from Ahriman's clutches, both during earthly life and after death, when they were preparing for a new earthly life. During life on Earth, Ahriman's power causes us to see physical, sensory existence as the only existence, which blocks our view to the spiritual world. In the spiritual world, ahrimanic power completely isolates us so that our interests are focused only on ourselves. People who are in Ahriman's power when they die are reborn as egotists.

Today, through spiritual science, we can describe life between death and a new birth as it exists when the ahrimanic influence has been overcome to a certain extent. This is how the author of this book has described it in other works and in the first chapters of this book [*An Outline of Esoteric Science*], and this is how it must be depicted to show what people can experience after death if they have acquired a purely spiritual view of what is actually present. Whether individuals experience this to a greater or to a lesser degree depends on the extent of their victory over Ahriman's influence. We are drawing ever closer to being all that we can be in the spiritual world. However, as we consider the course of human evolution, we must remain clear that other influences can restrict our potential.

Among the Egyptians, Hermes made sure that individuals prepared themselves during earthly life for fellowship with the Spirit of Light. However, their souls' spiritual gaze remained clouded after death, and their perception of the world of light remained faint, because the pattern of people's interests at that time between birth and death already permitted very little penetration of the physical, sensory veil. Such veiling of the spiritual world after death reached a peak among souls who entered the body-free state from incarnations during the Greco-Roman civilization. They had brought the cultivation of sensory, physical existence to full flower, thus condemning themselves to a shadowy existence after death. Inclined as he was toward the life of the senses, it was a feeling for the truth and not empty talk that made a hero of that age state: "Rather a beggar on Earth than a king in the realm of shades" (Homer).

All this was even more pronounced among Asian peoples who, instead of turning their gaze to spiritual archetypes, also made sensory representations the focus of their reverence and adoration. A large part of humanity was in this situation during the Greco-Roman cultural period. As we see, post-Atlantean humanity's mission of conquering the world of the senses necessarily led to estrangement from the spiritual world. The greatness of this age was thus bound up inevitably with its decline.

The human connection to the spiritual world was cultivated in the mysteries. During certain soul conditions, initiates were able to receive revelations of this world. They were more or less the successors of the Atlantean guardians of the oracles. They were able to see what had become veiled to others through the impact of Lucifer and Ahriman. Lucifer veiled the aspect of the spiritual world that had flowed uninvited into people's astral bodies until the middle of the Atlantean age. If the ether body had not been separated partially from the physical body, people would have been able to experience this area of the spiritual world as an inner soul revelation. Because of luciferic intervention, however, they could do so only during particular soul states. Thus a spiritual world appeared to them in astral array. In this way, supra-human beings revealed themselves, appearing as figures that consisted only of the higher members of the human makeup. These members bore astrally visible symbols of these beings' particular spiritual forces.

After Ahriman's intervention during the middle of the Atlantean age, another type of initiation was added to this one. Ahriman concealed completely the aspect of the spiritual world that, if this intervention had not taken place, would have appeared behind physical sense perceptions. Initiates owed the disclosure of this aspect to the fact that their souls had practiced all the faculties that human beings had acquired since that time, but to a far greater extent than needed to gain impressions of physical, sense-perceptible existence. Through this, the spiritual powers behind the forces of nature were revealed to those initiates, who were then able to speak of the spiritual beings behind the natural world. The creative powers of the forces at work in nature below the human level were disclosed to them. What had continued to work since the time of the Saturn, Sun, and old Moon phases of evolution—shaping the human physical, etheric, and astral bodies, as well as the mineral, plant, and animal kingdoms—constituted one type of mystery. These were the mysteries Ahriman tried to conceal. What had led to the sentient soul, mind soul, and consciousness soul was revealed in mysteries of a second type.

However, there was one thing that the mysteries could only prophesy: eventually, an individual would appear with an astral body in which consciousness of the Sun Spirit's world of light could manifest through the life body, in spite of Lucifer and without any special states of soul. This individual's physical body would have to make it possible for him to receive the revelations of the aspect of the spiritual world that Ahriman can conceal until the time of physical death. Physical death would be able to change nothing in this individual's life. In other words, it would have no power over him. In such an individual, the "I" would manifest in such a way that his complete spiritual life would simultaneously be present in physical life. This being is the bearer of the Spirit of Light, to whom initiates lifted themselves in one of two ways—by being led during special soul states either to the spirit of the supra-human element or to the essence of the powers of nature. Because initiates of the mysteries predicted that such a human being would appear in the course of time, they were the prophets of the Christ.

An exceptional prophet, in this sense, arose among the Hebrew people, who had acquired Near Eastern ethnic characteristics through natural heredity and gained Egyptian teachings through education. That prophet was Moses. His soul had been influenced so thoroughly by initiation that, in exceptional states of consciousness, it received the revelation of the being who formerly assumed the role of shaping human consciousness from the Moon in the normal course of Earth's evolution. In thunder and lightning, Moses saw not only physical phenomena, but also manifestations of that spirit. However, his soul had also been worked on by mysteries of the other kind. Thus, he had astral visions of the supra-human element becoming human through the "I." The being to come was disclosed to Moses from two sources as the highest form of the "I."

With the appearance of the Christ, the great prototype that had been prepared for humanity by the exalted Sun being appeared in human form. In certain respects, all mystery wisdom had to take on a new form at this point. Previously, this wisdom had existed only in order to make people capable of entering a state of soul in which they could perceive the domain of the Sun spirit *outside* of earthly evolution. From this point onward, mystery wisdom was given the task of making people able to recognize the Christ who had become human and to understand the natural and spiritual worlds out of this center of all wisdom.

At that moment in the life of Jesus Christ when His astral body first contained everything that Lucifer's intervention can conceal, He began to appear as the teacher of humanity, and human evolution on Earth began to be implanted with the potential to take up the wisdom that will allow the gradual attainment of Earth's physical goal. The other possibility, which can allow Ahriman's influence to be turned toward the good, was implanted in humanity at the moment of the event of Golgotha. From that point onward, human beings can take with them into death what frees them from isolation in the spiritual world. That event in Palestine is at the center of humankind's physical evolution, as well as that of the other worlds to which human beings belong. When the Mystery of Golgotha was accomplished, when the Christ had undergone death on the cross, he appeared in the world where souls lingered after death and limited Ahriman's power, illuminating the regions that the Greeks had called "the kingdom of shades" with a spiritual bolt of lightning, showing its inhabitants that light was meant to enter there again. What was accomplished on behalf of the physical world through the Mystery of Golgotha cast its light into the spiritual world.

Until this event, post-Atlantean human evolution had been a time of ascent for the physical world of the senses, as well as a time of decline for the spiritual world. Everything that flowed into the sensory world came from what had been present in the spiritual world since primeval times. Ever since the Christ event, however, those who lift themselves to the Christ mystery can take with them into the spiritual world what they have struggled to achieve in the sensory world. Then it flows from the spiritual world back into the earthly reality of the senses through reincarnating human beings who bring what the Christ impulse has become for them in the spiritual world between death and a new birth.

What flowed into humanity's evolution through the appearance of the Christ worked within it like a seed that could ripen only gradually. Until now, only the very smallest part of this profound new wisdom has flowed into physical existence, which is only just beginning its Christian evolution. During the ages since the Christ's appearance, Christian evolution has been able to reveal only as much of its inner essence as individuals and peoples were able to receive and absorb through their capacity for thought. This knowledge was first cast in a form that could be called a comprehensive ideal for life. As such, it opposed the forms of life that post-Atlantean humanity had developed.

Earlier, this book [*An Outline of Esoteric Science*] described the conditions prevailing in human evolution since the repopulating of the Earth in Lemurian times. We saw that, with regard to their souls, human beings may be traced back to various beings who came from other heavenly bodies and incarnated into the bodily descendants of the ancient Lemurians. The various human races arose from this fact. As a result of their karma, those reincarnated souls had widely diverging interests in life. As long as all of this was still in effect, the ideal of "universal humanity" could not exist. Humanity originated in a unity, but up to this point all of Earth's evolution led only to separation. The Christ concept supplied an ideal that counteracts all separation, because the forces of the exalted Sun being, who is the origin of each human "I," also lived in the human beings who bore the name of Christ. The Hebrew people still experienced themselves first and foremost as an ethnic group; the individual was a member of that group. To begin with, the fact that the ideal human being lives in Jesus Christ, untouched by divisive circumstances, was apprehended only as a thought, and Christianity became the ideal of all-embracing fellowship. Above and beyond all special interests and relationships, the feeling arose that each person's inner "I" has the same origin. Alongside all of our earthly ancestors, the common father of all human beings appears: "I and the Father are one" (John 10:30).

In Europe, the fourth, fifth, and sixth centuries C.E. paved the way in Europe for a cultural epoch that began in the fifteenth century and continues today. That fifth post-Atlantean epoch would gradually replace the fourth or Greco-Roman epoch. The peoples who became the vehicle for that age following various migrations and destinies had descended from the Atlanteans least touched by all that had occurred during the preceding four cultural epochs. They had not moved into areas where these cultures took root, but reproduced the cultures of Atlantis in their own way. There were many among them who largely retained the legacy of ancient dusk-like clairvoyance (the condition we described as halfway between waking and sleeping). They knew the spiritual world through personal experience and were able to communicate events in that world to others. A whole world of tales about spiritual beings and spiritual events was built up. Our ethnic treasures of fairy tales and legends developed originally from this sort of spiritual experience, because the shadowy clairvoyance of many people continued until the recent past. Others had lost their clairvoyance, but they developed their acquired abilities, which related to the physical world of the senses, according to feelings and sensations in harmony with such clairvoyant experiences.

Here, too, the Atlantean oracles had successors in the mystery centers that were everywhere. However, the secrets of initiation that developed in these mysteries were primarily ones leading to revelation of the spiritual world that Ahriman had blocked. That is, they disclosed the spiritual powers behind the forces of nature.

The various European mythologies contain the remnants of what the initiates of these mysteries could disclose to people. However, these mythologies also include the other secret, although in a less perfect form than the southern and eastern mysteries. Superhuman beings were also known in Europe, but people saw them as constantly doing battle with Lucifer's companions. They did in fact proclaim the God of Light, but in such a form that it was impossible to tell whether he would succeed in overcoming Lucifer. However, the figure of the Christ, who was to come, also illumined those mysteries. It was prophesied that His kingdom would succeed that of the other god of light. All the legends about the twilight of the gods and the like originated with this European mystery knowledge.

Those influences led to dualism in the human soul during the fifth cultural epoch. That split still exists and is evident in many different phenomena of life. Human souls did not retain a sufficient inclination toward the spirit from ancient times to preserve the connection between the spiritual and sense-perceptible worlds. That connection was retained only as feelings and sensations, but not as direct perceptions of the spiritual world. In contrast, people paid increasing attention to perceiving and controlling the sensory world. The intellectual forces that awakened in the previous (fourth) Atlantean period (the human forces that employ the physical brain as their instrument) were developed in the context of knowing and controlling the sensory world. Two worlds developed within the human breast, so to speak. One is turned toward physical, sense-perceptible existence, while the other is receptive to the revelation of the spiritual element, seeking to penetrate it through feeling and sensation, but without direct perception.

This split in the soul was prefigured when the teaching of the Christ flowed into these areas of Europe. People took this message of the spirit to heart, imbuing their sensations and feelings with it, but they were not able to build a bridge between it and what their sense-oriented intellect was exploring in physical existence. The divergence we witness today between physical science and inner spiritual knowledge is simply a consequence of this situation. The Christian mysticism of Eckhart, Tauler, and others was the result of imbuing feeling and sensation with Christianity, while the exclusively sense-oriented natural sciences and their effects on our life are the results of the soul's other predisposition. We owe all our accomplishments in the domain of outer material culture entirely to this separation of our capacities. Because of our one-sided orientation toward physical life, the faculties that use the brain as their instrument were enhanced to the point where modern science, technology, and so on became possible. This material culture could originate only among the peoples of Europe, because they were the Atlantean descendants who developed their inclination toward the physical, sense-perceptible world into specific faculties after that inclination had matured somewhat. They had previously allowed it to remain dormant, subsisting on their legacy of Atlantean clairvoyance and on the communications of their initiates. Outwardly, the spiritual culture was devoted wholly to these influences, but their sense for controlling the material world was gradually maturing.

Today, however, the sixth post-Atlantean cultural epoch is already dawning. Whatever is meant to arise at a future time in human evolution gradually matures during the preceding age. It is possible to begin now to discover the thread that will reconnect the two sides of the human breast: material culture and life in the spiritual world. On the one hand, this requires that we understand the results of spiritual perception; on the other, we must recognize the manifestations of the spirit in our observations of and experiences in the world of the senses. The sixth cultural epoch will develop fully the harmony between these two aspects.

From Rudolf Steiner, An Outline of Esoteric Science
(Anthroposophic Press, 1997) pp. 263–279.

3.

Anthropos:
Body, Soul, and Spirit

Body, Soul, and Spirit

THE ONLY VALID WAY for us to shed light on ourselves as human beings is by clearly grasping the significance of thinking within our overall being. The bodily instrument of thinking is the brain. We can see colors only by means of a well-formed eye; similarly, only an appropriately constructed brain can serve the purpose of thinking. The whole human body is built up in such a way that the brain, the organ of the spirit, is its crowning glory. We can understand the structure of the human brain only when we look at it in relationship to its function, which is to serve as the bodily basis for the thinking spirit. This is demonstrated by a comparative survey of the animal kingdom: the brains in amphibians are relatively small in proportion to the spinal cord; in mammals it is larger; and in human beings, it is largest of all in proportion to the rest of the body.

Numerous prejudices prevail against observations about thinking such as those being made here. Many people tend to underestimate thinking and to place more value on the warmth and depth of feelings or sensations. They even claim that it is not through sober thinking but through the warmth of feelings, through the direct power of sensations, that we ascend to higher knowledge. These people are afraid that clear thinking will deaden their feelings. This is certainly true of mundane thinking that is concerned only with utilitarian things, but exactly the opposite is true of thoughts that lead to higher levels of existence. No feeling and no enthusiasm on Earth can compare with the sensations of warmth, beauty, and exaltation that are enkindled by pure, crystal-clear thoughts relating to higher worlds. Our loftiest feelings are not the ones that happen by themselves, but the ones achieved through strenuous and energetic thinking.

The human body is built in such a way that it meets the requirements of thinking; that is, the same substances and forces that are also present in the mineral kingdom are put together in the human body in a way that allows thinking to appear. For purposes of the following discussion, we will call this mineral structure, formed in accordance with its function, "the physical body" of the human being.

This mineral structure, organized with the brain as its center, comes about through reproduction and achieves its mature form through growth. Reproduction and growth are characteristics that human beings have in common with plants and animals; they distinguish a living being from a lifeless mineral. Living things develop out of other living things by means of the reproductive cells; descendants are linked to their ancestors in the succession of generations. The forces through which a mineral comes into being are directed toward the substances composing it—a quartz crystal takes shape through forces inherent in the silicon and oxygen combined in it. But the forces that shape an oak tree must be looked for indirectly in the reproductive cells of the parent plants. Through reproduction, the form of the oak is maintained and passed on from ancestor to descendant in accordance with the inner, inborn dictates of life. People had a crude view of nature indeed when they believed that lower animals and even fish could take shape out of mud. A living being's form is reproduced through heredity, and how it develops depends on the parents it came from, or, in other words, on the species it belongs to. The substances that make it up are continually changing, but its species remains constant throughout its lifetime and is passed on to its descendants through heredity. The species is therefore what determines how the substances are put together. We will call the species-determining force the *life force.* Just as mineral forces express themselves in crystals, the formative life force expresses itself in the species, or forms, of plant and animal life.

As human beings, we perceive mineral forces by means of our bodily senses. We can perceive things only for which we possess the corresponding bodily sense. Without the eye there would be no perception of light, without the ear, no perception of sound. Of those senses in human beings, the very lowest organisms possess only a kind of "sense of touch"; they sense only the perceptible mineral forces in the way that human senses perceive them. The degree to which the other senses of higher animals have developed determines the richness and variety of their surroundings for them, the surroundings that human beings also perceive. Therefore, the organs that a living being possesses determine whether or not something present in the environment is also present for it as a perception or a sensation. For instance, what is present in the air as a certain kind of movement becomes the sensation of sound for human beings.

We do not perceive the manifestations of the life force by means of our ordinary senses. We see the colors of plants and smell their fragrance, but the life force is concealed from this kind of observation. However, our ordinary senses have as little right to deny the existence of the life force as a person born blind has to deny the existence of colors. Colors are present for a blind person after a successful eye operation, and in the same way the plant and animal species—not just the individual plants and animals—created by the life force are also present for those whose corresponding organ has opened up. A whole new world is disclosed to us once this organ has opened. From that point on, we perceive not only the colors, scents, and so forth of living things, we perceive their very life itself. In every plant and animal, we perceive the life-filled spiritual form in addition to the physical form. Since we need a name for this spirit form, we will call it the *ether* or *life,* body.

For investigators of spiritual life, the ether body is not merely a result of the physical body's substances and forces, but a real, independent entity that calls these same substances and forces to life. Speaking in the sense of spiritual science, we might put it like this: a body that is merely physical—a crystal, for example—owes its form to the material formative forces inherent in lifeless matter. A living body, however, cannot owe its form to these same forces, since it starts to decay immediately once life has abandoned it and it has been surrendered to physical forces alone [see "Note" page 132]. The life body is present at every moment of life as an entity that constantly maintains the physical body against decay. In order to see this life body, to perceive it in another living being, we need the awakened spiritual eye. We may be able to deduce the existence of the ether body on logical grounds without this spiritual eye, but we can "see" it with the spiritual eye, just as we see colors with the physical eye. Please do not take offense at the term "ether body," but take it simply as a name for what is described here. *Ether,* as the word is used here, has a meaning different from that used hypothetically by nineteenth-century physics.

In its structure, the human ether body, like the human physical body, is an image of its function. It, too, can be understood only in relation to the thinking spirit. The human ether body differs from that of plants and animals in being organized to support the thinking spirit. Just as we belong to the mineral world through our physical body, we belong to the world of life through our ether body. After death, the physical body disintegrates into the mineral world, the ether body into the world of life. The term "body" is used here to designate what gives a being of any kind its form, shape, or Gestalt. It should not be confused with the sense-perceptible form of the material body. As used in this book, the term "body" can also refer to something that takes on form in soul or in spirit.

The life body is still something external to us, but with the first stirring of sensation our inner self responds to the stimuli of the outer world. No matter how far we pursue what we justifiably call the "external world," we will never be able to find sensation. Rays of light penetrate into the eye, to the retina, where they stimulate chemical changes in what is called the visual purple in the rods of the retina. The effect of this stimulus then moves along the visual nerve to the brain, where further physical processes take place. If we could actually observe this happening, we would simply see physical processes like those that take place anywhere else in the external world. But if we are able to observe the ether body, we will perceive how a physical process taking place in the brain is also a life process. However, the sensation of the blue color that the recipient of the light rays experiences is still nowhere to be found; it comes about only in the recipient's soul. If the recipient's constitution consisted only of the physical body and the ether body, sensation could not take place. The activity through which sensation becomes a fact fundamentally differs from the working of the formative life force and elicits from it an inner experience. Without this activity, our response to external stimuli would be nothing more than a mere life process such as those we observe in plants. Picture human beings receiving impressions from all sides. Our sensations respond to all these impressions, so we also picture ourselves as the source of the sentient activity described above, which moves out in all the directions from which we receive impressions. We will call this source of activity the sentient soul. It is just as real as the physical body. If a person stands before me, and I disregard that person's sentient soul, imagining that individual merely as a physical body, it is as if I were imagining a painting as nothing more than its canvas.

With regard to perceiving the sentient soul, we must say something similar to what was said earlier about the ether body. Our bodily organs are blind to the sentient soul, and so is the organ by which life can be perceived as life, by which the ether body can be perceived. But by means of a still higher organ, the inner world of sensations can become a particular kind of suprasensory perception. As we develop this organ, we become able not only to sense the impressions of the physical and ether worlds, but also to see the sensations as such. At that point, another being's world of sensations is spread out before us like any outer reality. We must differentiate between experiencing our own world of sensations and perceiving that of someone else—of course anyone can look into his or her own personal world of sensations, but only a seer with an opened "spiritual eye" can see the inner sensations of another being. Unless we are seers, we can know the world of sensation only as something within ourselves, as the personal and hidden experiences of our own souls; but once one's "spiritual eye" is open, what would otherwise live hidden inside another being shines out, accessible to our outward spiritual gaze.

To avoid misunderstanding, it should be stated immediately that a seer does not experience inwardly the inner worlds of sensations of other beings. Those beings experience perceptions and sensations from their own inner perspectives, while the seer perceives a manifestation, or expression, of each person's world of sensations.

In its functioning, the sentient soul is dependent on the ether body, because it draws from the ether body what it then allows to light up as sensation. Moreover, because the ether body is the life within the physical body, the sentient soul is indirectly dependent on the physical body as well. Only a properly functioning and well-formed eye makes accurate color sensations possible. This is how the bodily nature affects the sentient soul. The sentient soul is thus determined and restricted in its activity by the physical body and lives within the limits set by our bodily nature. That is, the physical body, which is built up out of mineral substances and enlivened by the ether body, in turn sets the limits for our sentient soul. Those who possess the above-mentioned organ for "seeing" the sentient soul therefore recognize it as having limits set by the body.

However, the boundaries of the sentient soul do not coincide with those of the material physical body. The sentient soul extends beyond the physical body, even though the force that determines its limits proceeds from the physical body. This means that still another distinct member of the human constitution inserts itself between the physical and ether bodies, on the one hand, and the sentient soul on the other. This is the sentient or soul body. To say it another way, a portion of the ether body is finer than the rest, and this finer part forms a unity with the sentient soul, while the coarser part forms a kind of unity with the physical body. However, the sentient soul extends beyond the soul body.

For simplicity sake, we have chosen the term *sentient soul,* which is related to "sensing." But in fact, "sensing" is only one aspect of the soul's being. Our feelings of pleasure and displeasure, our drives, instincts, and passions, are all very close to our sensations. They are all similarly private and individual in character and similarly dependent on our bodily nature.

❋

Our sentient soul interacts with thinking, with the spirit, just as it does with the body. To begin with, thinking serves the sentient soul: we formulate thoughts about our sensations and thus explain the outer world to ourselves. For instance, a child who has been burned thinks about it and arrives at the conclusion that fire burns. We do not blindly pursue our drives, instincts, and passions; we think about them, thus creating opportunities to gratify them. This is the direction taken by our material culture, which is the sum of the services rendered to the sentient soul by thinking. Vast amounts of thought power are directed toward this end. Thought power has created ships, railroads, telegraphs, and telephones—all things that for the most part serve to satisfy the needs of sentient souls.

We have seen how the formative life force pervades the physical body. In a similar way, thought power pervades the sentient soul. The formative life force connects the physical body to its ancestors and descendants and, thus, places it in the context of natural laws having nothing to do with mere minerals. Similarly, thought power gives the soul a place within a system of laws to which it does not belong as mere sentient soul.

Through the sentient soul, we are related to the animals, in whom we can also recognize the presence of sensations, drives, instincts, and passions. Animals, however, follow these directly without weaving them into independent thinking, which transcends immediate experience.[1] This is also the case to a certain

---

1. Spiritual scientific statements must be taken very exactly, because they are of value only if the ideas are expressed precisely. For example, take the sentence, "animals follow these [perceptions, instincts, etc.] up directly without interweaving them with independent thoughts that go beyond their immediate experience...." If the modifiers "independent" and "that go beyond their immediate experience" are not fully taken into

extent with less developed human beings. As such, therefore, the sentient soul is different from the more highly evolved part of the soul that places thinking in its service. We may call this soul the "mind" soul, which is served by thinking.

The mind soul permeates the sentient soul. Anyone who possesses an organ for "seeing" the soul will see the mind soul as an entity distinct from the mere sentient soul.

❁

Through thinking, we are led beyond our own personal lives; we acquire something that extends beyond our own souls. We take it as a matter of course that the laws of thinking correspond with the universal order. We can feel at home in the universe because this correspondence exists, and it is a weighty factor in learning to recognize our own essential nature. We seek the truth in our soul; through the truth, not just the soul but also the things of the world express themselves. Truth recognized through thinking has an independent significance that refers to the things of the world and not just to our own souls. In my delight in the starry heavens, I am living inside myself, but the thoughts that I formulate about the orbits of the heavenly bodies have the same meaning for anyone else's thinking as they have for mine. It would be senseless to speak of "my" delight and pleasure if I myself were not present, but it is not at all senseless to talk about my thoughts without reference to me as

---

account, it would be easy to make the mistake of assuming that what is meant here is that no thoughts are present in the sensations and instincts of animals. However, true spiritual science is based on the recognition that the inner experience of animals, like everything else in existence, is permeated with thoughts, although these thoughts are not those of an independent "I" living within each animal. Instead, they belong to a collective animal ego that must be seen as a being that governs the individual animals from outside. This collective ego, unlike the human "I," is not present in the physical world but works on the animals from the soul world described [in *Theosophy*] on pp. 93ff. (Further details may be found in *An Outline of Esoteric Science*.) The point here is that, in human beings, thoughts acquire an independent existence; that is, we can have a direct soul experience of them as thoughts rather than experiencing them indirectly in sensation. —R. STEINER

a person. The truth I think today was also true yesterday and will be true tomorrow, even though it occupies my mind only for today. If understanding something gives me pleasure, this pleasure is meaningful only as long as it is active in me, but the truth of the understanding has a significance totally independent of my pleasure. In grasping the truth, the soul links up with something that possesses intrinsic value, a value that neither appears nor disappears with the soul's perception of it. The real truth neither comes into being nor passes away; its significance cannot be destroyed.

This is in no way contradicted by the fact that certain human "truths" are of only temporary value because they are recognized as partial or total errors in due time. We must realize that the truth, in itself, endures, even though our thoughts are only transient manifestations of eternal truths. Even if, like Lessing,[2] we say that we are content to strive eternally for the truth since the pure and perfect truth can surely exist only for a god, this does not deny the eternal value of the truth, but rather confirms it. Only something of eternal and intrinsic significance can evoke eternal striving and be the object of an eternal search. If the truth were not wholly independent in itself, if its value and significance came from the feelings of human souls, then it could not be a goal agreed on by all humankind. The very fact that we all strive for it confirms its independent nature.

This applies equally to what is truly good. What is morally right is independent of our inclinations and passions insofar as it does not submit to them but makes them submit to it. Desire and revulsion, likes and dislikes, are the property of each individual human soul, but duty stands higher than likes and dislikes, sometimes standing so high in people's estimation that they will give up their lives for it. The more we have ennobled our inclinations, our likes and dislikes, so that they submit without force or compulsion to what we recognize as our duty, the higher we stand as human beings. What is morally right, like what is true, has an intrinsic eternal value that it does not receive from the sentient soul.

---

2. Gotthold Ephraim Lessing, 1729–1781, German dramatist and critic.

By letting what is intrinsically true and good come to life within us, we rise above the mere sentient soul. The eternal spirit shines into the sentient soul, kindling in it a light that will never go out. To the extent that our soul lives in this light, it takes part in something eternal, which it links to its own existence. What the soul carries within itself as truth and goodness is immortal. This eternal element that lights up within the soul we will call *consciousness soul*.

We can speak of consciousness even in connection with the soul's lower stirrings. Even the most mundane sensation is already the object of consciousness, and to this extent animals must also be credited with having consciousness. But the very core of human consciousness, the "soul within the soul," so to speak, is what "consciousness soul" means here. The consciousness soul is different from the mind soul, which is still entangled in sensations, drives, emotions, and so forth. We all know how we accept our personal preferences as true, at first. But truth is lasting only when it has freed itself from any flavor of such sympathies and antipathies. The truth is true, even if all our personal feelings revolt against it. We will apply the term "consciousness soul" to that part of the soul in which truth lives.

Thus the soul, like the body, consists of three distinct members—the sentient soul, the mind soul, and the consciousness soul. Just as our bodily nature works from below upward to set limits on the soul, spirituality works from above downward to expand it. The more our soul is filled with what is true and good, the broader and more inclusive its eternal aspect becomes.

For anyone who can "see" the soul, the glow that proceeds from a human being whose eternal aspect is expanding is as real as a flame's radiant light is to the physical eye. To the seer, the visible bodily person is only a part of the whole human being, the coarsest structure in the midst of others that interpenetrate it and each other. The ether body as a life form fills out the physical body, and beyond the ether body we can distinguish the soul body or astral form projecting outward on all sides. Extending beyond this is the sentient soul, and then the mind soul that grows ever larger as it takes in ever more of the true and the good. If people lived solely out of their own inclinations, likes, and dislikes, the boundaries of their mind souls would coincide with those of their sentient souls.

This formation, amid which the physical body can be seen as if in a cloud, can be called the *human aura*. When the essential nature of the human being is seen in the way that this book attempts to describe, it is supplemented and enriched by the measure of the aura.

※

During our early development, a moment arrives for the first time when we each experience ourselves as independent beings, face-to-face with the rest of the world. For those who are sensitive, this is a significant experience. In his autobiography, the poet Jean Paul recounts this moment:

> Although I have never told anyone about it, I will never forget the experience of being present at the birth of my self-awareness. I can tell you the place and time exactly. One morning when I was a very small child, I was standing in the front door looking toward the woodpile on the left, when suddenly the inner vision, "I am an I," struck me like a lightning bolt from heaven. It has gone on shining ever since. My "I" had seen itself, for the first time and for all time. It is almost inconceivable that my memory could deceive me on this point, since no one else ever told me anything about it that I might have added to. It was an incident that took place veiled in my human holiest of holies, and its very novelty gave permanence to the mundane circumstances surrounding it.[3]

We all know that little children refer to themselves, by saying things like "Charlie's a good boy," or "Mary wants that," and we find it appropriate that they should speak about themselves as they would about someone else, since they are not yet aware

---

3. Jean Paul Friedrich Richter (1763–1825) first described this experience in *Wahrheit aus Jean Pauls Leben. Kindheitsgeschichte von ihm selbst geschrieben* ("The True Story of Jean Paul's Life: A Childhood Autobiography," Breslau, 1826–1828), book 1, p. 53.

of their own independent existence. Consciousness of self has not yet been born in them.[4]

Through this consciousness of self, an individual achieves self-definition as an independent being, separate from everything else, as "I."

By "I," a person means the total experience of one's being as body and soul. Body and soul are the vehicles of the "I," which works within them. Just as the physical body has its center in the brain, the soul has its center in the "I." Our sensations are stimulated from outside; our feelings assert themselves as effects of the outer world; our will relates to the outer world by manifesting in outward-directed actions. "I" being, however, our individual essence, remains invisible. It is very telling that Jean Paul describes becoming aware of his "I" as "an incident...veiled in [the] human holiest of holies," because we are each completely alone with our "I." Our "I" being is the self of each human being. We are justified in seeing the "I" as our true being and may, therefore, describe body and soul as the "garments" in which we live, as the bodily conditions under which we act. In the course of our development we learn to use these instruments more and more as servants of our "I."

This little word "I," as we use it in our language, is a name different from all other names. Appropriate reflection on the nature of this name opens up an approach to understanding human nature in a deeper sense. Any other name can be applied to the corresponding object by all of us in the same way. Everyone can call a table "table" and a chair "chair." But this is not the case with the name "I." No one can use it to mean someone else; we can call only ourselves "I." The name "I," if it designates *me*, can never reach my ear from outside. The soul can designate only itself as "I" from within, through itself. Thus,

---

4. Small children refer to themselves in the third person. Here it is not important how early children say "I," but at what point they can connect the appropriate idea with this word. Children hear the word from adults and may use it without grasping the idea of "I." In general, however, they start to use the word relatively late, and this in itself points to an important fact of development, namely that the *idea* "I" gradually unfolds out of a vague *feeling* of "I." —Rudolf Steiner

when we say "I" to ourselves, something begins to speak in us that has nothing to do with any of the worlds from which the above-mentioned "garments" are taken. The "I" gains increasing mastery over body and soul, which is expressed in a person's aura. The greater the mastery, the more differentiated, complex, and richly colored the aura becomes. How the "I" affects the aura is visible to the seer, but the "I" itself is not; it is "veiled in [the] human holiest of holies."

The "I" takes in the rays of the light that shines as eternal light in each human being. Just as we gather up experiences of body and soul in the "I," we also allow thoughts of truth and goodness to flow into it. Sense-perceptible phenomena reveal themselves to our "I" from one side, the spirit from the other. Body and soul give themselves over to the "I" in order to serve it, but the "I" gives itself over to the spirit in order to be filled by it. The "I" lives within the body and the soul, but the spirit lives within the "I." What there is of spirit in the "I" is eternal, for the "I" receives its nature and significance from whatever it is united with. To the extent that it dwells in a physical body, it is subject to mineral laws; through the ether body it is subject to the laws governing reproduction and growth; by virtue of the sentient and mind souls it is subject to the laws of the soul world. Moreover, to the extent that it receives the spiritual into itself, it is subject to the laws of the spirit. What is formed in accordance with mineral laws and the laws of life comes into existence and passes away again. The spirit, however, has nothing to do with becoming and perishing.

※

The "I" lives in the soul. Although the highest manifestation of the "I" belongs to the consciousness soul, it is also true that the "I" radiates outward from there, filling the entire soul and exerting its influence on the body through the soul. Within the "I," the spirit is alive and active. The spirit streams into the "I," taking it as its "garment" just as the "I" itself lives in the body and the soul. The spirit shapes the "I" from the inside out and the mineral world shapes it from the outside in. We will call the spirit that shapes the "I" and lives as "I" *spirit self,* since it appears as the human "I," the "self."

We can explain the difference between the spirit self and the consciousness soul as follows. The consciousness soul merely touches the autonomous truth that is independent of all sympathy and antipathy, but the spirit self carries this same truth inside itself, taken up, enclosed, and individualized by means of the "I" and taken into the individual's independent being. Through becoming independent and uniting with the truth, the "I" itself achieves immortality.

The spirit self is a revelation of the spiritual world within the "I," just as a sense perception, coming from the other side, is a revelation of the physical world within the "I." In what is red, green, light, dark, hard, soft, warm, or cold we recognize the revelations of the physical world; in what is true and good, the revelations of the spiritual world. Just as we call the revelation of physical things "sensation," we will call the revelation of spiritual things intuition.[5] Even a very simple thought already contains intuition, because we cannot touch it with our hands or see it with our eyes; we must receive its revelation from the spirit by means of the "I."

If a less-developed person and a more-developed person look at the same plant, something quite different happens in the "I" of the first from that of the second, even though the sensations of both are prompted by the same object. The difference is that one person can form much more complete thoughts about the object than the other. If objects revealed themselves only through sensation, there could be no progress in spiritual development. Members of less-developed cultures also experience nature, of course, but natural laws become apparent only to the intuition-fructified thinking of the more highly developed person. Even children experience

---

5. My books *How to Know Higher Worlds* and *An Outline of Esoteric Science* describe the true nature of intuition. Casual readers could easily imagine a discrepancy between how this term is used in those books and its use here. However, such a contradiction does not appear if we observe closely and note that the element from the spiritual world that discloses itself in its full reality to spiritual perception by means of intuition announces itself in its lowest manifestation to the spirit self, just as outer existence announces itself to the physical world by means of sensation. —R. STEINER

the stimuli of the outer world as incentives to their will, but the dictates of what is morally right become accessible to them only in the course of their development as they learn to live in the spirit and understand its revelations.

Just as there would be no sensations of color without the eye, there would also be no intuitions without the higher thinking of the spirit self. The sensation does not create the plant on which the color appears, nor does intuition create spiritual realities; it merely supplies information about them.

Through intuitions, the "I," awakening in our soul, receives messages from above, from the spiritual world, just as it receives messages from the physical world through sensations. In this way, the "I" makes the spiritual world part of its personal soul life, just as it does with the physical world by means of the senses. The soul, or rather the "I" that is beginning to shine within it, opens its doors on two sides, toward the physical world and toward the spiritual.

The only way the physical world is able to make its presence known to our "I" is by building up, out of its own substances and forces, a body in which a conscious soul is able to live and to take hold of the organs for perceiving the external physical world. Similarly, the spiritual world, with its spirit substances and spirit forces, builds up a spiritual body in which the "I" is able to live and to perceive spiritual realities by means of intuitions. (Obviously, the terms "spirit substance" and "spiritual body" are contradictions in terms if taken literally. They are used here only to direct our thoughts to the spiritual entity that corresponds to the physical human body.)

The physical body is built up within the physical world as a completely separate being, and the same is true of the spiritual body in the spiritual world. The human being likewise has an inside and an outside in the physical world, and the same is true in the spiritual world. Moreover, just as we take in substances from our physical surroundings and incorporate them into our bodies, we also take in spiritual substance from our spiritual surroundings and make it our own. This spiritual substance is eternal nourishment for human beings. We are born out of the physical world, and yet we are independent beings separate from the rest of the physical world. In the same way, we are born out of the spirit through the eternal laws of the good and the true, and yet we are separate from the spiritual world outside us. We will call this independent spiritual entity the "spirit body."

When we examine a physical human body, we find the same substances and forces that are found outside it in the rest of the physical world. The same is true of the spirit body—the elements of the outer spiritual world pulsate in it; the forces of the rest of the spiritual world are active in it. In the physical world, a living and sentient being is closed off within a physical skin, and the same applies to the spiritual world. A membrane closes off the spirit body from the undifferentiated spiritual world and makes the spirit body a self-contained spiritual being within that world, a being that intuitively perceives the spiritual content of the universe. We will call this spiritual membrane the *spiritual*, or *auric, membrane*. We must keep in mind, however, that this spiritual skin is constantly expanding to accommodate human development, and that the spiritual individuality of a human being (the auric membrane) is capable of unlimited expansion.

Inside the spiritual skin, the spirit body is alive and built up by a spiritual life force in the same sense that the physical body is built up by a physical life force. Therefore, just as we speak of an ether body, we must also speak of an ether spirit for the spirit body. We will call this ether spirit the life spirit. The spiritual constitution of the human being is thus subdivided into three members, the spirit body, the life spirit, and the spirit self.

For someone who can "see" in spiritual regions, this spiritual constitution is a perceptible reality—the higher, truly spiritual portion of the aura. A seer can "see" the spirit body as life spirit inside the spiritual skin, can see how the life spirit constantly grows larger by taking in nourishment from the outer spiritual world, and can also see how, as a result, the spiritual skin continues to expand, and the spirit body becomes larger and larger. Of course the spatial concept of "getting larger" is only an image of the actual reality. Nevertheless, in picturing this we are directed toward the corresponding spiritual reality. The difference between the human being as a spiritual being and as a physical being is that physical growth is restricted to a fixed size while spiritual growth can continue indefinitely. What is taken in as spiritual nourishment is of eternal value. It follows that the human aura is made up of two interpenetrating parts, one of which is given form and color by our physical existence, the other by our spiritual existence; the "I" separates the two. The physical relinquishes its distinctive character to build a body that allows a soul to come to life, while on the other side the "I" does the same, allowing the spirit to have a life within it. The spirit in turn permeates the soul and gives it a goal in the spiritual world. The soul is confined to physical existence through the physical body. Through the spirit body, it grows wings that give it mobility in the spiritual world.

❁

If we wish to comprehend the human being as a whole, we must imagine that each individual is made up of the components just described. The physical body builds itself from the world of physical substance in such a way that this structure meets the requirements of a thinking "I" being. This body is permeated by life force, thus becoming the ether body or life body. As such, it opens itself up to the outside in the sense organs and becomes the soul body. The soul body is permeated by, and forms a unity with, the sentient soul. The sentient soul not only receives the impressions of the outer world in the form of sensations but also has a life of its own that is fructified both by sensations from one side and by thinking from the other. Through this it can become the "mind soul." By being open to intuitions from above just as it is open to sensations from below, the sentient soul becomes the consciousness soul. This is possible because the spiritual world builds the organ of intuition into it, just as the physical body builds the sense organs for it. The senses transmit sensations to it by means of the soul body; similarly, the spirit transmits intuitions to it by means of the organ of intuition.

The spirit body and the consciousness soul are thus linked in an entity analogous to the linking of the physical body and the sentient soul in the soul body. That is, the consciousness soul and the spirit self form a unity in which the spirit body lives as the life spirit, just as the ether body forms the living bodily basis for the soul body. Moreover, just as the physical body is contained within the physical skin, the spirit body is also contained within the spiritual skin. As a result, the entire human being is subdivided into the following members:

A. Material, physical body
B. Ether body or life body
{ C. Soul body
{ D. Sentient soul
E. Mind soul
{ F. Consciousness soul
{ G. Spirit self
H. Life spirit
I. Spirit body

The soul body (C) and sentient soul (D) are a unity in earthly human beings, as are the consciousness soul (F) and the spirit self (G). This yields seven components of the earthly human being:

1. The material, physical body
2. The ether or life body
3. The sentient soul body
4. The mind soul
5. The spirit-filled consciousness soul
6. The life spirit
7. The spirit body

Within the human soul, the "I" flashes up, receives the impact of the spirit, and thus becomes the vehicle of the spirit body. Therefore, we each participate in three worlds: physical, soul, and spiritual. We are rooted in the physical world through the physical body of matter, the ether body, and the soul body; we blossom in the spirit world through the spirit self, life spirit, and spirit body. The stem, which roots at one end and flowers at the other, is the soul itself.

It is possible to give a simplified version of this subdivision of the human being that is in complete harmony with the original. Although the human "I" lights up in the consciousness soul, it also permeates the entire being of the soul, whose members on the whole are less clearly separated than the components of the bodily organization and interpenetrate one another in a higher sense. If we look at the mind soul and the consciousness soul as the two garments of the "I" that belong together, with the "I" as their central core, then the human being can be differentiated into physical body, life body, astral body, and "I" being with the term *astral body,* designating the union of the soul body and the sentient soul. This term is common in older literature and is here applied freely to the aspect of the human being beyond what is sense-perceptible. Although in a certain respect the sentient soul is also filled with forces by the "I," it is so intimately connected with the soul body that using a single term for the union of the two is justified.

When the "I" in turn imbues itself with the spirit self, the spirit self manifests so that the astral body is worked over from within the soul. What is active in the astral body to begin with are our drives, desires, and passions, to the extent that we perceive them, as well as our sense perceptions. Sense perceptions come about through the soul body, a member of our human constitution that comes to us from the outer world. Drives, desires, passions, and so on originate in the sentient soul to the extent that it is filled with forces by our inner self before this inner self gives itself over to the spirit self. When the "I" imbues itself with the spirit self, the soul in turn fills the astral body with forces of the spirit self. As a result, drives, desires and passions are illumined by what the "I" has received from the spirit. The "I" has then become master over the world of drives, desires, and so on by virtue of its participation in the spiritual world. To the extent that this mastery takes place, the spirit self appears within the astral body, which is transformed as a result. The astral body then appears as a twofold entity, one part transformed and the other not transformed. Consequently, we may call the spirit self, as manifested in the human being, a *transformed astral body.*

A similar process takes place when we receive the life spirit into the "I." The life body is transformed by being imbued with the life spirit. That is, the life spirit manifests in such a way that the life body becomes something different. Thus we can also say that the life spirit is the transformed life body.

And again, if the "I" then takes the spirit body into itself, it receives the strong force, which it uses to permeate the physical body. Of course, the part of the physical body that is thus transformed is not perceptible to the physical senses; the spiritualized part has become the spirit body. The physical body, as a physical phenomenon, is then perceptible to the physical senses, but to the extent it has been spiritualized, it must be perceived by spiritual faculties. To the outer senses, even the physical part that has been permeated by the spiritual appears to be purely physical.

With all of this as a basis, we can now subdivide the human being as follows:

1. Physical body
2. Life body
3. Astral body
4. The "I" as the soul's central core
5. Spirit self as transformed astral body
6. Life spirit as transformed life body
7. Spirit body as transformed physical body

Addendum

It may seem that the subdivisions of the human constitution presented in this book are based on purely arbitrary distinctions between parts within a monolithic soul life. To counter this objection, it must be emphasized that the significance of this phenomenon is similar to that of the appearance of the seven colors of the rainbow when light passes through a prism. What a physicist contributes to our understanding of light by studying this process and the seven colors that result is analogous to what the spiritual scientist does for our understanding of the makeup of the human soul. The soul's seven members are not abstract intellectual distinctions any more than are the light's seven colors. In both cases, the distinctions rest on the inner nature of the things themselves, the only difference being that the seven constituents of light become visible by means of an external device while the seven components of the soul become perceptible to a method of spiritual observation consistent with the nature of the human soul. The true nature of the soul cannot be grasped without knowing about this subdivision, because the soul belongs to the transitory world by virtue of three of our constitutional components—physical body, life body, and soul body—and has its roots in eternity through the other four constituent parts.

When the soul is seen as a unity, its transitory and eternal aspects are indistinguishably bound up with each other; but unless we are aware of the differentiations within it, we cannot understand its relationship to the world as a whole. Let me use another comparison. Chemists separate water into hydrogen and oxygen, two substances that cannot be distinguished when they are united in the form of water. However, each of these elements has an identity of its own and can form compounds with other elements. Similarly, at death our three lower constitutional components unite with the makeup of the perishable world, while our four higher members unite with the eternal. Refusing to consider this differentiation within the soul is like being a chemist who refuses to learn about decomposing water into hydrogen and oxygen.

NOTE

For a long time after compiling this book, I also spoke of what is here termed *ether body*, or *life body*, as the *body of formative forces*. I felt compelled to give it this name because I believed one could not do enough to try to prevent the identification of what I meant with the "life force" or "vital force" of an earlier stage of science. When it comes to refuting this outdated concept, as modern science does, I agree in some respects with those who would deny the existence of any such force. That term was used in an attempt to explain the unique way of working that inorganic forces took on within a living organism. However, inorganic activity is actually no different inside an organism from what it is outside in inorganic nature. Within an organism there is simply something additional present, something that is not inorganic, namely the formative activity of life whose basis is the ether body or body of formative forces. Recognizing the existence of the ether body in no way impinges on the legitimate task of science, which is to trace the effects of forces observed in inorganic nature into the world of living organisms. Spiritual science, however, also finds it justified not to imagine these effects as altered by a particular "vital force" within an organism. A spiritual researcher speaks of an ether body at the point at which an organism discloses something that a lifeless object cannot. In spite of all this, I do not find it necessary to replace the term *ether body* with *body of formative forces* in this book, since in this context anyone who so chooses will be able to avoid misunderstanding. Misunderstanding will only arise if this term is used in an incompatible context.

From Rudolf Steiner, Theosophy: An Introduction to the Spiritual Processes in Human Life and in the Cosmos *(Anthroposophic Press, 1994), pp. 31–62.*

4.

Spiritual Intelligence

1. How to Know Higher Worlds

Conditions

The capacities by which we can gain insights into higher worlds lie dormant within each one of us. Mystics, gnostics, and theosophists have always spoken of a world of soul and spirit that is as real to them as the world we can see with our eyes and touch with our hands. Listening to them, we can say to ourselves at every moment: "I know that I, too, can experience what they talk about, if only I unfold certain forces within me that today still lie dormant there." All we need to know is how to begin to develop these faculties for ourselves.

Only those who have already developed such powers for themselves can help us to do this. From the beginning of the human race, a form of training has always existed in which persons possessing higher faculties guide those who seek to develop these faculties for themselves. Such training is called *esoteric*, or mystery training, and the instruction one receives there is called *esoteric*, or *occult*, teaching.

By their very nature, these terms invite misunderstanding. Hearing them, we might easily be led to believe that those who provide this kind of training wish to form a privileged class of human beings who arbitrarily withhold their knowledge from others. We might even think that perhaps there is nothing much to this kind of knowledge. Were it genuine knowledge, we are tempted to think that there would be no need to make a secret of it and that it could be made public and its benefits shared by all.

Those initiated into the nature of esoteric knowledge are not in the least surprised that the uninitiated should think like this. After all, the secret of initiation can be understood only by those who have themselves, to some degree, undergone initiation into the higher mysteries of existence. How, we may well wonder, under these conditions, are the uninitiated to develop any human interest whatsoever in this so-called esoteric knowledge? Why and how should one seek for something of whose nature one can have no clear idea?

Such questions are based on a completely false idea of the nature of esoteric knowledge. In fact, esoteric, inner knowledge is no different from other kinds of human knowledge and ability. It is a mystery for the average person only to the extent that writing is a mystery for those who have not yet learned to write. Given the right teaching methods, anyone can learn to write, just as anyone can become a student of esoteric knowledge and, yes, even a teacher of it, by following the appropriate path. Ordinary knowledge and ability differ from esoteric knowledge in only one respect. One may lack the possibility of learning to write because of cultural conditions or the poverty into which one is born, but no one who seeks sincerely will encounter any barriers to attaining knowledge and abilities in the higher worlds.

Many believe that they must seek out masters of higher knowledge wherever such masters may be found and receive teachings from them. There is a twofold truth to this. On the one hand, if our aspiration to higher knowledge is sincere, we will certainly spare no effort and avoid no obstacle in our quest for an initiate who can lead us into the higher mysteries of the world. On the other hand, we can be certain that, if our striving for knowledge is sincere and worthy, initiation will find us whatever the circumstances. There is a universal law among initiates that the knowledge due a seeker cannot be withheld. However, there is another universal law that esoteric knowledge may not be imparted to those not qualified to receive it. The more perfect the initiate, the more strictly these two laws are observed.

The spiritual bond uniting all initiates is not outer; rather, the two laws just mentioned hold its members together. You may live in close friendship with one who has been initiated, but until you yourself have been initiated, something will always separate you from that initiate's inmost being. You may enjoy an initiate's full heart and love, but the initiate will not share the secret with you until you are ready. You may flatter or torment, but nothing will induce an initiate to betray anything that should not be revealed to you, at the present stage of your development, until you understand how to prepare a proper welcome for that secret in your soul. Specific methods prepare one to receive such secrets, which are traced with indelible, eternal letters in the spiritual worlds, where initiates preserve the higher secrets. In prehistoric times, temples of the spirit were outwardly visible, but today life has become so unspiritual that they no longer exist where we can see them with physical eyes. Yet spiritually they are present everywhere, and whoever seeks can find them. Only within the soul can one find the means of opening an initiate's mouth. But before one can receive the highest treasures of the spirit, one must develop definite inner qualities to a specific high degree.

We begin with a fundamental mood of soul. Spiritual researchers call this basic attitude *the path of reverence,* devotion to truth and knowledge. Only those who have acquired this fundamental mood or attitude can become students in an esoteric school. Anyone with any experience in this area knows that those who later become students of esoteric knowledge demonstrated this gift for reverence in childhood. Some children look up to those whom they revere with a holy awe. Their profound respect for such people affects the deepest recesses of their hearts and forbids any thoughts of criticism or opposition to arise. Such children grow into young people who enjoy looking up to something that fills them with reverence. Many of these young people become students of esoteric knowledge. If you have ever stood at the door of someone you revered, filled with holy awe as you turned the doorknob to enter for the first time a room that was a "holy place" for you, then the feeling you experienced at that moment is a seed that can later blossom into your becoming an esoteric student. To be gifted with the potential for such feelings is a blessing for every young person. We should not fear that such feelings of reverence lead to subservience and slavishness; on the contrary, a child's reverence for others develops into reverence for truth and knowledge. Experience teaches that we know best how to hold our heads high in freedom if we have learned to feel reverence when it is appropriate, and it is appropriate whenever it flows from the depths of the heart.

We will not find the inner strength to evolve to a higher level if we do not inwardly develop this profound feeling that there is something higher than ourselves. Initiates found the strength to lift themselves to the heights of knowledge only because they first guided their hearts into the depths of veneration and devotion. Only a person who has passed through the gate of humility can ascend to the heights of the spirit. To attain true knowledge, you must first learn to respect this knowledge.

We certainly have the right to turn our eyes toward the light, but we must earn this right. Spiritual life has its laws just as physical life does. Rub a glass rod with the appropriate substance and it becomes electrified; the glass rod will gain the power to attract small particles. This demonstrates a physical law. If one has learned some elementary physics, one knows that this is so. Similarly, if one knows the fundamentals of esoteric science, one knows that every feeling of *true* devotion developed in the soul produces inner strength, or force, that leads sooner or later to knowledge.

Whoever possesses an innate tendency toward feelings of devotion or has been fortunate enough to receive an education that cultivated such feelings is well prepared in later life to seek the way to higher knowledge. Those who do not bring this preparation with them will have to work at developing this devotional mood through vigorous self-discipline; if not, they will encounter difficulties after only the first few steps on the path of knowledge. Today, it is especially important to focus complete attention on this point. Our civilization is more inclined to criticize, judge, and condemn than to feel devotion and selfless veneration. Our children criticize far more than they respect or revere. Every feeling of devotion and reverence nurtures the soul's powers for higher knowledge, just as every act of criticism and judgment drives away those powers. This is not intended to imply anything against our civilization; our concern is not to criticize it. After all, we owe the greatness of our culture precisely to our ability to make critical, self-confident human judgments and to our principle of "testing all and keeping the best." Modern science, industry, transportation, commerce, law—all these would never have developed without the universal exercise of our critical faculty and standards of judgment. Yet the price of our gain in outer culture has been a corresponding loss in higher knowledge and spiritual life. Thus, we must always remember that higher knowledge is connected with revering truth and insight rather than with revering people.

We must be clear about one thing. Those immersed completely in the superficial civilization of our day will find it especially difficult to work their way to cognition of the higher worlds. To do so, they will have to work energetically upon themselves. In times when the material conditions of life were still simple, spiritual progress was easier. What was revered and held sacred stood out more clearly from the rest of the world. In an age of criticism, on the other hand, ideals are degraded. Reverence, awe, adoration, and wonder are replaced by other feelings; they are pushed increasingly into the background. Consequently, everyday life offers few opportunities for their development. Anyone seeking higher knowledge must create such feelings inwardly and instill them in the soul. This cannot be done by studying. It can be done only by living.

If we wish to become esoteric students, we must train ourselves vigorously in the mood of devotion. We must seek—in all things around us, in all our experiences—for what can arouse our admiration and respect. If I meet others and criticize their weaknesses, I rob myself of higher cognitive power. But if I try to go deeply and lovingly into another person's good qualities, I gather that force.

Disciples of this esoteric path must always bear in mind the need to cultivate such admiration and respect. Experienced spiritual researchers know the strength they gain by always looking for the good in everything and by withholding critical judgment. This practice should not remain simply an outer rule of life; it must take hold of the innermost part of the soul. It lies in our hands to perfect and gradually transform ourselves completely. However, this transformation must occur in our innermost depths, in our thinking. Showing respect outwardly in our relations with others is not enough; we must carry this respect into our thoughts. Therefore, we must begin our inner training by bringing devotion into our thinking. We must guard against disrespectful, disparaging, and criticizing thoughts. We must practice reverence and devotion in our thinking at all times.

Each moment that we spend becoming aware of the derogatory, judgmental, and critical opinions that remain in our consciousness brings us closer to higher knowledge. We advance even more quickly if, in such moments, we fill our consciousness with admiration, respect, and reverence for the world and life. Those experienced in these things know that such moments awaken inner forces that otherwise remain dormant. Filling our consciousness in this way opens our spiritual eyes. We begin to see things around us that we could not see before. We begin to realize that previously we saw only part of the world around us. We begin to see others in a way that is different from the way we saw them before.

Of course, this one rule of life does not enable us to perceive, for example, what we call the *human aura*. For this, still higher training is needed. Yet we cannot begin such training until we have undergone a vigorous training in devotion.

As esoteric students, we should embark upon "the path of knowledge" quietly and unnoticed by the outer world. Outwardly, no one should perceive any change in us. We continue to do our duties and attend to business just as before. Changes occur only within the soul, which is withdrawn from and invisible to the outer eye. Initially, a basic mood of devotion toward everything truly worthy of reverence suffuses our entire inner life. This one fundamental feeling becomes the center of one's soul life. The reverence in us quickens all the feelings in our soul, just as the Sun's rays give life to all living things.

At first glance, it is not easy to believe that feelings of reverence and respect are in any way connected with knowledge. This is because we tend to see cognition as an isolated faculty that has no real connection with anything else in our souls. Thus, we forget that it is the soul that knows. Feelings are to the soul as food is to the body. If we feed the body stones instead of bread, it will cease to function. It is the same with the soul. We nourish it with reverence, respect, and devotion. These make the soul healthy and strong, particularly for the activity of knowing. Disrespect, antipathy, and disparaging admirable things, on the other hand, paralyze and slay our cognitive activities.

For spiritual researchers these soul realities are visible in the aura. A soul that learns feelings of devotion and reverence changes its aura. Certain spiritual yellow-red or brown-red colors, as they may be called, disappear and are replaced by tones of blue-red. Our cognitive capacity increases. We now receive information about facts in our environment of which we were previously unaware. Reverence awakens a power of sympathy in the soul. This draws toward us qualities in the beings around us that would otherwise remain hidden.

What we attain through devotion becomes even more effective when another kind of feeling is added. This involves learning to surrender ourselves less to the impressions of the outer world and developing an active inner life instead. If we chase amusements and rush from one sensory impression to the next, we will not find a way to esoteric knowledge. Esoteric students should not become dull or unfeeling toward the outer world, but *a rich inner life* should orient us in response to impressions.

When those who are rich in feeling and deep of soul pass through a beautiful mountain landscape, they will experience it differently from those whose inner life is poor in feeling. Inner experience is only key to the beauties of the outer world. Depending on the inner lives we have developed, when we travel across the ocean, perhaps only a few inner experiences will pass through our souls, or we may sense the eternal language of the world spirit and understand the mysteries of creation. To develop a meaningful relationship to the outer world we must learn to work with our own feelings and ideas. The world around us is filled everywhere with the glory of God, but we have to experience the divine in our own souls before we can find it in our surroundings.

As students of esoteric knowledge, we are told to create moments in life when we can withdraw into ourselves in silence and solitude. In such moments, we should not give ourselves over to our concerns, which would lead to the opposite of our goal. Instead, during such moments, we should allow what we have experienced—what the outer world has told us—to linger on in utter stillness. In these quiet moments, every flower, every animal, and every action will disclose undreamed mysteries. It prepares us to receive new sensory impressions of the outer world with new eyes.

If we seek only to enjoy and consume one sensory impression after another, we blunt our capacity for cognition. If, on the other hand, we allow the experience of pleasure to reveal something to us, we nurture and educate our cognitive capacities. Before this can happen, we must learn to allow the pleasure (or impression) to linger on within while we renounce further enjoyment (new impression), assimilating and digesting with inner activity the past experience we have enjoyed.

Here we must face a great hurdle, and with it a great danger. Instead of working inwardly, we can fall into the opposite and indulge enjoyment to the full. We should not underestimate the boundless sources of error that opens for us here. For we must pass through a throng of tempters of the soul, all of whom seek to harden the "I" and enclose it within itself.

As students, it is our task to open the "I" to the world. Moreover, because the outer world can approach us only through sensory impressions, we must seek pleasure there. If we become indifferent to enjoyment, we become like plants that can no longer draw nourishment from their environment. On the other hand, if we stop at mere pleasure, we become enclosed within ourselves. We might have meaning for *ourselves*, but we will have none for the world. No matter how intensely we live in ourselves and how much we cultivate our "I," the world will cut us out. As far as the world is concerned, we will be dead. As esoteric students, we regard pleasure only as a means to become nobler for the sake of the world. Pleasure becomes a messenger, instructing us about the world. After we have taken in the teaching it provides, we move on to inner work. The purpose is not to accumulate learning as a private store of knowledge, but to place what we have learned in the service of the world.

One fundamental principle of esoteric science, taught in every form of training, must never be violated if we wish to achieve our goal. *Every insight that we seek only to enrich our own store of learning and to accumulate treasure for ourselves alone leads us away from our path. However, every insight that we seek, to become more mature on the path of human ennoblement and world evolution, brings us another step forward.* This fundamental law must always be observed. We cannot call ourselves genuine seekers of higher knowledge unless we make it the guiding principle for our lives. This truth of esoteric training may be summarized as follows. *Every idea that does not become an ideal for us kills a force in our soul. However, every idea that becomes our ideal creates forces of life within us.*

Inner Peace

At the beginning of esoteric training, the student is directed first to the path of *reverence* and to the development of an *inner life*. Spiritual science then provides *rules of practice* that, when observed, help us follow this path and develop an inner life. These rules of practice are not arbitrary but based on age-old experience and wisdom. They are given in a similar way wherever ways to higher knowledge are taught. All true teachers of spiritual life agree on the substance of these rules, though they may not always express them in the same words. Any seeming differences are minor and due to facts we need not discuss here.

No spiritual teacher exercises dominion over others by means of such rules. They do not wish to restrict anyone's autonomy.

Indeed, there is no better judge and guardian of human independence than a spiritual researcher. As we have said, a spiritual bond connects all initiates, and two laws hold this bond together. But when initiates leave their closed spiritual circle and appear in public, they are subject immediately to a third law. *Regulate each of your words and actions so that you do not interfere with anyone's free decisions and will.* Once we understand that a true teacher of spiritual life must be thoroughly permeated by this attitude, we know that we will lose none of our independence by following these rules of practice.

One of the first rules may now be put into words, somewhat as follows. *Create moments of inner peace for yourself and, in these moments, learn to distinguish the essential from the inessential.*

Here it is put into words, but originally all the rules and teachings of spiritual science were given symbolically in a sign language. Whoever would learn the full meaning and significance of these rules must first understand the symbolic language. Such understanding, however, depends on having taken the first steps in spiritual science. To take these steps, one must observe closely the rules presented here. The way stands open to anyone whose will is sincere. The rule concerning moments of inner peace is simple. Following it is also simple. However, the rule leads to results only when the practice of it is as sincere and rigorous as it is simple. Thus it will be plainly stated how this rule is to be followed.

As students of the spirit, we must set aside a brief period of time in daily life when we focus on things quite different from the objects of our daily activity. The kind of activity in which we engage must also differ from that of the rest of our day. This is not to say, however, that what we do in the minutes we have set aside is disconnected from the content of our daily work. On the contrary, we soon realize that, if approached correctly, such moments give us the full strength for completing our daily tasks. We need not fear that following this rule will take time from our duties. If one genuinely cannot spare more time, five minutes a day are enough. The important thing is how we use those five minutes.

In these moments we should tear ourselves completely out of our everyday life. Our thinking and feeling lives should have a different coloring from the usual. We should allow our joys, sorrows, worries, experiences, and actions to pass before the soul. Our attitude toward these, however, should be one of looking at everything we have experienced from a higher point of view. Consider how differently in ordinary life we perceive what other people have experienced or done from perceptions of what we ourselves have experienced or done. This must be so. We are still interwoven with what we experience or do, but we are mere onlookers of other people's experiences or acts.

In the time we have set aside for ourselves, then, we must try to view and judge our own experiences and actions as though they belonged to someone else. For example, imagine you have had a serious misfortune. You naturally regard your own misfortune differently from the way you would that of another. Such an attitude is quite justified; it is simply human nature. Indeed, it comes into play not only in exceptional circumstances but also in the events of everyday life. As students of higher knowledge we must find the strength to view ourselves as we would view strangers. We must face ourselves with the inner tranquillity of a judge. If we achieve this, our own experiences will reveal themselves in a new light. As long as we are still woven into our experiences and are within them, we remain as attached to the nonessential as we are to the essential. Once we have attained the inner peace of the overview, however, the nonessential separates from the essential. Sorrow and joy, every thought, every decision will look different when we face ourselves in this way.

It is as though we spent the whole day somewhere and saw everything, small and large, at close range, and then in the evening climbed a neighboring hill and enjoyed an overview of the whole place at once. Then the various parts of the town and their relationships to each other would appear very different from when we stood among them.

Of course, we cannot succeed in achieving such a transcendent perspective toward the daily experiences that destiny brings us, nor is it necessary to do so. However, as students of the spiritual life, we must strive to develop this attitude toward events that occurred in the past. The value of such inner, peace-filled self-contemplation depends less upon what one contemplates and more upon finding the inner strength that such inner calm develops.

In addition to what we may call the ordinary, everyday self, everyone also bears a higher self, a higher human being, within. This higher human being remains hidden until awakened. It can be awakened only as each individually awakens it inwardly. Until then, those latent higher faculties within each of us, which lead to suprasensory knowledge, remain hidden. We must continue to observe this rule seriously and faithfully until we experience the fruits of inner calm and tranquillity. For everyone who does this, a day will come when all around will become bright with spirit. Then a whole new world will be revealed to eyes we did not know we had.

Nothing needs to change in our outer lives because we begin to follow this rule. We perform our duties just as before. In the beginning, too, we endure the same sufferings and experience the same joys. We must not in any way become alienated from life. On the contrary, we gain the ability to live life more fully throughout the day, simply because we are acquiring a "higher life" during those moments we set aside. As the higher life increasingly manifests its influence in our established, ordinary lives, the calm of our contemplative moments begins to affect our daily existence. Our whole being becomes more peaceful. We act with greater confidence and certainty in all our activities. We do not lose composure in the face of all sorts of events. Gradually, as we continue on the path, we come increasingly to guide ourselves, as it were, instead of allowing ourselves to be led by circumstances and outer influences. Soon, we realize that the daily moments set aside become a great source of strength.

For example, we gradually cease to become angry about the things that used to annoy us; we no longer fear many things that used to frighten us. Instead, we acquire a whole new outlook on life. Before, we may have approached what we had to do with hesitation, thinking, *I don't have the energy to do this the way I would like to*. Now, however, such thoughts no longer occur to us. We are more likely to think, *I will gather my strength and work as well as I possibly can*. We suppress all thoughts that could make us tentative, because we know that hesitation can lead to a poor performance, or at least it does nothing to improve what we have to do. Thus, thought after thought, fruitful and beneficial to our life's affairs, begins to permeate our interpretation of life. Such new thoughts replace thoughts that previously weakened and hindered us. In the process, we begin to steer a safe and steady course through the ups and downs of life rather than being tossed about by them.

Such inner calm and certainty affect our whole nature. Our inner person grows, and with it, inner faculties that lead to higher knowledge. As we progress in this direction, we become increasingly able to control the effect that impressions from the outer world have upon us. For example, we may hear someone say something to hurt or anger us. Before we began esoteric training, this would have made us feel hurt or anger. Now, however, because we are on the path of inner development, we can take the hurtful or annoying sting out of another's words before it finds its way into our inner being. Another example: before beginning to follow this path, we may have been quick to lose our patience when we had to wait for something. But now, having started on the path and become students in a school of esoteric study, we imbue ourselves in our contemplative moments so fully with the realization that most impatience is futile that, whenever we feel any impatience, it immediately calls this realization to mind. The impatience that was about to take root thus disappears, and the time we would otherwise have wasted expressing impatience can now be filled with useful observations that we may make while we wait.

We should realize the scope and significance of all these changes. The "higher self" evolves continuously. Only the kind of inner calm and certainty described here can ensure that it evolves organically. If we do not master our lives but are ruled by life, the waves of outer life will press in upon the inner self from all sides, and we become like a plant trying to grow in the cleft of a rock.

Without more space, the plant will be stunted. Outer forces cannot create the space our inner being needs to grow. Only the inner calm we create in the soul can do this. Outer circumstances can change only our outer life; they can never awaken the "spiritual individual" within. As esoteric students, we must give birth to a new, higher being within us.

This higher self then becomes the inner ruler, directing the affairs of the outer person with a sure hand. As long as the outer being has the upper hand and guides us, the "inner" self remains its slave and cannot develop its powers. If other people can make me angry, I am not my own master; or better stated, I have not yet found the "inner ruler." In other words, I must develop the inner faculty of allowing the impressions of the outer world to reach me only in ways that I choose. Unless I do this, I cannot become a student of the esoteric.

Only a person striving sincerely for this ability can reach the goal. How far we advance in a certain amount of time is unimportant; it is important only that our seeking is sincere. Many work on themselves for years without noticeable progress, and then suddenly—if they have not despaired, but have remained unshakable—they attain the "inner victory." Of course, great strength is needed in many life situations to create such moments of inner peace. The more effort we need to exert, however, the more meaningful the achievement we accomplish. On the path to knowledge, it all depends on whether we can face ourselves and all our actions energetically, with inner truthfulness and uncompromising honesty, as if we were strangers to ourselves.

Yet the birth of our *own* higher self marks only one side of our inner activity. Something else is needed. When we view ourselves as strangers, it is still only *ourselves* that we contemplate. We see the experiences and actions connected to us by the particular course of life we have grown through. But we must go beyond that. We must rise to see the purely human level that no longer has anything to do with our own particular situation. We must reach the point of contemplating those things that concern us as human beings as such, completely independent of the circumstances and conditions of our particular life.

As we do this, something comes to life in us that transcends the personal or individual. Our view is directed toward worlds higher than those of our everyday life. We begin to feel that we belong to those higher worlds of which our senses and everyday activities tell us nothing. The center of our being shifts inward. We listen to the voices that speak within us during moments of serenity. Inwardly, we associate with the spiritual world. Removed from our daily round, we become deaf to its noise. Everything around us grows still. We put aside everything that reminds us of outer impressions. The soul is filled with quiet, inner contemplation and dialog with the purely spiritual world.

For students of the spirit, this quiet contemplation must become a necessity of life. At first, we are wholly absorbed in a world of thought. We must develop a *living feeling* for this silent thinking activity. We must learn to love what flows toward us from the spirit. Then we soon cease to accept this world of thought as less real than the everyday life surrounding us. Instead, we begin to work with our thoughts as we do with material objects. Then the moment approaches when we begin to realize that what is revealed to us in the silence of inner thinking activity is more real than the physical objects around us. We experience *life* speaking in this world of thoughts. We realize that thoughts are not mere shadow images, and that hidden *beings* speak to us through thoughts. Out of the silence, something begins to speak to us. Previously, we heard speech only with our ears; now words resound within our souls. An inner speech, an inner word, is revealed to us. The first time we experience this, we feel supremely blessed. The outer world is suffused with an inner light, and a second life begins for us. A divine, bliss-giving world flows through us. In thoughts, this soul life gradually broadens in life into "spiritual existence." In spiritual science, or gnosis, this is called *meditation* (contemplative reflection). Meditation, in this sense, is the way to suprasensory knowledge.

We should not lose ourselves in feelings in these moments of meditation. Nor should our souls be filled with vague sensations, which would only prevent us from attaining true spiritual insight. Our thoughts should be clear, sharp, and precise. We find a way to achieve this by not staying blindly in the thoughts that arise within. Rather, we should fill ourselves with high thoughts that more advanced, spiritually inspired souls have thought in similar moments. Here we should begin with writings that have grown out of meditative revelations. We may find such texts in works of mystical, gnostic, or spiritual-scientific literature. They provide the material for our meditations. Indeed, it is spiritual seekers who have set down the thoughts of divine science in such works. Through these messengers, the spirit has allowed these thoughts to be revealed to the world.

Practicing such meditation will transform us completely, and we begin to form new ideas about reality. Things assume a different value for us. Yet such transformation does not make us unworldly. In no way does it estrange us from our daily responsibilities. This path teaches us that our most trivial tasks and our most trivial experiences are woven together with great cosmic beings and world events. Once this interconnection becomes clear to us during moments of contemplation, we go about our daily round of activities with new and increased strength, because now we know that all our work and all our suffering are work and suffering for the sake of a great, spiritual, cosmic interrelationship. Thus, meditation produces *strength* for life, not indifference. Consequently, students of higher knowledge go through life with confidence, holding their heads high, regardless of what life may bring them. Previously, they did not know why they worked and suffered. Now they know.

Naturally, such meditative activity will lead to its goal more easily when practiced under the guidance of someone with experience, one who knows from personal knowledge how best to proceed. Therefore, we would do well to consider the advice and instructions of such people. We certainly will not lose our freedom or independence by doing so. Such guidance turns uncertain groping into work with a clear end. When we listen to those with knowledge and experience, we never ask for guidance in vain. Nevertheless, we must understand that we are seeking only the advice of a friend, not domination by someone who wants power over us. We will always find that those who truly know are the most humble and that nothing is more alien to them than any lust for power.

When we lift ourselves through meditation to what unites us with the spirit, we enliven something within that is eternal and not limited by birth and death. Once we experience this eternal part within us, we no longer doubt its existence. Meditation is thus the way to knowing and witnessing the eternal, indestructible, essential center of our being. Only meditation can lead us to this vision. Gnosis and spiritual science speak of the immortality of this essence and of its reincarnation. People often ask: Why do we know nothing of our experiences before birth and after death? This is the wrong question. We should ask: How do we attain such knowledge? Practiced properly, meditation opens the way to this knowledge. Meditation brings to life memories of experiences beyond birth and death. Each of us can attain such knowledge. We all have the capacities to see firsthand what true mysticism, spiritual science, Anthroposophy, and gnosis teach. We simply have to choose the right means. Only a being with ears and eyes can perceive sounds and colors. Nonetheless, even an eye cannot see without light to make phenomena visible. Spiritual science offers a method for developing our spiritual ears and eyes and a means of kindling spiritual light.

Three stages in this method of spiritual training may be distinguished:

1. *Preparation* develops the spiritual senses;
2. *Illumination* kindles spiritual light;
3. *Initiation* initiates our relationship with higher spiritual beings·

From Rudolf Steiner, How to Know Higher Worlds: A Modern Path of Initiation *(Anthroposophic Press, 1994), pp. 13–37.*

2. Trust in Thinking

Cognizing the Spiritual World

Insight into the results of spiritual science comes easier when, in ordinary soul life, you focus on what produces concepts that can be expanded and transformed such that they can then gradually approach the processes and beings of the spiritual world. This path requires patience. Without it, you will be tempted to imagine the spiritual world as too much like the physical, sensible world. Indeed, unless you walk this path patiently, you will be able to form neither a true picture of spirit itself nor of how it relates to human beings.

Spiritual events and beings press toward those who have prepared their souls to perceive them. But they impose themselves upon us in a way that is completely different from the way physical facts and beings do. We may, however, gain an idea of this very different mode of appearance if we contemplate the process of memory.

Long ago, or perhaps more recently, you experienced something. Then, at a certain moment, occasioned by this or that, a memory of the event rises out of the substrate of your soul life. You know that what has arisen corresponds to an experience, and you relate it to that experience. But *in the present,* in the moment of remembering, you have nothing more of the experience than a remembered image.

Imagine an image arising in your soul that is like a memory image, but is not a picture of something you experienced before. It expresses something foreign to your soul. This gives you some idea of how the spiritual world first appears in the soul that has been sufficiently prepared. Because the spiritual world first appears in the soul in the form of images, people who are insufficiently familiar with the workings of the spiritual world will always object, saying that all supposed spiritual experiences are nothing more than vague memory images, which the soul does not recognize and so takes to be revelations of a spiritual world. One cannot deny that it is certainly difficult to differentiate between illusions and reality in this realm. Indeed, many people who believe they have had perceptions of the suprasensory world have in fact merely seen only memory images that they do not recognize.

To see clearly in the spiritual world, a person must learn about the many possible sources of illusion. For instance, you may have once seen something so fleetingly that its impression did not fully enter your consciousness. Later, a very vivid image of it—perhaps in a highly altered form—arises within you. You may well then swear that you never saw it before, that you have had a genuine inspiration. This is one reason why it is quite understandable that the results of suprasensory vision seem highly questionable to those unfamiliar with the special features of spiritual research. In my book *How to Know Higher Worlds*, I explain the gradual development of spiritual vision. If you read that book carefully, you will certainly be prepared to distinguish between illusion and spiritual reality.

Nevertheless, it must still be said that spiritual experiences occur, at least in the beginning, as images. They rise as pictures from the depths of prepared souls. The important thing is to have the right relationship to those pictures. In fact, they have value for suprasensory perception only if the way in which they present themselves *shows* that they are not to be taken literally. If we take them as they appear literally, they have little more value than common dreams. We must consider them as if they were letters of the alphabet laid out before us. We do not focus upon the form of the letters. Rather, we read in them what is expressed through them. Just as something written does not need to be described in terms of the form of the letters, so the images that form the contents of the suprasensory vision do not require to be understood *as pictures*. Of themselves, they make us turn completely away from their pictorial nature and lead the soul toward the suprasensory process or being they express.

You cannot complain that a text from which you can learn something new consists only of well-known letters of the alphabet. Similarly, you cannot object because the images in suprasensory consciousness contain only things borrowed from normal life—which, to an extent, they do. What those images borrow from normal life is unimportant for genuine suprasensory consciousness. The important thing for suprasensory consciousness is *what* the images express.

To cognize the spiritual world, you must first prepare your soul to see the pictures that arise in the spiritual field of vision. At the same time, you must carefully develop the attitude that you will not remain with the images but will, rather, relate them in the right way to the suprasensory world. True suprasensory vision, therefore, has not only a capacity to see an inner world of images; it also has another capacity, one comparable to *reading* in the sensory world.

When you begin, you must imagine the suprasensory world as lying completely outside normal consciousness. Nothing at all of ordinary consciousness can enter that world. The soul is *touched*—contact with the spiritual world is established—when the powers of soul life are strengthened by meditation. Through these soul powers, pictures arise from the flux of soul life.

In themselves, these images are like a great tableau, woven entirely by the soul itself. To be precise, they are woven from powers the soul has gained in the sensory world. The images woven in the soul can be compared only to memory. The clearer we are about this, the better we shall understand clairvoyant consciousness, for then we shall have no illusions about its pictorial nature. On the contrary, we will develop a proper feeling for the way we should relate to the images of the suprasensory world. That is, we will learn to *read* through the images.

Of course, we are brought much closer to the nature and processes of the sensory world through our sensory impressions than we are to the suprasensory world through clairvoyantly seen images. Indeed, we could even say that those images are, initially, a kind of curtain that the soul places between itself and the suprasensory world when it feels touched by that world.

It is important that you find your way to suprasensory experience step by step. Experience gradually provides a proper interpretation, a right reading. More importantly, suprasensory experience, the vision itself, will demonstrate that what you see has nothing to do with memory images drawn from ordinary experiences. People make many absurd assertions in this area, having been convinced (or at least believing they have been convinced) that they have had certain suprasensory insights. How many there are who, convinced of the reality of repeated earthly lives, relate certain images that arise in their souls to experiences of a previous earthly existence. You should always be suspicious when such images seem to point to a previous earthly life that, in one way or another, is like one's present life or when they allow you to use an imagined earlier life to make it easier to understand *rationally* your present life.

When a *true* impression of a previous earthly life arises in *real* suprasensory experience, it is usually one that would be impossible to think up based upon all the desires and goals of your present life. For instance, you may receive an instantaneous impression of a prior earthly life in which you possess faculties or the like impossible in your present life. Such images that accompany our more important spiritual experiences rarely come from memories of ordinary life; usually, they are images we would never have thought of ordinarily.

This is true to an even greater extent in the case of genuine impressions from the purely suprasensory worlds. For example, it is often impossible to form images from ordinary life that relate to the existence between earthly lives—that is, to the period between your last death and your present birth on Earth. From that state, you can learn that while you were in the spiritual world you developed interests in people and phenomena that completely contradict the corresponding interests you developed during earthly life. You recognize that in earthly life you are often led to develop affection for something that you avoided during your spiritual life between death and birth. Everything about the life between death and birth that could arise from memories is necessarily different from the impression you receive from real perception of the spiritual world.

Naturally, when I offer such descriptions, those who are unfamiliar with spiritual research may disagree, saying, "I can see you are very fond of this idea, but human nature is complex. Every interest, every affection has its opposite secretly mixed into it. It comes to you at a certain moment, in connection with something specific. You call it a prebirth experience, but maybe it can be explained through natural facts in the subconscious soul."

Generally, we cannot say much against such an argument because it is certainly correct in many cases. It is not easy to gain *unassailable* knowledge through suprasensory consciousness. It is true that someone who is supposed to be a spiritual researcher can mistakenly attribute a subconscious memory to a spiritual experience of prebirth life. Nevertheless, it is also true that spiritual-scientific training leads to a level of self-knowledge *that includes the subconscious soul* and that, in this way, genuine spiritual science can free itself from illusions in this regard.

Here we need affirm only that *true* suprasensory insights are those in which, *in the act of cognition*, we can *differentiate* between what the suprasensory worlds provide and what imagination provides. The capacity to differentiate is acquired through experience in suprasensory worlds. Consequently, we can differentiate between perception and fantasy, just as we are able to differentiate between a poker that is red-hot to the touch and one that is hot only in our imagination.

From Rudolf Steiner, A Way of Self Knowledge and the Threshold of the Spiritual World *(SteinerBooks, 2006), pp. 11–17.*

3. The Foundation Stone Meditation

Human soul!
You live in the limbs,
that carry you through the world of space
into Spirit's ocean being.
Practice *spirit recollection*
in the soul's depths,
where, in the powerful
world creator's being,
your "I" gains being
in the "I" of God;
then, you will truly *live*
in human cosmic being.

For the Father spirit of the heights reigns
in the world's depths, begetting being.
Spirits of power,
let what echoes in the depths
ring out from the heights,
saying:
Humanity's being is born from the Divine.

Spirits hear this in the east, west, north, south.
May human beings hear it.

Human Soul!
You live within the beat of heart and lung,
which leads you through time's rhythm
into the feeling of your own soul's being.
Practice *spirit awareness*
in serenity of soul,
where surging
deeds of world becoming
unite your "I"
with the "I" of the world;
then, you shall truly *feel*
in the soul's inner working.

For the Christ will reigns in the spheres around us,
shedding grace upon souls in the world's rhythms.
Spirits of light,
let what is formed in the west
be kindled in the east,
saying:
In Christ, death becomes life.

Spirits hear this in east, west, north, south.
May human beings hear it.

Human Soul!
You live within the silence of the head,
where, from our eternal foundations,
cosmic thoughts unveil before you:
Practice *spirit beholding*
in peace of thought,
where for your free willing
the gods' eternal aims
shed cosmic beings' light
on your innermost "I."
Then, you will truly *think*
in the foundations of the human spirit.

For Spirit's cosmic thoughts reign
in the world's being, beseeching light.
Spirits of soul,
let what is heard in the heights
be sought in the depths,
saying:
The soul awakens in Spirit's cosmic thinking.

Spirits hear this in east, west, north, south.
May human beings hear it.

At the turn of time
cosmic spirit light descended
into Earth's stream of being.
Night's darkness
had run its course;
Day-bright light
streamed into human souls—
light
that warms
poor shepherds' hearts;
light
that illumines
the wise heads of kings.

Divine light,
Christ Sun,
warm through
our hearts,
illumine
our heads
so that what
we would create
from our hearts
and guide from our heads,
in sure willing,
may be good.

From Rudolf Steiner, Start Now! A Book of Soul and Spiritual Exercises *(SteinerBooks, 2004), pp. 239–242.*

5.

Christ and Other Exalted Beings

Christ, the Virgin Sophia, and the Holy Spirit

We have reached the point of discussing the change that takes place in the human astral body through meditation, concentration, and other practices given in the various methods of initiation. We have seen that the astral body is thus affected so that it develops in itself the organs needed to perceive in the higher worlds, and we have said that, up to this point, the principle of initiation is really the same everywhere, though the forms of practices fully conform to the particular cultural epochs. The main difference appears with the occurrence of what must follow. The student cannot actually perceive in the higher worlds unless the organs that have been formed out of the astral part impress, or stamp, themselves upon the ether body, or the etheric element.

The ancient name for refashioning the astral body indirectly through meditation and concentration is *catharsis*, or *purification*. Its purpose is to rid the astral body of all that hinders it from becoming harmonious and orderly, which enables it to acquire higher organs. The astral body is endowed with the seed of these higher organs; it is only necessary to evoke the forces already present. We have said that the most varied methods can be used to bring about this catharsis. Students can go quite far in this matter of catharsis if, for example, they have gone through and experienced inwardly everything in my book *Intuitive Thinking as a Spiritual Path: A Philosophy of Freedom*, feeling that the book was a stimulation and reaching the point of actually being able to reproduce the thoughts as presented there. Those who have the same relationship to this book that a virtuoso (in playing a selection on the piano) has with the composer of a piece—that is, one reproduces the whole inwardly and naturally according to one's ability—then, through the strictly established sequence of thought of this book (for *it is* written in this way), catharsis will become highly developed.

The important point in matters such as this book is that we practice all the thoughts so that they become active. In many books today, merely by changing the system a little, statements earlier in a book can be said later just as well. In *Intuitive Thinking as a Spiritual Path*, however, this is not possible. Page 150 could not be placed fifty pages earlier in the subject any more than a dog's hind legs could be exchanged with the forelegs. The book is a logically arranged organism, and the effect of working out the thoughts in it is a kind of inner training. Thus, there are various methods of bringing about catharsis. If a person has not been successful in doing this after going through this book, one should not assume that what has been said is untrue; rather, one has not studied it properly or with sufficient energy or thoroughness.

Now something else must be considered. Once this catharsis has taken place, and the astral organs have formed in the astral body, it must all be imprinted upon the ether body. In pre-Christian initiation, it was done as follows. Once the student had undergone suitable preparatory training (frequently lasting for years), one was told that the astral body had been developed enough to have astral organs of perception, and that they could now become aware of their counterpart in the ether body. At this point, the student was subjected to a process that today is not only unnecessary (at least for our cultural epoch), but also is not really feasible. The student was put into a lethargic state for three-and-a-half days and, during that time, was treated in such a way that the astral body left the physical and ether bodies (which occurs every night in sleep), and even the ether body was lifted out of the body to some degree.

Nonetheless, they made certain that the physical body remained intact and that the student did not die in the process. The ether body was liberated from the forces of the physical body that act upon it. It had become elastic and plastic, so to speak. When the sensory organs formed in the astral body sank down into the ether body, it received an imprint from the whole astral body. The student was then returned to a normal state by the chief priest, the astral body and "I" were reunited with the physical and ether bodies, a procedure that the chief priest understood well. Then, not only did the student experience catharsis, but also what is called *illumination*, or *photismos*. At that point, one could not only perceive everything physically perceptible in the surrounding world, but also employ spiritual organs of perception, indicating the ability to see and perceive the spiritual. Initiation essentially involved two processes: purification (purging) and illumination.

Next, human evolution entered a phase in which it became increasingly impossible to draw the ether body out of the physical without a great disturbance in all its functions. This was because the tendency of post-Atlantean evolution was to cause the ether body to attach more closely to the physical body. Thus, it became necessary to practice other methods of initiation in such a way that, without separating the physical and ether bodies, the astral body—having become sufficiently developed through catharsis and able on its own to return to the physical and ether bodies—could imprint its organs on the ether body, despite the hindrance of the physical body.

It was necessary for stronger forces to become active in meditation and concentration, so that there would be a strong impulse in the astral body to overcome the power of resistance of the physical body. Initially, there was an actual, specifically Christian initiation in which the student had to undergo the procedure I described in my previous lecture as "the seven steps."[1] Once one had gone trough these feelings and experiences, the astral body was affected with such intensity that it molded its organs of perception (perhaps only after years, but sooner or

---

1. Lecture of May, 30, 1908, in Hamburg, entitled "Christian Initiation." The seven steps, or exercises, correspond to Christ's Passion: 1) washing of the feet; 2) scourging; 3) crowning with thorns; 4) stigmata; 5) death and descent into Hell; 6) interment and resurrection; 7) ascension.

later nevertheless) and then impressed them upon the ether body, thus making of the student one of the illumined. This kind of initiation, which is specifically Christian, could not be described fully unless I were able to lecture on its particular aspects every day for perhaps two weeks instead of just a few days. But that is not the important thing. Previously, you were given certain details of the Christian initiation. In this lecture, we wish only to become familiar with its principle.

By meditating continually upon passages of the Gospel of John, the Christian student is able to attain initiation without the lethargic sleep for three-and-a-half days. Each day, we allow the first verses of the Gospel of John to work on us, from "In the beginning was the Word" to "full of grace and truth" (John 1:1–14). These become a very significant meditation. They have inner force because this Gospel does not exist simply to be read and understood merely through the intellect; instead, it must be experienced fully and felt inwardly. It is a force that comes to the help of initiation and works for it. Then the "washing of the feet," the "scourging," and other inner processes will be experienced as astral visions, corresponding fully to the descriptions in the Gospel, beginning with chapter 13.

The Rosicrucian initiation, though based on a Christian foundation, works more with other symbolic ideas that produce catharsis, primarily *imaginative* pictures. This is another modification that had to be used, because humankind had proceeded a step in evolution, and the methods of initiation must conform to what has gradually evolved.

We must understand that, once students have attained this initiation, they are fundamentally different from what they had been. Previously, they were connected only with phenomena of the material world, but now they have the possibility of associating with events and beings of the spirit world. This assumes that such individuals have acquired knowledge in a far more real sense than in the abstract, dry, and prosaic sense that one usually associates with knowledge. Those who acquire spiritual knowledge discover that the process is quite different. It is a complete realization of that beautiful expression, "Know yourself." However, the most dangerous thing in terms of knowledge is to misunderstand these words, and today this occurs only too frequently. Many people construe the words "know yourself" to mean one should no longer look at the physical world but gaze only into one's own inner being, looking for everything spiritual there. This is a very wrong understanding of the saying and not at all what it means.

We must understand clearly that, from a certain perspective, true higher knowledge is also an evolution one has attained toward another, which had not been attained previously. Those who practice self-knowledge by mere self-absorption see only what they already possess. They gain nothing new, but only come to know their lower self in the present sense of the word. One's inner nature is just one aspect needed for knowledge; another necessary part must be added. Without both aspects, there is no real knowledge. Through our inner nature, we can develop organs by which we gain knowledge. However, just as the eye, as an external sensory organ, must look outwardly at the Sun and would not perceive it by looking inwardly, likewise the inner organs of perception gaze outwardly. In other words, *to perceive, they gaze into an outer spiritual reality.*

The concept "knowledge" had a much deeper and a more genuine meaning when spiritual phenomena were better understood than they are today. Read in the Bible "Adam knew his wife," or this or that patriarch "knew his wife." One does not need to look very far to understand that this expression means "to fructify." When we consider the saying "know yourself," in the Greek it does not mean that we stare into our own inner being, but that we *fructify* ourselves by what flows into us from the spirit world. "Know yourself" means "fructify yourself" with the substance of the spiritual world.

This requires two steps. Specifically, we must prepare ourselves through catharsis and illumination, and then we open our inner being freely to the spirit world. In this sense, we may liken our inner nature to the female aspect and the outer spiritual nature to the male. The inner being must be made available to receiving the *higher self.* Once this happens, the higher human self flows into us from the spiritual world. We may ask: Where is this higher human self? Is it within the personal human being? No, it is not there. During the Saturn, Sun, and Moon periods, the higher self was diffused over the entire cosmos. At that time, the cosmic "I" was spread out over all of humankind. Now, however, we must allow it to work upon us. We must permit this "I" to work upon our previously prepared inner nature.

Our human inner nature, or astral body, must be cleansed, purified, ennobled, and subjected to catharsis, and then we may expect the external spirit to flow into us for illumination. This will happen after we have been prepared ourselves so that we have subjected our astral body to catharsis, thereby developing our inner organs of perception. The astral body, in any case, has progressed so far that when it now dips into the ether and physical bodies, illumination, or *photismos,* is the result. In fact, the astral body imprints its organs upon the ether body, making it possible for the human being to perceive a surrounding spiritual world. It becomes possible for one's inner being, or astral body, to receive what the ether body is able to offer to it—what the ether body draws from the entire cosmos, the cosmic "I."

This cleansed and purified astral body bears none of the impure impressions of the physical world inwardly at the moment of illumination, but only the organs of perception of the spiritual world. In esoteric Christianity this is called the "pure, chaste, and wise Virgin Sophia." Through all that is received during catharsis, the student cleanses and purifies the astral body so that it becomes transformed into the Virgin Sophia. Moreover, when the Virgin Sophia encounters the cosmic, or universal "I," which leads to illumination, the student is surrounded by spiritual light. Even today, in esoteric Christianity this second power that approaches the Virgin Sophia is called the "Holy Spirit." Therefore, according to esoteric Christianity, it is correct to say that, through his processes of initiation, Christian esotericists attain the purification and cleansing of the astral body. They make the astral body into the Virgin Sophia and are illumined from above. If you prefer, one may say "overshadowed by the 'Holy Spirit,' or cosmic, universal 'I.'"

Moreover, those who have been illumined in this way and who have, according to esoteric Christianity, received the "Holy Spirit" into themselves, speak afterward in a different way. How do they speak? When they speak of Saturn, Sun, and Moon or about the various members of the human being or about the processes of cosmic evolution, they are not expressing *their own* opinions, which do not even come under consideration. When they speak of Saturn, *Saturn itself* speaks through them. When they speak of the Sun, the solar spirit being speaks through them. They become the instrument; the personal "I" has been eclipsed, which means that at such moments it has become impersonal and it is the cosmic, universal "I" that is using the human "I" as an instrument to speak.

Thus, in true esoteric teaching that arises from esoteric Christianity, we should not speak of *views* or opinions, because, in the highest sense of the word, this is incorrect; there is no such thing. According to esoteric Christianity, those who speak with the right attitude of mind toward the world will, for instance, be able to say: if I were to tell people that there are two horses outside, it is unimportant that one of them pleases me less than the other and that I consider one horse to be worthless. The important point is to describe the horses to others and give the facts. Likewise, observations in the spiritual worlds must be described regardless of personal opinions. In every spiritual-scientific system of teaching, only the sequence of facts must be related, and this must have nothing to do with the opinions of the one who relates them.

Consequently, we have acquired two concepts in their spiritual significance. We have come to know the nature of the Virgin Sophia, which is the purified astral body, and the nature of the "Holy Spirit," the cosmic, universal "I," which is received by the Virgin Sophia and can then speak out of the purified astral body. There is something else to be attained, an even higher stage, which is the ability to help someone else—the ability to give others the impulse to accomplish both of these. People of our evolutionary period can receive the Virgin Sophia (or purified astral body) and the Holy Spirit (illumination) as described, but only Jesus Christ could give to the Earth what was needed to accomplish this. He implanted in the spiritual part of the Earth the forces that make it possible for this to happen at all. This has been described in the Christian initiation.

You may wonder how this happened. To understand this, first we must understand a purely historical fact, the custom of giving names that, when the Gospels were written, was different from current custom. Those who interpret the Gospel today do not understand the principle of giving names when the Gospels were written, and they speak incorrectly as a result. It is indeed very difficult to describe the principle of giving names at that time, yet we can make it comprehensible, though only roughly. Imagine that we meet a man and, instead of holding onto a name that does not fit him (the one given in today's usual abstract way), we notice his most distinguishing characteristics. We notice the most prominent attribute of his character, and we are able to discern clairvoyantly the deeper foundations of his being. Then we name him according to the most important qualities that we believe should be attributed to him. If we were to follow such a method of giving names, it would be, at a lower, more elementary stage, similar to what was done by those who gave names in the way of the writer of the Gospel of John.

To clarify that writer's way of giving names, consider this. The author of John's Gospel observed the physical, historic Mother of Jesus in her most prominent characteristics and thought: *Where can I find a name for her that most perfectly expresses her true being?* Then, because she had reached the spiritual heights upon which she stood by means of her earlier incarnations, and because in her outer personality she appeared to be a counterpart, a revelation of what esoteric Christianity calls the *Virgin Sophia*, he called the Mother of Jesus the *Virgin Sophia*. This is what she was always called in the esoteric places where esoteric Christianity was taught. Exoterically, he leaves her entirely unnamed, in contrast to the others, who chose for her the secular name of Mary. He could not use the secular name; in the name, he had to express the profound, cosmically historic evolution.

He does this by indicating that she cannot be called Mary. Moreover, he places her sister Mary at her side, the wife of Cleophas, and calls her simply the *Mother of Jesus*. Thus, he shows that he does not wish to mention her name, and that it cannot be revealed publicly. In esoteric circles, she is always called *Virgin Sophia*. It was she who represented the *Virgin Sophia* as a manifested historical personality.

If we wish to go further into the nature of Christianity and its founder, we must consider yet another mystery. We should understand clearly how to distinguish between the ones esoteric Christianity calls *Jesus of Nazareth* and *Jesus Christ,* the Christ dwelling in Jesus of Nazareth. This means that, in the historical personality of Jesus of Nazareth, we are dealing with a highly developed human being who passed through many incarnations and, following a cycle of high development, was reincarnated again. He is one who, because of this, was attracted to a mother so pure that the writer of the Gospel could call her *Virgin Sophia*.

Thus, we are dealing with Jesus of Nazareth, a highly developed human being who had progressed far in his evolution in previous incarnations and, in that incarnation, began at a highly spiritual stage. The other evangelists were not as highly illumined as the writer of this Gospel was. The actual sensory world was more available to them, a world in which they saw their master and the Messiah moving about as Jesus of Nazareth. The mysterious spiritual relationships—or at least those of the heights into which the writer of the Gospel of John could see—were hidden from them. Therefore, they emphasized the fact that the Father lived in Jesus of Nazareth—the Father who had always existed in Judaism and who was transmitted down through the generations as the "God of the Jews." Moreover, they expressed this when they said, "If we trace the ancestry of Jesus of Nazareth back through the generations, we can prove that the same blood flows in him that flowed through those generations." The evangelists provide precise genealogical tables and, according to them, they show different stages of evolution at which they stand.

For Matthew, it was important to show that Jesus of Nazareth is a person in whom Father Abraham lives. The blood of Father Abraham flowed down through the generations as far as Jesus. Thus, he traced the genealogical tables back to Abraham. He had a more materialistic view than Luke did. It was important to Luke not just to show that the God who lived in Abraham was also present in Jesus. He also wished to show that the ancestry, or line of descent, can be traced back even further, to Adam, and that Adam was a son of the very Godhead, meaning that he belonged to a time when humanity had just made the transition from a spiritual to a physical state. Both Matthew and Luke wished to show that this earthly Jesus of Nazareth has his being only in what can be traced back to the divine Father power. This was not important to the writer of the Gospel of John, who was able to see into the spirit world. The words "I and Father Abraham are one" was not important to him, but that an eternal exists in the human being in every moment of time and was present in him before Father Abraham. He wanted to show this. In the beginning was the Word that is called the "I AM." He was, before all external phenomena and beings; he was in the beginning. For those who preferred to describe Jesus of Nazareth and were able to describe only him, it was a matter of showing how the blood flowed down through the generations from the beginning. To them, it was important to show that the same blood that flowed down through the generations also flowed in Joseph, the father of Jesus.

If we could speak esoterically, we would, of course, need to discuss the idea of the so-called virgin birth, but this can be discussed only in the most intimate circles. It belongs to the deepest of mysteries, and the misunderstanding connected with this idea arises because people do not know the meaning of "virgin birth." The assumption is that it means there was no father, but this is not it. Something much more profound and mysterious is behind it, compatible with what the other disciples wanted to show: that Joseph *is* the father of Jesus. If they were to deny this, then all the trouble they took to show this as a fact would have no meaning. They wanted to show that the ancient God exists in Jesus of Nazareth. Luke, especially, wanted to make this very clear. He traced the whole ancestry back to Adam and then to God. How could he have come to such a conclusion if he had wanted only to say that such a genealogical tree exists, but that Joseph actually had nothing to do with it. It would be very strange if people were to take the trouble to represent Joseph as a very important person and then leave him out of the whole affair.

In the event of Palestine, we are dealing only with this highly developed person, Jesus of Nazareth, who had passed through many incarnations and had developed himself so highly that he needed such an extraordinary mother as the Virgin Sophia.

However, we are also dealing with another mystery. When Jesus of Nazareth was thirty years old, he had advanced to a certain stage because of what he had experienced in his present incarnation and was able to do something that it is possible in exceptional cases.

We know that human beings are made up of physical, ether, astral, and "I" being. The fourfold human is the human being who lives here among us. For those at a certain high stage of evolution, it is possible at a certain point to draw the "I" out of the three other bodies and abandon them, while leaving them intact and entirely unharmed. The "I" then "goes" into the spiritual worlds as the three bodies remain behind. We encounter this process at times in cosmic evolution. At some especially exalted, enraptured moment, the "I" of an individual departs and enters the spirit world (under certain conditions this can be extended for a long period), and because the three bodies are so highly developed by the "I" that lived in them, they are suitable instruments for an even higher being, who takes possession of them. In the thirtieth year of Jesus of Nazareth, the being we have called the Christ took possession of his physical, ether, and astral bodies. This Christ being could not incarnate in an ordinary child's body, but only in one that had been prepared by a highly developed "I," because the Christ being had never been incarnated in a physical body. Thus, after the thirtieth year, we are dealing with the Christ within Jesus of Nazareth.

What actually happened? The corporeality of Jesus of Nazareth, which he had left behind, was so matured and perfected that the *Sun Logos* (the being of the six Elohim we described as the spiritual solar being) was able to penetrate into it. It could incarnate for three years in this corporeality and become flesh. Thus entered the Sun Logos, the Holy Spirit, who can shine into human beings through illumination. The universal, cosmic "I" entered, and for three years the Sun Logos spoke through the body of Jesus. The Christ spoke through the body of Jesus during these three years. This is indicated in the Gospel of John and in the other Gospels by the descent of the dove, or Holy Spirit, upon Jesus of Nazareth.

Esoteric Christianity says that, at that moment, the "I" of Jesus of Nazareth left his body and that, from that point on, the Christ was in him and speaking through him to teach and work. This was the first event, according to the Gospel of John. We now have the Christ within the astral, ether, and physical bodies of Jesus of Nazareth, where he worked as described until the Mystery of Golgotha. What occurred on Golgotha? Let us consider this important moment when the blood flowed from the wounds of the crucified Savior. To help you better understand me, I will compare what occurred with something else.

Imagine a container filled with water. We dissolve salt in the water, and the water becomes transparent. Moreover, because we have warmed the water, we have made a salt solution. Now let us cool the water. The salt precipitates, and we see the salt condense below to form a deposit on the bottom of the container. This is the process for those who see only with physical eyes. Those who see with spiritual eyes see something else happening. As the salt condenses below, the spirit of the salt flows up through the water and fills it. The salt can condense only after the spirit of the salt leaves it and becomes diffused in the water. Those who understand such matters know that, wherever condensation occurs, spiritualization also occurs. Whatever condenses below in this way has a spiritual counterpart above. In the case of the salt when it condenses and is precipitated below, its spirit flows upward and disseminates.

It was not only a physical process that occurred when the blood flowed from the wounds of the Savior, but was accompanied by a spiritual process—the Holy Spirit that was received at the Baptism united with the Earth. The Christ himself flowed into the very being of the Earth. From then on, the Earth was changed, and this is the reason for saying to you, in earlier lectures, that if the Earth had been viewed from a distant star, one would have seen that its whole appearance was altered by the Mystery of Golgotha. The Sun Logos became part of the Earth, formed an alliance with it, and became the spirit of the Earth. He achieved this by entering the body of Jesus of Nazareth in his thirtieth year and by remaining active there for three years, after which he remained on Earth.

Most important is that this event should affect true Christians. It must provide something through which we may gradually develop the beginnings of a purified astral body in the Christian sense. There had to be something there for Christians, whereby they could make the astral body increasingly like a Virgin Sophia and, through it, inwardly receive the Holy Spirit that was able to spread out over the whole Earth, but that could not be received by those whose astral bodies did not resemble the Virgin Sophia. There had to be something with the power to transform the human astral body into a Virgin Sophia. What is this power? It is the fact that Jesus Christ trusted the disciple whom he loved (the writer of the Gospel of John) with the mission of describing truly and faithfully, through his own illumination, the events of Palestine so that human beings might be affected by them.

For those who allow what is written in the Gospel of John to affect them sufficiently, their astral body will begin the process of becoming a Virgin Sophia and becoming receptive to the Holy Spirit. Gradually, through the strength of the impulse that emanates from this Gospel, it will become susceptible of feeling the true spirit and later of perceiving it. This mission, this charge, was given to the writer of the Gospel by Jesus Christ. You need only read the Gospel. The Mother of Jesus—the Virgin Sophia in the esoteric meaning of Christianity—stands at the foot of the Cross, and from the Cross, the Christ says to the disciple whom he loved: "Henceforth, this is your Mother," and from this hour the disciple took her to himself. This means: "The force that was in my astral body and made it capable of bearing the Holy Spirit, I now give over to you; you shall write down what this astral body has been able to acquire through its development." "And the disciple took her unto himself," which means he wrote the Gospel of John. And this Gospel of John is the Gospel in which the writer has concealed powers which develop the Virgin Sophia. At the Cross, he was entrusted with receiving that force as his mother and with being the true, genuine interpreter of the Messiah. This means, in fact, that if you live wholly in accordance with the Gospel of John and understand it spiritually, it has the power to lead you to Christian catharsis and to give you the Virgin Sophia. Then, the Holy Spirit, united with the Earth, will grant you illumination, or *photismos*, according to the Christian meaning.

The most intimate disciples experienced something in Palestine that was so powerful that, from that time on, they possessed at least the capacity of perceiving in the spiritual world. The most intimate disciples had received this capacity into themselves. Perceiving in the spirit, in the Christian sense, means that one transforms the astral body to such a degree through the power of the event of Palestine that what one sees need not be present externally or physically perceptible. One possesses something through which to perceive in the spirit. There were such intimate students. Through the Event of Palestine, the woman who anointed the feet of Jesus Christ in Bethany received the powerful force needed for spiritual perception, and she is one of those who first understood that what lived in Jesus was present after his death—that it had been resurrected. She possessed that faculty.

One might ask: What is the source of such a possibility? It arose through the development of her inner sensory organs. Are we told this in the Gospel? Indeed, we are told that Mary Magdalene was led to the grave, that the body had disappeared, and that she saw two spiritual forms there. These two spiritual forms can always be seen for a certain time after death when the corpse is present. On one side is the astral body, and on the other side is what gradually separates from it as ether body and passes over into the cosmic ether. Wholly apart from the physical body, two spiritual forms are present that belong to the spiritual world.

> Then the disciples went away again unto their own home. But Mary stood without at the sepulcher weeping: and as she wept, she stooped down and looked into the sepulcher and saw two angels in white sitting, the one at the head, and the other at the feet, where the body of Jesus had lain. (John 20:10–12)

She beheld this because she had become clairvoyant through the force and power of the event of Palestine. Further, she beheld something else: the Risen Christ. Was it necessary for her to be clairvoyant to see the Christ? If you saw a man in physical form a few days ago, do you not think you would recognize him if he appeared before you?

> And when she had thus said, she turned herself back, and saw Jesus standing, and knew not that it was Jesus. Jesus said to her, Woman, why do you weep? Whom do you seek? She, supposing him to be the gardener... (John 20:14–15)

Moreover, to tell us as exactly as possible, it was not said only once, but again at the next appearance of the Risen Christ, when Jesus appeared at the sea of Gennesareth.

> But when the morning was now come, Jesus stood on the shore, but the disciples knew not that it was Jesus. (John 21:4)

Esoteric students find him there. Those who had received the full force of the event of Palestine could grasp the situation and see that it was the Risen Jesus who could be perceived spiritually. Although the disciples and Mary Magdalene saw him, yet there were some among them who were less able to develop clairvoyant power. One of these was Thomas. It is said that he was not present the first time the disciples saw the Lord, and he declared he would have to lay his hands in His wounds, he would have to touch physically the body of the Risen Christ. You ask: What happened? The effort was then made to assist him to develop spiritual perception. And how was this done? Let us take the words of the Gospel itself:

> And after eight days again his disciples were within, and Thomas with them: then came Jesus, the doors being shut, and stood in the midst, and said, Peace be unto you. Then he said to Thomas, reach forth your fingers and behold my hands, and reach out your hand and thrust it into my side; and be not faithless, but believing. (John 20:26–27)

You will see something if you do not rely on the outer appearance but are imbued with inner power. This inner power that should arise from the event of Palestine is called "Faith." It is no ordinary force, but an inner clairvoyant power. Permeate yourself with inner power and you will no longer need to consider only what you see outwardly as real. Blessed are they who are able to know what they do not see outwardly.

We see that we are dealing with the full reality and truth of the Resurrection and that only those who have developed the inner power to perceive in the spirit world can understand it fully. This will make the last chapter of the Gospel of John comprehensible to you. Again and again it is shown there that the closest followers of Jesus Christ have reached the stage of the Virgin Sophia, because the event of Golgotha had been consummated in their presence. But when they had to stand firm for the first time and actually to witness a spiritual event, they were still blinded and had to find their way. They did not know that he was the same one who had been among them earlier. Here is something we must grasp with the most subtle concepts. A grossly materialistic person would say that the Resurrection is undermined. The miracle of the Resurrection is to be taken quite literally, for he said: "Lo, I am with you always, even unto the end of the world"—even until the end of the age, until the end of the cosmic age.

He is present and will come again, though not in a form of flesh but in a form that those who have been sufficiently developed through the power of the Gospel of John can actually perceive, and, possessing the power to perceive him, they will no longer be unbelieving. The mission of the anthroposophic movement is to prepare those who have the will to allow themselves to be prepared for the return of the Christ on Earth. This is the cosmic historical significance of spiritual science: to prepare humankind and to keep our eyes open for the time when the Christ will appear again actively among humanity during the sixth cultural epoch, so that what was indicated to us in the marriage at Cana may be accomplished for a great part of humanity.

Therefore, the worldview gained from spiritual science appears like an execution of the Christian testament. To be led to real Christianity, people of the future will have to receive the spiritual teaching that spiritual science is able to give. Many may still say today that spiritual science actually contradicts true Christianity. But those are the little "popes" who form opinions about things they know nothing of and who make a dogma out of "What I do not know does not exist."

Such intolerance will grow in the future, and Christianity will experience the greatest danger specifically from those today who believe they can be called good Christians. The Christianity of spiritual science will experience serious attacks from the "Christians" in name, because all views must change before a true spiritual understanding of Christianity can come about. Above all, the soul must become increasingly conversant with and understanding of the legacy of the one who wrote the Gospel of John, the great school of the Virgin Sophia, and John's Gospel itself. Only spiritual science can lead us deeper into this Gospel.

These lectures could offer only examples to show how spiritual science can introduce us to the Gospel of John, for it is impossible to explain the whole of it. We read in the Gospel itself: "And there are also many other things that Jesus did that, if every one should be written, I suppose that even the world itself could not contain the books that should be written" (John 21:25). Just as the Gospel itself cannot go into all the details of the event of Palestine, likewise is it impossible for even the longest course of lectures to present the full spiritual substance of the Gospel. Therefore, we must be satisfied with these indications for now and content ourselves with the thought that, through just such indications in the course of human evolution, the true testament of Christianity becomes executed.

Let us allow all this to affect us to the degree that we may possess the power to hold on to the foundation we recognize in the Gospel of John, especially when others say to us: the concepts you are giving are too complicated. There are so many concepts that we must make our own first in order to comprehend this Gospel—the Gospel is for the simple and naïve, and we dare not approach them with too many concepts and thoughts. There are many who say this today. Perhaps they refer to another saying: "Blessed are the poor in spirit, for theirs is the kingdom of heaven." One can merely quote such a saying as long as one does not understand it, because it really means: "Blessed are the beggars in spirit, for they shall reach the kingdom of heaven within themselves." This means that those who are like beggars of the spirit and who desire to receive more and more of the spirit will find in themselves the kingdom of heaven.

Today, the idea is all too prevalent that all things religious mean primitive and simple. People say: we acknowledge that science possesses many complicated ideas, but we do not grant the same to faith and religion. Faith and religion, say many "Christians," must be simple and naïve; they demand this. And many rely on a view that is perhaps rarely quoted, but today haunts the minds of people. Voltaire, one of the great teachers of materialism, expressed it thus: those who wish to be prophets must find believers, for what they assert must be believed, and only the simple, always repeated in simplicity, find believers.

This is often true of prophets, both true and false. They trouble themselves to say something and repeat it again and again, and the people come to believe it simply because it is repeated constantly. Representatives of spiritual science do not want to be such prophets; they do not wish to be prophets at all. Moreover, it may frequently be said that not only do they repeat, but that they also always elucidate matters from other perspectives and discuss them in other ways. When people make such statements, however, they are not really at fault. Prophets hope that people will believe in them. Spiritual science, on the other hand, does not wish to lead people to *belief* but to *knowledge*.

Let us, therefore, take Voltaire's statement in a different way. He says that *the simple is believable* and is the concern of the prophet. Spiritual science says: *the diverse whole is knowable.* Let us try to understand better that multiplicity is a part of spiritual science; it is not a creed but a path to knowledge. Consequently, it bears within it the diverse whole. Let us not avoid gathering much to help us understand the Gospel of John, one of the most important Christian documents.

We have tried to assemble the most varied material that allows us to understand increasingly the profound truths of this Gospel. To understand how the physical mother of Jesus was an outer manifestation, or image, of the Virgin Sophia; to understand the spiritual importance of the Virgin Sophia for the student of the mysteries, whom the Christ loved; to understand how, for the other Evangelists (who view the bodily descent of Jesus as important), the physical father plays his significant role when it was a matter of the external imprint of the God idea in the blood; and to understand the significance that the Holy Spirit had for John—the Holy Spirit through which the Christ was begotten in the body of Jesus and lived therein during the three years, symbolized for us by the descent of the dove at the baptism by John.

If we understand this, we must call the father of Jesus Christ the "Holy Spirit who begot the Christ in the bodies of Jesus." Then, if we can comprehend something from all sides, we will find it easy to understand why the disciples who were less highly initiated could not give us such a profound picture of the events of Palestine, as did the disciple whom the Lord loved. Moreover, if people today speak of the synoptic Gospels as the only authoritative Gospels for them, this shows only that they are unwilling to make an effort to understand the true form of the Gospel of John. People resemble the God they understand. If we try to create a feeling, an experience, from what we can learn from spiritual science about the Gospel of John, we will find that this Gospel is not a textbook but a force that can become active within our souls.

If these short lectures have aroused the feeling in you that this Gospel contains not only what we have been discussing here, but also that, indirectly, through the medium of words, it contains a force that can develop the soul itself, then the real purpose of these lectures has been understood correctly. Not only was something intended for the intellectual capacity of understanding, but also that what takes a roundabout path through this intellectual understanding may condense into feelings and inner experiences, and that these feelings and experiences shall be a result of the facts that have been presented here. If, in a certain sense, this has been understood correctly, we will also comprehend what is meant when it is said that the anthroposophic movement has the mission of raising Christianity into wisdom, and to understand Christianity correctly and indirectly through spiritual wisdom. We will understand that Christianity is just at the beginning of its activity and that its true mission will be fulfilled once it has been understood in its true spiritual form. The more these lectures are understood in this way, the more they have been comprehended in the sense intended.

From Rudolf Steiner, The Gospel of St. John *(Anthroposophic Press, 1962), lecture in Hamburg, May 31, 1908, pp. 174–192.*

6.

Reincarnation, Karma, and the Dead

Destiny and Reincarnation of the Spirit

The soul lives and acts in the middle, between body and spirit. Impressions reaching the soul through the body are fleeting and present only as long as the body's organs are open to phenomena of the outer world. My eyes perceive the color of a rose only as long as they are open and face the rose. The presence of both the outer-world object and the bodily organ is needed for an impression, sensation, or perception to occur.

However, what I recognize in my spirit as true about the rose does not pass with the present moment. This truth does not at all depend on me; it would be true even if I had never experienced that rose. Whatever I may recognize through the spirit is grounded in an element of the soul's life that connects the soul to a universal content, a content that reveals itself in the soul but is independent of its transitory bodily basis. Whether this content is imperishable in every respect does not matter, but it is important that it is revealed in such a way that the soul's independent, imperishable aspect is involved, not its perishable physical basis. The soul's enduring aspect comes into view as soon as we become aware of experiences that are not limited by its transitory aspect. Here, too, the important point is not whether such experiences first enter consciousness through transitory bodily processes, but whether they contain something that, although it lives in the soul, nevertheless possesses a truth independent of any transitory perceptual processes.

The soul stands between the present and the permanent, in that it occupies the center ground between body and spirit.

However, it also mediates between the present and the permanent. It preserves the present for remembrance, wresting it away from perishability and giving it a place in the permanence of its own spiritual nature. The soul also puts the stamp of permanence on the temporal and temporary, since it does not simply surrender to fleeting stimuli, but also determines matters on its own initiative, incorporating its own essence into its actions. Through memory, the soul preserves yesterday; through action, it prepares tomorrow.

If my soul were unable to hold the red color of the rose through memory, it would have to perceive the red repeatedly to be aware of it. However, whatever remains after the external impression is gone, whatever my soul can retain, can again become a mental image, or representation, independent of the external impression. Through this ability, my soul turns the outer world into its own inner world by retaining the outer world through memory and continuing to lead an inner life with it, independent of any impressions acquired in the past. Thus, the soul's life becomes a lasting result of transitory impressions made by the outer world.

Actions, however, also acquire permanence once they have been impressed on the outer world. When I cut a branch from a tree, something that occurs because of my soul changes the course of events in the outer world. Something different would have occurred to the branch if I had not intervened through my action. I have invoked a series of consequences that would not have existed without me, and what I have done today will remain in effect tomorrow. It persists through my action, just as yesterday's impressions persist for my soul through memory.

In our ordinary consciousness, we do not usually form a concept of "becoming persistent through action" in the way that we form a concept of memory, of persisting as a result of observation or perception. However, is the "I" not linked just as strongly to a change in the world that results from its own action as it is to a memory that results from an impression? The "I" assesses new impressions differently according to the memories it does or does not have, of one thing or of another. As an "I" being, however, it also begins another relationship with the world that depends on whether it has performed one action or another. Whether I made an impression on someone else through something I have done depends on the presence or absence of something in the relationship of the world to my "I" being. I am a different person in my relationship to the world after I have made an impression on my environment. We do not notice this as easily as we notice how the "I" changes by gaining a memory, but this is only because, as soon as a memory is formed, it unites with the overall life of the soul, which we have always regarded as our own, while the external consequence of an action, released from this soul life, continues to work through aftereffects that are different from what we can recall about the action. Despite this, we must acknowledge that something exists now in the world as a result of our completed action, something whose character has been affected by the "I."

Thinking this through carefully, we must ask: Could it be that the results of our actions, whose character has been impressed on them by the "I," tend to return to the "I" just as an impression preserved in memory comes to life again when evoked by an outer circumstance? What is preserved in memory is waiting for a reason to reappear. Could it be the same with things in the outer world that have been made persistent by the character of the "I"? Are they waiting to approach the soul from outside, just as a memory waits for a reason to approach from inside? This is posed here only as a question, since these results, laden with the character of our "I," may well never have any reason or opportunity to meet our soul again. However, if we follow this line of thought carefully, we can immediately see that such results could exist and, by their very existence, determine the relationship of the world to the "I."

Now let us investigate whether anything in human life suggests that this conceptual possibility points to an actual fact.

❁

Looking first at memory, we can ask how it arises. Clearly, the process differs from the way sensation or perception arises. Without eyes, I could not have the sensation of blue. However, my eyes do not give me any memory of the blue. My eyes cannot provide the sensation unless something blue is in view at the moment. My bodily nature would allow all impressions to sink back into oblivion if something was not also taking place in the relationship between the outer world and my soul—that is, the formation of a present mental image through the act of perception, with the result that, through inner processes, I may later have a mental image again of something that originally caused a mental image from *outside*.

Those who have practiced observation of the soul will realize that it is wrong to say that, if I have a mental image today, that mental image will show up again tomorrow in my memory, having remained somewhere inside me in the meantime. On the contrary, the mental image that I have right now is a phenomenon that passes with the present moment. If memory intervenes, however, a process occurs in me that is caused by something additional that occurred in the relationship between me and the outer world, something other than the evoking of the present mental image. The old mental image has not been "stored" anywhere; the one my memory recalls is new. Remembering means the ability to visualize something new; it does not mean that a mental image can return to life. What appears today is different from the original mental image. This is important because, in the field of spiritual science, it is necessary to form more exact concepts about certain things than we do in ordinary life, or even in conventional science. Remembering means experiencing something that is no longer present, linking a past experience to one's present life. This happens in every instance of remembering. Suppose I encounter a man I recognize because I met him yesterday. He would be a stranger to me if I were unable to link the image formed through yesterday's perception to today's impression of him. Today's image is given to me by perception through my sensory system. Who conjures yesterday's image into my soul? It is the same being in me who was present at both yesterday's and today's encounters.

Throughout this discussion, we have called this being the "soul." Without this trusted keeper of the past, each outer impression would be new for us. The soul imprints on the body the process by which something becomes a memory. However, the soul must first imprint and then perceive that imprint, just as it perceives something external. In this way, the soul preserves memory. As keeper of the past, the soul continually collects treasures for the spirit.

I owe my ability to distinguish right from wrong to the fact that, as a human being, I am a thinking being capable of grasping truth in my spirit. Truth is eternal. Even if I were to continually lose sight of the past, making each impression new to me, the truth could always reveal itself to me again in phenomena. The spirit in me, however, is not restricted to impressions of the moment. My soul broadens the spirit's field of vision to include the past, and the more my soul can add to the spirit from the past, the richer the spirit becomes. The soul passes on to the spirit what it has received from the body.

At every moment of its life, therefore, the human spirit carries two very different elements: first, the eternal laws of truth and goodness; second, recollection of past experiences. All that it does is influenced by these two factors. Thus, if we want to understand a human spirit, we must know two different facts about it: how much of the eternal has been revealed to it, and how many treasures it holds from the past. Such treasures do not remain in an unchanged form for the spirit. The impressions we gain from experience gradually fade from memory, but their fruits do not. For example, we do not remember all the experiences we went through as children when we learned to read and write, but we would be unable to read and write now if we had not had those experiences and if their fruits had not been preserved in the form of abilities. This is how the spirit transforms its treasure of memories. It abandons to fate anything that can lead only to images of individual experiences, keeping only the power to heighten its own abilities. We can be sure that not a single experience goes to waste, since the soul preserves each one as a memory, and the spirit extracts from each whatever it can use to enhance its abilities and enrich its life. The human spirit grows as these experiences are worked over and assimilated. Thus, although we do not find our past experiences preserved in the spirit as though in a vault, we do find their effects in the abilities we have acquired.

❋

Thus far, we have considered the spirit and the soul only between birth and death, but we cannot leave it at that. That would be like considering the human body only within these same confines. Of course much can be discovered within these limits, but we would never be able to explain the human form through what exists between birth and death. This *Gestalt* cannot build itself directly from mere physical substances and forces, but must descend from another form, or *Gestalt,* like itself that has come about through reproduction. Physical substances and forces build the body during its lifetime, while the forces of reproduction enable it to produce another body of the same form, one that can carry the same life body. Every life body repeats its immediate ancestor, therefore the form of the life body is never arbitrary but inherited. The forces that have made my human form possible came from my ancestors.

However, the human spirit also assumes a specific form, or *Gestalt* (these words are used here in a spiritual sense). Human spiritual forms differ as much as they possibly can; no two individuals have the same spiritual form. Our observation in this area must be as calm and objective as it is on the physical plane. We cannot maintain that the spiritual differences in people result only from environmental differences, upbringing, and so on. Two people from similar environments and of similar educational backgrounds can still develop in very different ways. We are forced to admit that they must have begun life with very different endowments.

Here we are faced with an important situation that, if we fully recognize its implications, illumines the essential nature and constitution of the human being. Of course, if we choose to focus only on the material aspect of events, we could say that the individual differences in human personalities result from genetic differences in the reproductive cells from which they develop. If we consider the laws of heredity as discovered by Gregor Mendel and developed by others, this perspective can indeed seem very plausible and scientifically justified. Such a view, however, demonstrates only a lack of insight into how we actually relate to our experience. Careful observation of the pertinent details will show that outer circumstances affect different people in different ways through something that never interacts directly with their material development. A precise researcher in this area will see that what proceeds from material potentials is separate and distinct from what may originate in our interaction with our experiences, but forms only because the soul itself enters the interaction. Clearly, the soul relates to something in the outer world that, through its very nature, has no connection to genetic potentials.

In our physical form, or *Gestalt*, we differ from animals, our fellow creatures on Earth. Within certain limits, however, all human beings have a similar form; there is only one human genus and species. No matter how great the differences among races, tribes, peoples, and personalities, in all physical respects the similarity between two human beings is always greater than that between a human being and an animal of any species. Everything expressed in the human species is determined by heredity, passed from one generation to the next. Our human form is connected to this heredity. Just as a lion inherits its physical form only from its lion ancestors, we inherit ours only from our human ancestors.

The physical similarity between human beings is obvious to the eye, while the difference between human spiritual forms is equally clear to an unbiased spiritual view. This is shown by the very obvious fact that human individuals have biographies. If we were no more than members of our species, individual biographies would be impossible. A lion or a pigeon is of interest only as a member of the lion or pigeon species, and we understand everything essential about the individual by describing the species. It is unimportant whether we are dealing with a parent, child, or grandchild; the interesting aspect is common to all three generations. The significance of human individuals, however, begins where we are no longer merely members of a genus and species but become individuals. I cannot grasp the essential nature of Mr. John Doe by describing his son or his father; I must know his particular life story. If we think about the nature of biography, we can see that each human being is an individual genus with regard to the spirit.

Of course, when *biography* is defined as no more than a superficial list of events and experiences, we could argue that we could write a biography of a dog as we would that of a person. However, if a biographer captures a person's uniqueness, it will be clear that the biography of one human being corresponds to the description of an entire animal species. Clearly, something resembling a biography can be written about an animal, especially an intelligent one, but that is not the point. A human biography corresponds to the description of an animal species rather than to the biography of an individual animal. Some people will always try to refute statements like this by saying that those who work with animals (say, zookeepers) are well aware of individual differences between animals of the same species. Such comments, however, demonstrate only an inability to distinguish individual differences from those that can be acquired *only* through individuality.

Just as genus and species can be understood in a physical sense only when we understand that they are determined by heredity, the individual spiritual being can be understood only by means of a kind of *spiritual heredity*. I have my physical human form because I descended from my human ancestors. However, what is the source of what my biography expresses? As a physical human being, I repeat the form of my ancestors, but what do I repeat as a spiritual human being? If we insist that my biography must simply be accepted as it is, that it needs no further explanation, we might as well claim to have seen a hill out there where lumps of matter stuck themselves together to form a living human being.

As a physical human being, I descended from other physical human beings; I have the same form as the rest of the human genus. This shows that the characteristics of a genus are acquired within it through heredity. As a spiritual human being, however, I have my own particular form, just as I have a personal biography. Therefore, I must have acquired this form only from myself. Moreover, since I came into this world not with general predispositions of soul, but with very specific predispositions that determined the course of my life as shown by my biography, my work on myself must not have begun at birth. I had to have existed as a spiritual individual before my birth. I was certainly not present in my ancestors, because as spiritual individuals they are different from me, and their biographies cannot explain mine. Rather, as a spiritual being, I must be the repetition of one whose biography can explain mine.

The only other conceivable possibility would be that I have only a spiritual life before birth (or conception) to thank for shaping the substance of my biography. However, this idea could be justified only if we assume that what works on a human soul from its physical surroundings has the same character as what the soul receives from a purely spiritual world. This assumption, however, contradicts precise observation. What exerts a determining influence on a human soul from its physical surroundings works on it in the same way that a new experience works on a similar earlier experience in our physical life. To observe these relationships correctly, we must learn to perceive that some impressions in human life work on the soul's potentials in the same way that standing before something still to be done works on what we have already practiced repeatedly in physical life. Rather than affecting abilities acquired through practice in the course of this life, these impressions affect *potential* abilities of the soul. If we achieve insight into these things, we arrive at the idea of earthly lives that must have preceded this one. In thinking about it, we can no longer be content with assuming that this life is preceded only by purely spiritual experiences.

Schiller carried a physical form inherited from his ancestors, which could not have grown from the Earth. The same is true of Schiller as a spiritual individuality. He must have been the repetition of another spiritual being whose biography accounts for his, just as human reproduction accounts for his physical form. The human physical form is a repetition or reembodiment, over and over again, of what is inherent in the human genus and species. Similarly, a spiritual individual must be a reembodiment or reincarnation of one and the same spiritual being, for as a spiritual being, each person is his or her own species.

One could argue that this discussion is simply an arrangement of thoughts and could demand outer proof as one does in the physical sciences. It must be noted, however, that reincarnation of the spiritual human being is not part of the domain of outer physical facts, but takes place only in the spiritual world, and that, of all our ordinary mental powers, only thinking can access this realm. If we refuse to trust the power of thinking, we can never explain higher spiritual facts to ourselves. For anyone whose spiritual eye is open, however, the previous train of thought is just as compelling as any process that occurs in front of our physical eyes. Those who find a "proof" constructed according to ordinary scientific knowledge more persuasive than what has been presented about the significance of biography may be great scientists in the usual sense, but they are far from the methods of true spiritual research. An attempt to explain a person's spiritual attributes as inherited from the parents or other ancestors is evidence of a very dubious bias indeed. Those who are guilty of assuming that Goethe, for example, inherited anything essential to his nature from his father and mother will probably not respond to reason, since they harbor a deep dislike of unbiased observation. Their materialistic persuasion prevents them from seeing relationships between phenomena in the right light. What has been presented so far provides the prerequisites for tracing our essential being beyond birth and death.

Within the limits of birth and death, human beings belong to the three worlds of bodily, soul, and spirit nature. The soul is the link between body and spirit, permeating the body's third member, the soul body, with the capacity for sensation and (as the consciousness soul) pervading the first spiritual member, the spirit self. Throughout life, therefore, the soul participates in both body and spirit, which is expressed in all aspects of its existence. The organization of the soul body determines the extent to which the sentient soul can develop its capacities. On the other hand, the consciousness soul's own life determines the extent to which the spirit self can develop within it. The better the soul body's development, the better the sentient soul can develop its interaction with the outer world. The more the consciousness soul supplies the spirit self with nourishment, the richer and more powerful the spirit self becomes. During life, the spirit self is supplied with this nourishment through worked-over and assimilated experiences, and through their fruits, as has been demonstrated. Naturally, this interaction between soul and spirit can take place only where the two intermingle, that is, in the joining of the spirit self and the consciousness soul.

Let us look first at the interaction between the soul body and the sentient soul. As we have seen, the soul body is the most finely formed aspect of our bodily nature, but it still belongs to and depends on this bodily nature. In one respect, the physical, ether, and soul bodies form a whole. Thus, the soul body is also subject to the laws of physical heredity, through which the body receives its form, but because it is the most ephemeral aspect of our physical nature, it must also show the most ephemeral manifestations of heredity. Human physical bodies differ only slightly on the basis of race, nation, and family, and although individual ether bodies vary more, they still show a great similarity. However, when it comes to the soul body, the differences are very great. What we perceive as a person's outer personal uniqueness is expressed in the soul body, which also carries whatever personal uniqueness is passed from ancestors to descendants.

It is true that the soul, as described, leads a full and independent life of its own. It closes itself off with its likes and dislikes, emotions and passions. It is active as a whole, however, and the sentient soul, too, bears the stamp of this whole. Because the sentient soul permeates and "fills" the soul body, the soul body takes shape according to the nature of the soul and is then able, through heredity, to transmit the predecessor's inclinations, passions, and so on to the descendants. Goethe's saying, "From my father I get my build and my tendency to take life seriously; from my mother, my happy disposition and delight in storytelling," is based on this fact. His genius, however, did not come from either of his parents. This gives us an idea of the kinds of soul qualities that are, in effect, turned over to the line of physical heredity.

The substances and forces of the physical body are present in the very same way in outer physical nature all around us; we continually take them in and give them back again. Over the course of a few years, all the substances that make up the physical body are renewed. They are continually renewed, yet always assume the form of a human body, because the ether body holds them together. The form of the ether body is not determined solely by processes between birth (or conception) and death, but also depends on the laws of heredity that extend beyond birth and death. Because the soul body can be influenced by the sentient soul, characteristic soul qualities can also be transmitted through the line of heredity. In other words, the soul affects the process of physical heredity.

What about the interaction between soul and spirit? During life, the spirit is connected to the soul as described earlier. The soul receives the gift of living in truth and goodness from the spirit, which enables it to express the spirit itself in its life, its inclinations, drives, and passions. The spirit self brings the eternal laws of truth and goodness to the "I" from the spirit world. By means of our consciousness soul, those laws are linked to the soul's individual life experiences. Those experiences are transitory, but their fruits last. The fact that they have been linked to the spirit self makes a lasting impression on it. If the human spirit then approaches such an experience and finds it similar to another that it has already been linked to in the past, it recognizes something familiar in it and knows that it must act differently toward this than if it were encountering the experience for the first time. This is the basis of all learning. The fruits of learning are the abilities we acquire. In this way, the fruits of our transitory life are imprinted on our immortal spirit.

Are we in some way aware of these fruits? What is the source of the potentials described as characteristic of the spiritual human being? Surely, they can be based only on the various abilities people bring with them when they begin their earthly journey. In some respects, these capabilities are like those we can acquire during our lifetime. Consider the case of a genius, for instance. As a boy, Mozart could write a long piece of music from memory that he had heard just once. He could do this only because he was able to survey the whole thing as a whole. During our lifetime, we can all broaden our capacity (within certain limits) to gain an overview of things and understand their interrelationships. We then possess new abilities. Lessing, for example, said that, through his gift for critical observation, he had acquired something very close to genius. If we are not inclined to view such abilities, rooted in innate potential, as miracles, we must see them as the fruits of what the spirit self has experienced through a soul. They have been impressed upon the spirit self, and since it did not happen in this lifetime, it must have happened in a previous one.

Each human spirit is a species in it own right. Just as individual human beings pass on their characteristics, the spirit passes on its characteristics within its species—that is, within itself. *In each life the human spirit appears as a repetition of itself, with the fruits of its experiences in earlier lifetimes.* Thus, this lifetime is the repetition of others, and brings with it what the spirit self has gained in its previous life. When the spirit self takes in something that can develop into fruit, it imbues itself with the life spirit. Just as the life body reproduces the form of a species from generation to generation, the life spirit reproduces the soul from one personal existence to the next.

Thus far, this discussion has shown that certain processes in human life can be explained in terms of repeated Earth lives. The full significance of this idea can be realized only through the kind of observation that stems from spiritual insights such as those acquired by following the path to knowledge described at the end of this book [*Theosophy*]. It should be pointed out that ordinary observation, guided properly by thinking, can lead us to this idea, though initially it will leave the idea in a shadowy state, unable to defend it adequately against arguments that arise from imprecise observation and guided improperly by thinking. On the other hand, anyone who comes to this idea through ordinary thoughtful observation is preparing for suprasensory observation by beginning to develop something required before suprasensory observation can begin, just as we must have eyes before physical observation is possible. Those who argue that we can convince ourselves of the reality of suprasensory perception by conceiving an idea like this only prove themselves incapable of taking up the truth through independent thinking. They convince themselves of their own assertions.

❦

In this way, the soul's experiences become lasting, not only within the confines of birth and death, but also beyond death. However, the soul imprints these experiences not only on the spirit lighting up within it, but also on the outer world through means of its actions, as was shown. A person's actions yesterday are still present today through their effects.

Related to this, the metaphor of sleep and death gives us a picture of the connection between cause and effect. Sleep has often been called "death's younger brother." I get up in the morning, and the continuity of my activity has been interrupted by the night. Under normal circumstances, I cannot resume my activity arbitrarily; I must connect to what I did yesterday if my life is to have order and continuity. Yesterday's actions have become the conditions that regulate what I do today. Through my actions yesterday, I created my destiny for today. I disengaged from my own activity for a while, but it belongs to me and pulls me back after I have withdrawn from it for a time. My past is still connected to me, living on in my present and following me into my future. If the effects of my actions yesterday were not intended to be my destiny today, I would have to be recreated out of nothing instead of simply waking up this morning. It would be just as absurd as building a house for myself and not moving into it.

But we are not created anew each morning, nor is the human spirit created anew at the beginning of its earthly life. We must try to understand what really does happen when we set out on this journey. A physical body appears, having received its form through heredity. The body becomes the vehicle for a spirit repeating an earlier life in a new form. Between the two, leading its own self-contained life, is the soul. It is served by its likes and dislikes, its wishes and desires, and places thinking in its service. As the sentient soul, it receives impressions from the outer world and carries them to the spirit, which extracts and preserves their fruits. In a sense, the soul is a mediator whose purpose is accomplished in playing this role satisfactorily. The body forms impressions for the soul, which reshapes them into sensations, stores them in the memory as mental images, and passes them on to the spirit to be made lasting. It is the soul that makes us belong to this earthly life. Through the body, we belong to the physical human genus. With our spirit, we live in a higher world. The soul binds the two worlds together for a time.

When entering the physical world, the human spirit finds itself not in an unfamiliar setting, but in one that carries the imprint of its actions. Something in this new setting belongs to the spirit, bears the stamp of its being, and is related to it. Just as the soul once conveyed impressions of the outer world to the spirit to be made lasting, as the spirit's organ, it also transformed its spirit-given faculties into actions that, through their effects, are equally lasting. The soul actually flowed into those actions. The human soul lives on in a second independent life through the effects of its actions. This gives us a basis for examining how the processes of destiny enter life. Something happens to us, "bumps into us," and enters our life as if by chance—or so we tend to think at first. However, we can become aware that each of us is the result of many such "chance" events. If I take a good look at myself at the age of forty and refuse to be content with an empty, abstract concept of the "I" as I ponder my soul's essential nature, I could easily conclude that I am no more and no less than what I have become through what has happened to me until now as a matter of destiny. I would probably have been a different person if, at twenty, I had experienced a different series of events than what did happen to me. I will then look for my "I" in its developmental influences that come from within, as well as in what exerts a formative influence on my life from outside. I will recognize my own "I" in what "happens to me."

If we give ourselves impartially to such a realization, we need to take only one more step in our intimate observations of life before we can see something in what comes to us through certain experiences of destiny and takes hold of the "I" from outside, just as memory works from inside to allow past experiences to light up again. In this way, we can begin to recognize an experience of destiny as a past action of the soul finding its way to the "I," just as a memory is a past experience that is invoked by outer circumstances and finds its way into our minds as a mental image.

The idea that the results of its own actions may meet the soul again has already been discussed as a possibility. However, a meeting of this sort cannot come about within the confines of a single life on Earth because this life has been organized and prepared in such a way as to bring about the action in question. The experience is intertwined with the accomplishment of the action. It is as impossible for a specific consequence of this action to return to the soul as it is for us to remember an experience when we are still in the middle of it. Rather, what comes into question here is our experience of consequences that meet the "I" when it does not have the aptitudes it had during the lifetime in which the action was performed—that is, it is possible to focus only on consequences that come from other earthly lives. As soon as we sense that some seemingly coincidental experience is as closely related to the "I" as anything that takes shape out of the inner being of the "I," we must conclude that in such an experience of destiny we are confronting consequences that come from earlier lives on Earth. As we can see, an intimate, thought-guided approach to life leads us to adopt the idea (odd as it may seem to ordinary consciousness) that what we experience as destiny in one lifetime is related to our actions in previous earthly lives. Again, the full significance of this idea can be realized only through suprasensory knowledge, without which it remains vague at best. But here, too, the idea acquired through ordinary consciousness prepares one's soul for witnessing its full truth through genuine suprasensory perception.

However, only a part of my action is out in the world; the other part is in me. We can take a simple analogy from the field of biology to clarify the relationship between an "I" and its actions. In certain caves in Kentucky, there are animals that were able to see when they first ventured in but have lost their sight through prolonged life in darkness. Their eyes stopped functioning; the physical and chemical activity that occurs in seeing no longer happens for them, and the stream of nutrients that once supported that activity has been redirected to other organs. By now, those animals can live only in caves. Through their original action of migrating into the caves, they determined the conditions under which they must live today. Their migration became a part of their destiny, or fate. A being of the past linked itself to the results of its own actions. This is also true for the human spirit. Only through activity could the soul transmit certain capabilities to the spirit; those capabilities correspond directly to actions. An action by the soul gives it the strength and potential for another action, which is the direct fruit of the first. The soul bears this as an inner necessity until the second action is completed. We could say that, through an action, the need to carry out its consequence is impressed on the soul.

Through actions, each human spirit has truly prepared its own destiny. The human spirit finds itself linked in each new lifetime to what it did in the previous one. We may wonder how that could be, since the reincarnating spirit finds itself in a world very different from that left behind. The way we conceive of the chain of destiny when we ask such a question, however, clings to external and superficial aspects of life. If my area of activity is shifted from Europe to America, I will also find myself in very new surroundings, and yet my life in America will still depend on how I lived in Europe. If one was a mechanic in Europe, one's life in America will be quite different from what it would if one had been a banker. In the first instance, one will probably be surrounded by machinery again in America; in the second, by the trappings of the banking business. In each case, one's former life determines one's surroundings, as each life extracts from the surrounding world the phenomena related to it, so to speak. It is the same for the spirit self. In a new life, it must surround itself with the phenomena with which it was related in its previous life.

That is why sleep is a helpful image for death, because during sleep we are withdrawn from the arena in which our destiny awaits us. While we sleep, events in that arena continue without us, and for a while we have no influence over the course they take. Nevertheless, how we live the next day still depends on the effects of what we did the day before. In reality, our personalities are reembodied anew each morning in the world of our actions. It is as though whatever we were separated from during the night is spread out around us during the day. The same is true for our actions in earlier incarnations. They are connected to us as our destiny, just as living in dark caves is connected to the animals who lost their sense of sight by migrating into caves. Just as these animals can live only in the surroundings in which they find themselves, surroundings into which they have inserted themselves, a human spirit can live only in the environment it has created for itself through its actions. The ongoing stream of events makes sure that, when I awake in the morning, I find myself in a situation that I created the previous day. Similarly, my reincarnating spirit's relationship to the objects in the surroundings sees to it that I enter an environment corresponding to my actions in the previous life.

From all this, we can form an idea of how the soul is incorporated into the overall organization of a human being. The physical body is subject to the laws of heredity. The human spirit, however, must reincarnate repeatedly, and its law means having to carry the fruits of previous lifetimes into the following ones. Our souls live in the present, although the present life is dependent on our previous lives, since each incarnating spirit brings its destiny with it from previous incarnations, and this destiny determines its present life. The impressions our souls will be able to receive, the desires that can be fulfilled, the joys and sorrows, the other human beings we will meet—all of this depends on the nature of our actions during earlier incarnations of the spirit. People to whom our souls were connected in one lifetime will necessarily encounter us again in a later one, because the actions that occurred between us have consequences. Souls that have been associated will venture into reincarnation at the same time. Thus, the life of the soul is a product of the spirit's self-created destiny.

The course of a human life within the framework of life and death is determined in three ways, and therefore we are also dependent on three facts that go beyond birth and death.

1. The *body* is subject to the laws of *heredity*.
2. The *soul* is subject to self-created *destiny* or, to use an ancient term, its *karma*.
3. The *spirit* is subject to the laws of *reincarnation*, or repeated earthly lives.

The interrelationship of body, soul, and spirit can also be expressed as follows: The spirit is immortal; birth and death govern our bodily existence according to the laws of the physical world; and the life of the soul, which is subject to destiny, mediates between body and spirit during earthly life. These three worlds to which we belong will be the subject of the next section of this book [*Theosophy*], since some familiarity with them is needed for all further knowledge of the essential nature of the human being.

If our way of thinking deals with life's phenomena and does not hesitate to follow thoughts resulting from living, vital observation through to their final ramifications, we can indeed arrive at the idea of repeated earthly lives and the law of destiny through mere logic. It is true that, for a seer with opened spiritual eyes, past lives are present as direct experience, like reading from an open book, but it is equally true that the truth of all of this can come to light for anyone with an active, observant reasoning ability.

Addendum

The statements in this chapter on reincarnation and karma are an attempt to convey the extent to which human life and destiny point, in and of themselves, to the idea of repeated earthly lives. The intent was to do this by thoughtfully considering the course of human life without referring to spiritual scientific ideas as presented in other chapters. Of course the very idea of reincarnation and karma will seem rather questionable to people who accept only those ideas that assume the existence of a single earthly life as being well founded. The purpose of this chapter is to show that such ideas cannot lead to an understanding of why one's life takes a particular course. We must look for different ideas that may appear to contradict our usual ones. The only reason for not looking for them would be a fundamental refusal on our part to apply the same thoughtful consideration with which we investigate physical processes to processes that can be grasped only inwardly. Such refusal would mean that, for example, we dismiss the fact that an event of destiny resembles what we experience when our memory encounters an event related to something we actually recall. But if we try to see how a stroke of destiny is actually experienced, we can distinguish between the real situation and what may be said about such an experience from an external point of view that merely denies any vital connection between this stroke of destiny and one's "I." From this perspective, a stroke of destiny seems to be either a coincidence or something determined externally. And since in fact some strokes of destiny actually are making their first impact on a human life, so to speak, revealing their results only later on, there is an even greater temptation to generalize without considering any other possibility.

We begin to consider other possibilities only after life has educated our cognitive abilities and brought them into line with what Goethe's friend Knebel once wrote in a letter:

> On close observation, we will find that most people's lives contain a plan that seems laid out for them either in their own character or in the circumstances that guide them. No matter how changeable and varied their situations may be, in the end a certain wholeness, or inner coherence, is apparent.... The hand of a specific fate, no matter how hidden its working, is still clearly to be seen, whether moved by outer causes or by inner impulses. Often, in fact, we are moved in its direction for quite conflicting reasons. No matter how confused the course of a life may be, a plan and a direction still show through.[1]

---

1. Karl Ludwig von Knebel (1744–1834), in *K. L. v. Knebels literarischer Nachlass und Briefwechsel* (*K. L. von Knebel's Literary Legacy and Correspondence*), ed. K. A. Varnhagen von Ense and T. Mundt, 2nd ed., 1840, vol. 3, p. 452.

Objecting to an observation of this sort is easy, especially for those unwilling to consider the inner experiences from which it arises. However, the author of this book believes that, in what he has said about destiny and repeated Earth lives, he has accurately delineated the boundaries within which it is possible to form ideas about the causes that shape human life. He has pointed out that the conviction to which these thoughts lead is only outlined by them, that all they can do is prepare us in thought for what must ultimately be discovered through spiritual research. In itself, however, as long as this thought preparation does not exaggerate its own importance or attempt to prove anything, but only trains our soul, it entails an inner effort that can make us unbiased and receptive to facts we would simply take as foolish without it.

From Rudolf Steiner, Theosophy: An Introduction to the Spiritual Processes in Human Life and in the Cosmos *(SteinerBooks, 1994), pp. 63–91.*

7.

ARTS

The Suprasensory Origin of the Arts

In order to meet the requirements of evolution, humankind must achieve an expansion of consciousness in all areas of life. People today relate their actions only to events that occur between birth and death; events between birth and death is all we wonder about. Before our life can become healthy again, however, we will need to take an active interest in more than just this particular period of life, which in any case we spend under exceptional circumstances. Our life encompasses not just what we are and do between birth and death, but also what we are and do between death and rebirth. In the present age of materialism, we are relatively unaware of the influence of the life we spent between death and rebirth prior to the present life we entered by way of conception and birth. We are equally unaware of how things that occur during our present life in the physical body point toward the life we will lead after death. Here we will point to a number of processes that show how certain cultural areas will acquire a new relationship to the whole of human life because human consciousness must and will also extend to embrace our life in the suprasensory worlds.

I believe that a certain question may arise in our minds if we consider the entire scope of our artistic life. Let us take a look at suprasensory life from this viewpoint. This will lead us to something we will be able to put to good use later when we turn our attention toward social life.

The generally recognized "fine arts" are sculpture, architecture, painting, poetry, and music. Based on our anthroposophic life and knowledge, we are currently [1920] in the process of adding to these the art of eurythmy. The question I have in mind, which might occur in connection to our artistic life, is this: What is the actual positive reason for introducing art into our lives? It is only during our materialistic age that art has come to deal with the immediate reality of life between birth and death. Of course, we have forgotten the suprasensory origin of art, so our aim now is to copy, more or less, what our senses see out in nature. Those who have a deeper feeling for nature, on the one hand, and for art on the other will certainly not be able to agree with such naturalism, whereby art copies nature. We must question repeatedly whether even the best landscape painter, for example, can in any way conjure the beauty of a natural landscape on canvas. Faced with even a very well executed, naturalistic landscape painting, anyone of sound taste must have the feeling I expressed in the prologue of my first mystery drama *The Portal of Initiation:* no copy of nature will ever equal nature itself. People of refined feeling will inevitably find something repellent in naturalism. They will surely see in the aspect of art that transcends nature in some way and attempts (at least in the way the subject is portrayed) only justification to supply something other than what nature itself can present to us. But how do we come to create art in the first place? Why do we transcend nature in sculpture or poetry?

If we develop a sense of connectedness with all things, we see how in sculpture, for instance, artists work to capture the human form in a very particular way. Through the way they mold the form, they attempt to express something specifically human. We see that their statues cannot simply incorporate the natural human form as it stands before them, imbued with the soul and with the breath and flush of life, with everything we can see in the human being in addition to the form itself. However, I think that sculptors of human figures will gradually achieve an elevated and very particular way of feeling. There is no doubt in my mind that the Greek sculptors had this; it has simply been lost in today's naturalistic age.

It seems to me that sculptors who work on the human form have a different feeling while shaping the head than they do while forming the rest of the body. In the sculptor's work, sculpting the head and sculpting the rest of the body are very different. To exaggerate, I might say that, in working to sculpt the human head, sculptors have the feeling of being constantly drawn in by the medium, as if it were trying to absorb them; in fashioning the rest of the body, however, they have the feeling of pushing into it from outside, of pressing and poking it everywhere without justification. They have the feeling that they are fashioning the body and modeling its shapes from the outside. In shaping the body, they feel that they are working from the outside in, whereas in fashioning the head they feel that they are working from the inside out. It seems to me that this feeling is specific to sculpture. It was certainly still felt by Greek artists and has been lost only in our naturalistic age, now that we have become enslaved by the model. If we direct ourselves toward the suprasensory in our intention to sculpt the human form, we must wonder where such a feeling comes from.

Much deeper questions are connected to all this, but before I go into it any further, there is something else I would like to mention. Consider the strong feeling of inwardness we get when experiencing sculpture and architecture, despite the fact that they appear to be fashioned outwardly from physical materials. In architecture, we have an inner experience of dynamics, of how a pillar supports a beam or leads into the form of its capital. We have an inner experience of outer form. In the case of sculpture, our experience is similar.

This is not true of music, however, and especially not with poetry. In the case of prose, we can just about manage to retain the words in our larynx, but in the case of poetry it seems very clear to me (to put it rather drastically again) that words cast in iambic or trochaic rhythms and put into rhyme soar, so that we have to chase them. They populate the atmosphere around us more than that within us. We experience poetry much more externally than, for example, architecture or sculpture. The same is probably true of music when we apply our feeling to it. Musical tones also enliven our entire surroundings. We forget space and time, or at least space, and are lifted out of ourselves in a moral experience. We do not have the urge to chase the figures we create, as we do poetry; rather, we have the feeling we must swim out into an indeterminate element spread out everywhere, and that in the process we are dissolving.

You see how we begin to distinguish certain nuances of feeling in connection with the whole essence of art. These feelings are specific in character. I believe that what I have just described to you can be appreciated by those who have a subtle appreciation of art. However, this is not true when we view a crystal or some other natural mineral, or a plant, an animal, or even an actual physical human being. Our feelings and sensations with regard to the whole outer world of physical nature as perceived by our senses are very different from the feelings and sensations that arise in relation to our experiences of various types of art as described.

Suprasensory knowledge can be described as a transformation of ordinary abstract knowledge into seeing knowledge that points to experiential knowledge. It is nonsense to require the same sort of logical, pedantic, narrow-minded proof of matters in higher realms that is desirable in the coarser realms of science, math, and so on. If you "live into" the feelings that arise when you enter the world of art, you gradually come to remarkable inner states of soul. Specific and subtle states of soul arise when you inwardly experience tracing the dynamics and mechanics in architecture or the rounded forms of sculpture. One's inner feeling life follows a remarkable path. As you move along it, you are confronted by a soul experience similar to memory. When you experience recall or memory, you notice how much your inner sensing of architecture and sculpture resembles the inner process of memory, although remembering happens on a higher level. In other words, by way of your feeling for architecture and sculpture, you gradually approach the soul experience known to spiritual research as remembering prebirth conditions. In fact, the way you live in relationship to the entire cosmos between death and a new birth—feeling yourself move as soul–spirit, or spirit–soul, in directions that intersect the paths of certain beings and maintain an equilibrium with others—such experiences are remembered subconsciously for the time being, and architecture and sculpture reproduce this.

If we reexperience this singular situation in sculpture and architecture and do so with inner presence of mind, we discover that our real purpose in sculpture and architecture is simply to conjure, in the physical, sensory world experiences we had in the spiritual world before conception and birth. When we do not build houses merely according to utilitarian principles, but make them architecturally beautiful, we fashion their dynamic proportions as they arise from our recollections of the experiences of equilibrium and rhythmically moving forms that we had in the time between death and our new birth.

Thus, we discover how human beings came to develop architecture and sculpture as forms of art. Our experiences between death and rebirth were floating around in our soul. We wanted somehow to bring them forth and have them stand visibly before us, and so we created architecture and sculpture. We can attribute the fact that humanity brought forth architecture and sculpture in the course of cultural evolution to the fact that life between death and rebirth continues to work and that, within us, we will it to be so. Just as a spider spins, human beings desire to reproduce and give form to their experience between death and a new birth. Prenatal experiences are carried into the world of the physical senses. What we see when we survey the architectural and sculptural works of art created by humanity is simply an embodiment of unconscious recollections of our life between death and rebirth.

Now we have a realistic answer to the question of why human beings create art. If we were not suprasensory beings who enter this life through conception and birth, we would surely not engage in either sculpture or architecture.

And we know what singular connections exist between two (or, say, three) successive lives on Earth. In its formative forces, what is now your head is a transformation of the body (not including the head) that you had in your previous incarnation, while your present body will transform itself into your head in your next incarnation. The human head, however, has a completely different meaning. The head is old; it is the former body transformed. The forces experienced between a person's most recent death and present birth shaped this external form of the head, but the body is the carrier of forces that are now brewing and will take on form in the next incarnation.

This is why sculptors have a different feeling about the head that they do about the rest of the body. In the case of the head, sculptors feel somewhat as if it were trying to pull them into itself, because it is formed from the previous incarnation by forces embedded in its present form. In the case of the body, sculptors feel more as if they would like to press themselves into it while modeling it, because the body contains the spiritual forces that lead beyond death and into the next incarnation. Sculptors have a keen sense of this radical difference in the human form between what belongs to the past and what belongs to the future. The art of sculpture expresses the formative forces of the physical body and how they carry over from one incarnation to the next. On the other hand, what lies more deeply (in the ether body, which is the bearer of our equilibrium and of our dynamic forces) manifests more strongly in the art of architecture.

You see, it is impossible to grasp human life as a whole without looking at suprasensory life and without seriously answering the question of how we come to develop architecture and sculpture. The unwillingness of people to look at the suprasensory world stems from the fact that they also do not try to look at the things of this world in the right way.

Generally speaking, how do people feel about the arts that reveal a spiritual world? It is much like a dog's attitude toward human speech. A dog hears human speech and seems to hear it as barking. Except for particularly intelligent performing animals (such as the one that excited a lot of interest a while ago among people concerned with such useless tricks), a dog does not understand the meaning in the sounds. This illustrates people's attitude toward the arts that speak of the suprasensory world we once experienced. We do not see what they actually reveal.

Consider poetry, which emerges clearly for those who can feel their way into it. Keep in mind, however, that ninety-nine percent of the poetry written is unnecessary for human happiness on this globe and is not true art. The real art of poetry emerges from the whole human being. And what does poetry do? It is not content to stop at prose, but shapes it by bringing meter and rhythm into it. It does something that ordinary prosaic people consider superfluous to their way of life, adding form to something that would convey the intended meaning even without the form. If you listen to a truly artistic recitation of poetry and begin to sense what the poet has made out of the prose content, you will rediscover the remarkable character of this sensation. We cannot experience the mere content of a poem, its prose, as poetry. What we experience as poetry is how the words sweep along in iambus, trochee, or anapest, and how the sounds are repeated in alliteration, assonance, or other forms of rhyme. We experience many other qualities in the ways that prosaic content has been given form. This is what we must bring out in recitation. However, when people today recite in a way that brings out only the prose, however profound, they imagine they are being artistic.

Now, if you can really look at this special nuance of feeling that comprises your feeling for poetry, you will reach the point of saying that this does indeed go beyond ordinary feeling, because ordinary feeling adheres to things in the world of the senses, whereas shaping things poetically does not. I expressed this earlier by saying that, when words have been given poetic form, they live more in the atmosphere around us, or that we want to rush outside of ourselves to really experience the poet's words.

This happens because in poetry we are giving form to something that cannot be experienced between birth and death. We are giving form to something that is of the soul, something we can do without if we only want to live between birth and death. It's quite easy to live your entire life with only a dry prosaic content. But why do we feel the need to add rhythm, assonance, alliteration, and rhyme to this dry prosaic content? Because we have more within us than we need to make it to our death, and we want to provide a form for this excess while we are still living.

Thus we anticipate the life that will follow death. Because we already carry within us what is to follow after death, we feel the urge not only to speak but to speak poetically. Therefore, just as sculpture and architecture are connected with life before birth, with the forces that we carry with us from our prebirth life, so poetry is connected with life after death, with the forces that are already present in us for our life after death.

It is primarily the "I" being, as it lives this life between birth and death and then passes through the gates of death and continues to live, that already carries within it the forces that give expression to the art of poetry. And the astral body, already alive here in the world of sound, is what shapes the world of sound into melody and harmony, which we do not find in life in the external physical world. This astral body already contains within it what it will experience after death. You know that the astral body we carry within us lives on only for a while after death before we lay it aside. Nevertheless, this astral body contains the actual element of music. It contains it in the way it experiences music in its life-element, the air, between birth and death. We need air if we are to have a medium for experiencing music.

After death, when we reach the point of laying aside the astral body, we also lay aside everything of a musical nature that reminds us of this life on Earth. But at this cosmic moment music is transformed into the music of the spheres. We become independent of what we formerly experienced as music through the medium of the air; we lift ourselves up and live our way into the music of the spheres. What we experience here as music in the air is the music of the spheres up there. The reflection of this higher music makes its way into the element of air, condensing into what we experience as earthly music. We imprint it on our astral body, on what we give form to and reexperience as long as we have an astral body. When we lay aside our astral body at death, the musical experience in us switches to the music of the spheres. In music and poetry we anticipate what our world and our existence will be after death. We experience the suprasensory world in two directions. This is how these four forms of art present themselves to us.

What about painting? There is another spiritual world that lies behind the world of our senses. Materialistic physicists and biologists claim that atoms and molecules are behind the world of the senses. It is not molecules and atoms, however, but spiritual beings. It is a world of spirit, the reality we pass through between falling asleep and waking up. That world, which we bring with us out of sleep, is what really inspires us as we paint, giving us the ability to depict on canvas or murals the spiritual reality surrounding us spatially. For this reason, we must take great care to paint out of color rather than out of line, because the line is a lie in painting. The line always belongs to the memory of life before birth. If we are to paint in a state of consciousness that has expanded into the world of spirit, we must paint what comes from color. And we know that color is experienced in the astral world. When we enter the world we pass through between falling asleep and waking up, we experience this element of color. And when we want to create color harmonies and put color on canvas, what urges us on is the experience of pushing what we have gone through between falling asleep and waking up into our waking physical bodies, allowing it to flow into our waking physical bodies. This is what we attempt to paint on our canvases.

Here again, what appears in painting is a depiction of something suprasensory. In each case, the arts point to the suprasensory. To anyone with an appropriate sense of it, painting reveals the spiritual world that borders and permeates us spatially. This is the reality in which we find ourselves between going to sleep and waking. Sculpture and architecture bear witness to the spiritual reality in which we live between death and a new birth, music and poetry of the life we will go through after death. This is how our participation in the spiritual world makes its way into our ordinary earthly life.

If we have a narrow-minded view of the arts we create during life and see them as being connected only to the period between birth and death, we actually deprive artistic creativity of all meaning. For artistic creativity most certainly means carrying suprasensory spiritual worlds into the physical world of the senses. We bring architecture, sculpture, painting, music, and poetry into the world of physical experience simply because we feel the pressure of what we carry within us from pre-earthly existence, because when awake we feel the pressure of what we carry within us as a result of our spiritual life during sleep, and because we feel the pressure of something already in us that will shape us after death. That people usually do not speak about suprasensory worlds simply stems from the fact that they do not understand the world of the senses, either. And above all, they do not understand something that was once known to the spiritual culture of humanity before it was lost and became an external phenomenon, namely art.

If we learn to understand art, it becomes a real proof of human immortality and of life before birth. This is what we need in order to expand our consciousness beyond the horizon of birth and death, so that we can link what we have during life on the physical Earth to the life that transcends the physical plane.

If we work creatively out of such knowledge as the spiritual science of Anthroposophy, which aims to understand the spiritual world and to receive it into our ideas and thoughts, into our feelings, perceptions, and will, it will prepare the ground for an art that synthesizes in some way what precedes birth and what follows death.

Consider the art of eurythmy, through which we move the human body. What exactly are we moving? We are moving the human organism by making its limbs move. The limbs, more than any other part of the human body, pass into the life of the next incarnation. They point to the future, to what comes after death. But how do we shape the limb movements we bring forth in eurythmy? In the sense realm and in the suprasensory realm we study how the larynx and all the speech organs have been brought over from the previous life and shaped by the intellectual potentials of the head and the feeling potentials of the chest. We directly link what precedes birth with what follows death. In a certain sense, we take from earthly life only the physical medium, the actual human being who is the tool or instrument for eurythmy. But we allow this human being to make manifest what we study inwardly, what is already prepared in us as a result of previous lives. We transfer this to our limbs, which are the part of us where life after death is being shaped in advance. Eurythmy shapes and moves the human organism in a way that furnishes direct external proof of our participation in the suprasensory world. In having people do eurythmy, we link them directly to the suprasensory world.

Wherever art is developed on the basis of a truly artistic attitude, it bears witness to our connection to the suprasensory worlds. And if in our time we human beings are called upon to take the gods into our own soul forces, so to speak, so that we no longer wait in pious faith for the gods to give us one thing or another, but try instead to take action as though the gods were living in our active will, then the time has indeed come, if humankind will only experience it, when we must take the step from external, objectively formed arts to an art that will assume different dimensions and forms in the future, an art that portrays the suprasensory world directly. How could it be otherwise? Spiritual science itself wants to present the suprasensory directly, so it is bound to use its resources to create an art of this kind.

As for its educational applications, people who are educated along these lines will gradually come to find it quite natural to believe that they are suprasensory beings, because they move their hands, arms, and legs in such a way that the forces of the suprasensory world are active in them. It is the soul of the human being, the suprasensory soul, that begins to move in eurythmy. It is the living expression of the suprasensory that comes to light in eurythmy movements.

Everything spiritual science brings us is really in inner harmony with itself. On the one hand, it brings us these things so that we may more deeply and intensely comprehend the life we are engaged in, so that we may learn to turn our gaze to the living proof of the reality of existence before birth and after death. On the other hand, it introduces our suprasensory element into the will. This is the inner cohesiveness behind anthroposophically oriented spiritual scientific striving. This is how spiritual science will expand human consciousness. It will no longer be possible for people to make their way through the world as they have been doing in the age of materialism, when they have been able to survey only what takes place between birth and death. Although they may also believe in something else that promises bliss and redemption, they can form no concept of this "something else." They can only listen to sentimental sermons about it; in actuality it is empty of content. Through spiritual science, human beings are meant to receive real content from the spiritual world once again. We are meant to be released from the life of abstraction, from the life that refuses to go beyond the perceptions and thoughts that lie between birth and death, from a life that at most takes in some indefinite verbal indications of the spiritual world. Spiritual science will infuse us with a consciousness that will widen our horizon and enable us to be aware of the suprasensory world even as we live and work in the physical world.

It is true enough that we go through the world today knowing at, say, the age of thirty that the foundation for what we are now was laid in us when we were ten or fifteen. This much we can remember. If we read something at age thirty, we remember that the present moment is linked to the time twenty-two or twenty-three years ago when we were learning to read. But what we do not notice is that between birth and death we constantly have pulsing within us the experiences we underwent between our last death and our present birth. Let's look at what has been born out of these forces in architecture and in sculpture. If we understand this correctly, we will also be able to apply it to our lives in the right way and to achieve once again a sense of how prose is fashioned into the rhythm, meter, rhyme, alliteration, and assonance of poetry, even though this may be considered superfluous to ordinary prosaic life. Then we will form the right link between this special nuance of feeling and the immortal kernel of our being which we carry with us through death. We will say that it would be impossible for anyone to become a poet unless all human beings possessed the actual creative element of the poet, namely the force that already resides within us but does not become outwardly alive until after death.

This draws the suprasensory into our ordinary consciousness, which must expand again if humanity does not intend to sink further into the depths we have plunged into as a result of a contracted consciousness that makes us live only in what happens between birth and death, allowing us at most to hear preaching about what is present in the suprasensory world.

You see, we encounter spiritual science everywhere, whenever we speak about the most important cultural needs of our time.

From Rudolf Steiner, Art as Spiritual Activity: Rudolf Steiner's Contribution to the Visual Arts, *Michael Howard, ed. (Anthroposophic Press, 1998), lecture in Dornach, September 12, 1920, pp. 237–249.*

8.

SOCIETY

INTERIOR OF SOCIETY

IT IS VERY SIGNIFICANT TODAY that certain people feel compelled to speak of the human situation and try, through feelings and perceptions at least, to peer into the heart of social affairs. To show this significance, I would like to begin with a few statements from the address that Kurt Eisner[1] gave to a gathering of students in Basle shortly before his death. Some of you may have heard these statements, but they are very important for understanding the symptomatic nature of certain matters today. Referring to his previous remarks, he began:

> I hear, do I not? And I see clearly enough that, deep down, there is a longing in our lives that strives for expression in a way that recognizes clearly that life, as we must live it today, is no more than an obvious invention of some evil spirit. Imagine a great thinker living some two thousand years ago and knowing nothing of our time, dreaming of how the world would look in two thousand years. Even with the most vivid imagination, one would have been unable to think of a world such as the one in which we are condemned to live. In truth, existing conditions are the only utopia in the world, and the substance of our desires, the longing of our spirit, is the deepest and final reality, and everything else is horrible. We are simply confusing dreaming and waking. It is up to us to shake off this ancient dream of today's social existence. One glance at the war—can you imagine anyone with human intelligence inventing anything of the

---

1. Kurt Eisner (1867–1919) was a socialist politician and premier of Bavaria. He was assassinated.

sort? If this has not been what we call "reality," then perhaps it was a dream, and we are now waking.

Just think of it; in trying to understand the present, this man was driven to use the idea of dreaming and to ask himself whether it might be better to call today's reality a bad dream instead of actual reality.

So we have this remarkable case (and consider just how typical it is) of a thoroughly modern person, someone who considered himself a herald of a new age, regarding outer sense reality not altogether as *maya,* or a dream (as does, for instance, the Hindu view), but feeling compelled in face of today's exceptional events, to raise the question (regardless of the sense, but to raise it) whether we are not actually dreaming this reality. Indeed, the whole tenor of Eisner's address shows that he was using more than a turn of phrase when he said that this present reality can be nothing else but something inflicted upon humankind by an evil spirit.

Let us take some of the topics to which we have devoted our minds in the course of our anthroposophic work, especially the fact that in general we try to look at outer sensory reality not as the whole of reality but as being connected with suprasensory reality, without which it would be incomplete. This outlook, however, is no more than a tiny spark in the currents of thought of the present age, which to a large extent is flooded by materialistic thinking—yet we see that a man such as Kurt Eisner who, from his perspective, gave this spark no credit (at least not during his lifetime), is driven by the facts of his time to the one and only comparison he can make: outer reality, in its present appearance at least, is a dream. Faced with this current reality, he is forced to admit that he can express only in terms of the universal truth of the unreal nature, the *maya* quality of outer sensory reality on its own.

Now, let us go more deeply into some of the matters we have been considering over the past weeks, which included the social question. Let's look at how the trend of events in recent centuries has brought people increasingly to the point of denying the actual spiritual, or suprasensory, world and supporting that denial as much as possible. You may argue that people in some quarters talk a lot about the suprasensory world. There are still numerous churches, if not always full, that resound with words at least that claim to announce the spirit. After all, today and yesterday evening we have been hearing the tolling of bells almost non-stop, which is supposed to express spiritual life as presented to the world. Yet we experience something else in addition to this. If, in the immediate present, an attempt is made to listen to the words of Christ in our present age, then it is precisely the adherents of the traditional religious communities who most fiercely attack this form of spiritual revelation. Very few people today want a real spiritual life, which relies not just on faith or ancient tradition, but on today's direct spiritual findings.

In the light of this, does it not seem as if modern humanity needs to be pushed—not by an evil cosmic spirit, perhaps, but by a *good* cosmic spirit—to recall the spiritual side of existence? By being doomed to experience sense-perceptible reality of this kind, isn't a truly modern person forced to say that it resembles a dream, and that even a great thinker of two thousand years ago could not have imagined the sort of scenario that appears today as outer reality?

In any case, here is a modern person compelled to form ideas about reality that differ from those currently popular. I know that a great number of our anthroposophic friends have found it rather difficult to understand these particular ideas about reality, the importance of which I have been stressing today. But you will not be able to cope with life as it is unless you have the good will to accept such difficult ideas. What sort of thoughts do people form today in the following area? People hold a crystal in their hands and think of it as a real object. Then they hold a rose picked from a bush and call that, too, a real object. They call both of them real objects in the same sense. Yet, are they both real in the same sense? Scientists, whether from seats of learning or in laboratories or clinics, all speak of reality, in that they consider things real inasmuch as they are real in the sense of a crystal or a picked rose. However, is there not a considerable difference, an enormous difference, between these two objects, since the crystal retains its form through long ages of time, whereas the rose loses its form and dies a relatively short while after it has been picked? It does not have the same level of reality that the crystal has. Once it is dug up, even a rosebush does not have the same level of reality as it did when it was in the earth. So we must eventually view phenomena of the world in a way that is different from today's way of seeing them from outside. We should not call a rose or a rosebush "real." At the most, we cannot speak of reality unless we consider the whole Earth, with the rosebush and every flower on it as a strand of hair growing out of this reality.

From this, you can see that, in external sensory reality, phenomena can cease to be real in the true sense of the word once they are separated from their foundation. Moreover, this means that we must start searching *within* apparent outer reality, the great illusion, for the true realities. Mistakes of this kind are common in the study of nature today. However, those who make this sort of mistake and have gotten into this habit through the centuries will find it very difficult to think about social matters in a way that accords with reality. The great difference between human life and nature is that anything in nature that is no longer fully real, such as a picked rose, soon dies. Something that is not a reality can have the appearance of reality, yet is false in itself.

We can very well incorporate something that is not reality in itself as a reality in social life. In this case, although it is not bound to die off quickly, it will gradually turn into a source of grief for humanity. Nothing can become a blessing if it has not been experienced first and thought through as a complete reality before being embedded into the social organism. When we assume human labor can be a commodity (and I have often said this), it is not just a sin against the social order, but also a sin against truth itself. In apparent outer reality it can be made to seem so, but this illusion of reality will cause suffering in the human social order and set the stage for upheavals and revolutions in the social organism.

To summarize, what needs to become part of the way people think today is that not everything manifested in the outer appearance of reality, which we see in a limited way, is certain to be true reality; it may be a living lie. Moreover, this distinction between living truths and living lies should be engraved deeply into conscious minds today. The social organism will be restored to health as more people become deeply serious about this distinction, and as more people feel that we must open our eyes to facts that are not living lies but living truths.

It is not easy to know whether an external object is in fact real. Imagine a being from a planet on which the conditions are different from those on our Earth. That being never encountered the difference between a rose growing on a bush and a crystal. If you were to present such a being with a crystal and a rose, it may be assumed that the two were equally real. That being would then be surprised to find the rose withering so quickly, while the crystal remained the same. Here on Earth, we know about these differences because we have observed such things over a longer period. But we cannot follow everything as we can with a rose, seeing in outer reality whether something is real or not real. In life we are presented with phenomena that require us to create a foundation for our judgment if we are to visualize their true reality. What sort of foundation is this—especially when dealing with social life?

In the two preceding lectures I shared a few observations about this foundation, and today I will add more. From my books, you are familiar with my descriptions of the spiritual world—the world that human beings experience between death and a new birth. You know that, when we refer to this life in the suprasensory spiritual world, we need to be aware of the way souls relate to one another. Human beings do not have a body there and are not subject to the physical laws of the world in which we live between birth and death. Thus, we speak of the play of force or forces from soul to soul. In my book *Theosophy,* you can read that in the soul world, between death and a new birth, we need to speak about forces of sympathy and antipathy among souls. Such activity is completely inward. Through antipathy, one soul confronts another, and through sympathy pain is soothed. Harmony and disharmony arise between the souls' innermost experiences. This relationship between the innermost experiences of one soul and another constitutes reality in the suprasensory world. What one soul can experience in another soul in this material world during physical life is merely a reflection of those suprasensory events—what remains of them, so to speak.

This reflection, however, must be judged in the proper light. We can ask, in terms of social life: How should we judge what we live through here between birth and death when compared to suprasensory life? Having often thought about the need for a threefold social order, our attention is drawn immediately to the central sphere, often described as the political state. Those today who have reflected on this political state have tried constantly to understand what it is. But you know, people today have materialistic ideas and really lack a proper basis to consider something of this nature. Furthermore, in recent times all sorts of things have been fused together with the modern state according to the various class interests, making it almost impossible to discern whether the state is a reality or a living lie. There is a vast difference between the views of the German philosopher Hegel and the contrasting outlook that Fritz Mauthner (author of a philosophical dictionary) has recently made known. Hegel regards the state more or less as the realization of God on Earth, wheras Mauthner says that the state is a necessary evil, though indispensable and essential to social life. These are the radically opposed views of two prominent men of recent times.

A great deal that formerly occurred instinctively is now being raised into consciousness, and therefore all kinds of people have attempted to form ideas of what the state should be like and how it ought to be shaped. These ideas have appeared in every shade of the spectrum. On the one hand, there are those who fight without getting down to the essentials, yet they want to give it a form that gives those who have the most complaints the least chance of speaking out. Moreover, others want to make radical changes that enable people to create a satisfactory existence. The question is: How can we, in fact, form a view of the state's reality?

Observe impartially what can come into play among individuals in the state and compare this with my description of what comes into play among souls in suprasensory existence. This is the only way to perceive the state's potential reality.

Relationships based on the fundamental forces of sympathy and antipathy in the human soul during suprasensory existence have the most inward nature, whereas human relationships based on state politics have the most external quality. Such relationships are based on the law, which is the realm in which people confront one another in the most remote ways. If you follow through on this thought, you will understand that the state is the exact opposite of suprasensory life. The state is truest to its own nature when it is the complete opposite of suprasensory life—the less it presumes in any way to include anything of suprasensory life, the more it focuses on mutual human relationships based on the most external matters, in which everyone is equal in the eyes of the law. We become more and more profoundly convinced of the fact that it is the state's real nature to cover only the areas that belong to our life between birth and death and to the most external realm of our existence.

If that is the case, we have to ask: If the state is an image of suprasensory life, solely because it represents its opposite, how does the suprasensory realm find its way into the rest of our lives in the material world?

In the previous lecture, I spoke of this from another perspective. Today I would like to add that the antipathies that develop in the suprasensory world during the period between death and birth leave traces that we bring with us through birth into physical existence. These come face to face with everything that lives in so-called spiritual culture. This is what draws people together in religious communities and other common cultural interests, so that they can bring balance into the traces of antipathies that have lingered on from the life before birth.

All our spiritual culture should be a realm for itself, because it echoes our pre-earthly life and, so to speak, sends us into the sensory world equipped to form a kind of remedy for the remaining antipathies from the suprasensory world. This is why it is so bad when people create splits in their spiritual–cultural life instead of uniting with one another, as we should in spiritual life.

The echoes of the antipathies left over from spiritual life before birth churn about in the depths of the human soul and prevent our goals from coming to realization. What we should aim for is true spiritual harmony, real spiritual collaboration. Where there should be harmony, cliques arise. This inclination toward sectarianism and schisms is a sign of the remaining antipathies from which all spiritual life arises and for which spiritual–cultural life should really become the cure. We should recognize that spiritual life has an inner connection to our pre-earthly life and is, in a sense, related to suprasensory life. We should, therefore, not be tempted to set up this spiritual–cultural life as anything but an independent activity outside the jurisdiction of the state, which is not an echo in the same sense but a counterimage of suprasensory life. We cannot really understand the essence of both the state and spiritual–cultural life unless we consider suprasensory life as well as our life of the senses. Reality requires both, because the life of the senses on its own is no more than a dream.

Economic life is different. In economic life, people work for others because they find it to their advantage. The economy arises from needs and involves satisfying needs by producing all the physical things that can satisfy both natural human needs and the more delicate, still-instinctive needs of the soul. In economics, something develops on an unconscious level that works on beyond death. The work people do for one another out of egoistic economic needs brings about, under the surface, the creation of certain sympathies that we must develop further during life after death. In the same way that spiritual–cultural life is a kind of cure for the remains of antipathies that we bring into earthly life from our pre-earthly existence, what happens beneath the surface of economic life is filled with potential for creating sympathies that will develop after death. Again, this is an aspect of the way we can learn from the spiritual world to recognize the need for a threefold social order.

Of course, people cannot reach this point of view unless they work to gain a spiritual scientific basis for understanding the cosmos. However, for those who do this, it will become increasingly clear that, if the social organism is to be sound, it must be divided into these three branches. When compared, they each have a distinct relationship to suprasensory reality, which, as

I said, complements the sensory world and, together with it, makes up true reality.

Over the past few centuries, however, no one has discussed the aspects of outer physical existence that manifest in spiritual–cultural life, the life of the state, and economic life. People have continued to churn out old traditions without understanding them. They have lost the habit of taking a direct way, through an active soul life, into the land of the spirit, in search of the light that can illumine physical reality, without which our physical reality cannot be understood properly. The leading circles among humanity have of course set the tone for this non-spiritual life, and this accounts for the deep gulf between the social classes, a gulf that can be found at the very foundations of our life today and to which we really should awaken.

Perhaps I may persist in calling to mind how before July and August 1914 the people who belonged to the leading classes—the former leading classes—were full of praise for the heights of our civilization, as they called it. They spoke of how thought could be conveyed over long distances at lightning speed by the telegraph and telephone systems, as well as other fabulous achievements of modern technology that have brought such wonderful progress to civilization and culture. But this life of civilization and culture was based on the very foundations that have produced the frightful catastrophes of today. Prior to July and August 1914, European state leaders, especially those of Central Europe (and documents prove this), declared countless times that, according to the current situation, peace in Europe is assured for a long time to come. This is actually what state leaders (especially those of Central Europe) said in their party speeches. I could show you speeches made as late as May 1914, in which it was said that diplomatic measures have achieved the kind of interrelationships among the various states that give us the chance to believe in a lasting peace. This was in May 1914.

However, if you saw through the situation at the time, you would have had to speak differently. In my lectures in Vienna at the time, before the war, I stated what I have repeated often in recent years: we are living in the midst of something that must be called a cancer of our human social life, a carcinoma of the social order. This carcinoma has now burst, becoming what people call the World War.

At that time, the comment that we are living in a carcinoma, or social tumor, was taken to be mere words, because the World War was yet to come. They had no idea that they were dancing on a volcano. The reaction remains the same today when one points out the other volcano, which is real enough and awaiting us in what is only now manifesting in what people have long called "the social question." Because people are so fond of being asleep to reality, they do not realize that, within this very reality, the real forces exist that alone can turn it into true reality.

This is why it is so difficult to impress on people today the urgent need to work toward a threefold social order, for a healthy social organism must be divided into three branches. Why is the thinking behind this demand for a threefold social order different from other ways of thinking? Other ways of thinking, in fact, involve the invention of what might be the best social world order for us and what we ought to do to get there.

Notice the difference between this kind of thinking and the kind at the foundation of the threefold social organization. The threefold social order does not start by asking: What is the best way of arranging the social organism? On the contrary it starts with reality by asking how we can classify human beings themselves so that they take their place in the social order in an unrestricted way and work together toward what is right. This way of thinking does not hinge on principles, theories, or social dogmas, but on the nature of the human being. It says: place people in the environment of a threefold social order, and they themselves will say how it should be organized. This way of thinking takes its lead from what is truly human and not from abstract theories or abstract social dogmas.

If people were to live in isolation they would never develop human speech. Human speech can arise only in a social community. On the same premise, human beings do not, on their own, develop a social way of thinking, nor would they have any social perceptions or social instincts. Only in the right community is it possible to bring social life into today's events.

Nonetheless, a great many things contradict this. Owing to the rise of materialism in recent centuries, humankind has taken leave of reality and become alienated from it. In their inner being, people have become lonely, and most lonely of all are those who have been torn from life and become connected with nothing but barren machines, with the factory on the one hand and soulless capitalism on the other. The human soul itself has become barren. Out of this soul void, however, something can struggle to break free from a human being's individual personality. Out of the individual's being, spiritual thoughts and perceptions of the suprasensory world can arise—perceptions that also shed light on the outer world of nature. Precisely when we are truly lonely, we are thrown back entirely on ourselves, and we are in the best state of mind as individuals to gain knowledge of our relationships with the world of nature and the world of spirit. What we should acquire in the way of social thinking is the opposite of this. Unless we reflect on this, we cannot properly assess the significant moment of history in which we are living. Humanity needs to go through this historic moment of loneliness in world evolution, so that, out of their loneliness of soul, people can develop spiritual life. The loneliest of all were the great thinkers who seemed to live in the heights of total abstraction, yet in their abstractions they were simply seeking a path to the suprasensory world.

Human beings, of course, must not only seek the path to the suprasensory world and to nature, but out of their own thoughts they must seek the path leading to social life. However, because social life cannot be developed alone but only through truly experiencing others, the lonely people of today are not the best suited to develop social thinking. Just when they reached the point of wanting to attain something worthwhile through their inner forces, the results of their efforts turned out to be antisocial, not social thinking at all. People's present inclinations and longings are the result of spiritual forces reached in loneliness, and they are given a false direction by the overwhelming influence of ahrimanic materialism. The importance of this will really strike you if you ask yourself something that fills many people today with horror. Suppose you ask: Whom would you call the Bolshevists? People will say Lenin and Trotsky. Well, I know of another one—not living in the immediate present though—and he is none other than the German philosopher Johann Gottlieb Fichte. You may have encountered quite a lot about Fichte's idealistic and spiritual way of thinking, but this is less likely to have made you aware of the sort of person Fichte was than would his well-known views expressed in his booklet on a closed economy.

Compare the way Fichte thinks of how the social order ought to be arranged for the masses with what Trotsky or Lenin write, and you will discover a remarkable agreement. You will then begin to become distrustful of merely regarding a thing and judging it by outer appearances. You will be tempted to ask: What is, in fact, behind this? If you look at it more closely and try to understand what is behind it, you will arrive at the following: You will investigate the distinctive spiritual orientation of the most radical minds of today. You may look into the particular soul characteristics of people such as Trotsky and Lenin, their special way of thinking and forms of thought, and then you ask: How have such people become possible? The answer is to imagine them in a different social setting and then in ours, which has for centuries developed into what it is in the light (or more exactly, the darkness) of materialism. Imagine Lenin and Trotsky in a different social order. How might they have turned out when developing their spiritual forces in a different way? They might have become profound mystics. In a religious atmosphere, what lived in their souls might have developed into a profound mysticism. We can see what it became under the influence of modern materialism.

If you look into *The Closed Commercial State* by Johann Gottlieb Fichte, you see the social ideal of a person who truly was trying his utmost to travel the highest paths of knowledge and who developed the kind of thinking that tended constantly toward the suprasensory world. However, when he tried to work out a social ideal for himself, although it came entirely from his heart, we see that the very thing that suits us when we pursue for ourselves the highest ideals of knowledge is a handicap when applied to the kind of social thinking needed for working in social life.

The sort of spiritual work Fichte did must be done alone, whereas social thinking has to be worked out within a community of other human beings, where the primary task of the thinker is to consider how the social organism might be laid out so that people may work together in the right way to establish a social existence within the social realm itself. This is why I never tell you, or tell the people of today, how you should deal with private property in relation to the means of production, or with communal property in terms of the means of production. Rather, one has to say: try to work toward dividing the social organism into its three spheres. Then, whatever is affected by capital will be managed by the cultural sphere, and human rights will be administered by the political state. The area of rights and the organizational sphere will dovetail properly into the economic sphere. Thus socialization will occur that, in accordance with certain legal concepts, will insure that whatever people earn over and above their needs will be channeled constantly into the spiritual–cultural system. It returns again to the spiritual–cultural sphere.

Today, this arrangement applies only in the realm of intellectual property, where nobody finds it strange. Individuals cannot hold on to their intellectual property for their descendants for more than a certain period (thirty years at most after death), when it becomes public property. We ought to think of this as a possible model for returning surplus profit to the social organism, even when it is the result of individual effort, as well as returning what is covered by the capitalist system. The only question is: Return into which areas? Into the area that can take care of the individual capacities of people, whether spiritual or otherwise; into the spiritual–cultural realm. Things will be managed this way when people take their rightful place in the social organism. This is where this way of thinking leads. I could imagine these things being done differently in each century. In such matters, no arrangements are valid forever. In our era, however, people have become accustomed to judging matters from a materialistic point of view, so nothing is seen any longer in the right light.

I have frequently pointed out that labor has become a commodity. Ordinary work contracts are based on this. They are based on the amount of work the laborer does for the employer. A healthy relationship cannot arise when a contract is settled in terms of so much labor, because labor must be treated as a question of rights and settled by the political state, based on the goods produced being divided among those who do the physical and intellectual work. The contract can be made solely on the goods produced and not on the relationship of laborer and employer. This is the only way to put the matter on a healthy footing.

Nonetheless, people ask: What is the source of the social evils associated with capitalism? It is said that they arise from the capitalist economic system. But no evils can arise from an economic system. They arise, first, because we have no real labor laws to protect labor and, second, because we fail to notice that the way the workers are denied their due share amounts to a living lie. But why are they being deprived? Not because of the economic system, but because the social order itself allows the possibility of the individual capacities of the employer to be rewarded unjustly at the expense of the workers. The division of the proceeds ought to be made in terms of goods, for these are the joint products of the intellectual workers and physical laborers. However, if by virtue of your individual capacities you take something from someone that you have no right to take, what have you done? You have cheated that person; you have taken advantage. If you just look these circumstances straight in the face, you realize that the trouble is not capitalism itself, but the misuse of intellectual, or spiritual, capacities. Here you have the connection with the spiritual world. When you begin by making the spiritual organization healthy, so that spiritual, intellectual capacities are no longer permitted to take advantage of those who have to labor, you bring health to the social organism as a whole. It all depends on the ability to see the right thing to do in every case.

To do this, people need guidelines. Today we have reached the time when proper guiding principles can come only from spiritual life. Therefore, we have to give serious attention to this spiritual life. It has to be pointed out repeatedly that today it is not enough to declare continually that people should recapture a belief in the spirit. Yes, plenty of prophets are beginning to speak of the need to believe in the spirit. However, the point is not merely to say: In order to be cured of the present unhealthy conditions, people will have to turn away from materialism and back to the spirit. No mere belief in spirit is a cure today. However, many illustrious prophets go round repeating that people must become spiritual.

Prophets say that, in the past, Christ has been a concern only for our private life, but that now Christ should enter the public life of the state. Such statements have absolutely nothing to offer. Mere belief in the spirit is unimportant compared to becoming filled with the spirit to the point of bringing spirit into outer material reality. Today, it is important to speak of the kind of spirit that can truly master material reality and to explain how we should organize society instead of telling people to believe in the spirit. The non-spiritual nature of today is not the result of a failure to believe in the spirit but a failure to establish the kind of connection with the spirit that allows spirit to take hold of real-life matters.

Lack of faith in the spirit does not arise solely from denying the spirit; it can also come from the assumption that matter is unspiritual. How many people are there today who imagine they are highly superior when they say: See how non-spiritual outer material existence is; we should withdraw from it and turn away from external material life to a secluded life of spirit. Down here is material reality, in which you use the coupons in a ration book. Then you sit down to meditate, and off you go to the spiritual world. Two beautifully distinct ways of living, sharply distinguished. This is not what it is all about, however. It is essential that spirit should become so strong in people's innermost souls that it does not merely aspire to talk about things such as grace and salvation, but goes right into what we need to do in outer material reality, enabling spirit to flow into this external material reality. To acquire the habit of talking about the spirit comes very easily to people, and in this connection some people can contradict themselves in an extraordinary way. Anzengruber illustrates this through his dramatic personification of the human being who denies God.[2] Special emphasis is given to the denial by using the words: "I am an atheist as truly as there is a God in heaven." There are no small numbers of inconsistent people around today, even though they may not draw attention to themselves in such a striking way. Nevertheless, today it is common to use expressions such as that of Anzengruber.

This sort of thing certainly conveys a warning not to think that mere belief in the spirit is enough, but to try more than anything else to find the spirit in a way that will make us strong enough to penetrate outer material reality. Then people will stop using the word *spirit* in every sentence and show and instead, through the way they regard things, bring spirit into their observation. It is essential today that we view matters in the light of the spirit, and not just talk about spirit. People need to understand this, so that Anthroposophy is in no way confused with all the superficial talk about spirit so popular today. Again and again, when some worldly, Sunday-afternoon preacher merely speaks in a better style than usual, someone will say that it sounds just like Anthroposophy. In fact, it is usually just the opposite. This is precisely what we have to keep a wakeful eye on. This is what it is all about.

If you understand this then you will be very close to the understanding that such a well-intended statement (I might say a statement spoken out of a presentiment of tragic death) as the one I quoted from Kurt Eisner is especially valuable because it strikes one as being someone's confession: "To be honest, I don't really believe in a suprasensory element; at least, I do not wish to give it any active attention. Yet those who speak about the world of the suprasensory have always said: the reality we perceive here with our senses is only the half of reality; it is like a dream. I have only to look at the form this sensory reality has assumed in today's social life, and it does indeed look much like a dream. Indeed, one is forced to say that this reality is clearly the invention of some evil spirit."

This is certainly a remarkable confession. But could it mean something else? Could this terrible and tragic way of presenting

---

2. Ludwig Anzengruber (1839–1889), Austrian writer.

today's reality be the educative gesture of a good spirit, urging us to seek true reality in what appears to be a scary nightmare, to seek the wholeness of reality, which is compounded of the sense-perceptible dimension and the suprasensory dimension? We must not take an exclusively pessimistic view of the present time. We can also draw the strength from it to achieve a kind of vindication of contemporary existence. In this case, we should never again allow ourselves to stop short at the level of the sensory perceptible, but will have to find the way out of it to the suprasensory level.

Anyone who refuses to seek this way out would have to be pretty dim-witted not to say: this kind of reality is the invention of an evil spirit! But anyone who musters the will to rise from this sort of reality to spiritual reality will also be able to speak in terms of our being taught by a good spirit. Moreover, despite all that we see today, we may rest assured that humankind will find its way out of today's tragic destiny. Of course, we must respond to the clear pointer calling us to play our part in social healing.

From Rudolf Steiner, The Esoteric Aspect of the Social Question:
The Individual and Society *(Rudolf Steiner Press, 2001),
lecture in Zurich, March 9, 1919, pp. 67–89.*

9.

Education

The Fundamentals of Waldorf Education

After the collapse of Germany in 1918, a movement toward social renewal was born in Stuttgart, with the aim of lifting the country out of the chaos of the times and guiding it toward a more hopeful future. At the time, one of the oldest friends of the anthroposophic movement, Emil Molt, conceived the idea of beginning the Waldorf school in Stuttgart. Mr. Molt was in a position to implement that idea almost immediately, for he was in charge of an industrial enterprise employing a large number of workers. Thanks to the excellent relations existing between the management of that enterprise, the Waldorf-Astoria Cigarette Factory, and its workers, it proved possible to attract all of the workers' children to the school. In this way, more than two years ago, the Waldorf School was founded, primarily for working-class children.

During the past two years, however, the school has grown almost from month to month. Today we have not only the original students of the Waldorf school—whose guidance was put into my care—but also many other children from all social classes and backgrounds. Indeed, the number of students who have found their way into the Waldorf school from all quarters of the population is now considerably larger than the original number of founding students, the children of the factory workers. This fact shows the Waldorf school to be in practice a school for children of all types, coming from different classes and cultures, all of whom receive the same teaching, based on our own methods.

The idea of the Waldorf school grew out of the anthroposophic movement, a movement that, nowadays, attracts a great deal of hostility because it is widely misunderstood. In tonight's talk, and by way of introduction, I will mention only one such misunderstanding. This misunderstanding asserts that it is the aim of Anthroposophy or spiritual science, particularly in its social aspects, to be revolutionary or somehow subversive, which is not at all the case. I must emphasize this because it is of special importance for our pedagogical theme. As anthroposophic spiritual science seeks to deepen and fructify the many branches of science that have developed in the cultural and spiritual sphere during the last three or four centuries, it has no intention whatever of opposing modern science in any way. Nor does it wish to introduce amateurism into modern science. It only wishes to deepen and to widen the achievements of modern science, including modern medicine.

Likewise, the education arising from anthroposophic spiritual science does not wish to oppose the tenets of recent educational theory as put forward by its great representatives. Nor does it wish to encourage amateurism in this field. Acknowledging the achievements of modern natural science, anthroposophic spiritual science has every reason to appreciate the aims and the achievements of the great educators at the end of the nineteenth and the beginning of the twentieth centuries. Anthroposophy has no wish to oppose them. It wishes only to deepen their work by what can be gained through anthroposophic research. It wishes to stand entirely on the ground of modern pedagogical thinking. However, it does find it necessary to expand the scope of modern pedagogical thinking and I shall endeavor to give a few outlines of how this is to be done.

Though the Waldorf school takes its starting point from anthroposophic spiritual science, it is nevertheless not an ideological school—and this I hope will be accepted as an important fact. The Waldorf school is not in the least concerned with carrying into the school anthroposophic dogma or anthroposophic convictions. It seeks to be neither ideological nor sectarian nor denominational, for this would not be in character with anthroposophic spiritual science. Unfortunately, the opposite is often erroneously believed.

The Waldorf school, which has its roots in Anthroposophy, is a school applying specific methods and classroom practices, as well as pedagogical ideas and impulses drawn from anthroposophically oriented spiritual science. When we founded the school, we were simply not in a position to insist on such radical demands as are frequently made by some modern educators who maintain, for instance, that, if one wants to educate children properly, one has to open boarding schools or the like in the country, away from cities. There are many such endeavors today, and we have no objection to them. We understand fully the reasoning behind their demands. In the Waldorf school, however, we are not in the same happy position. We had to accept a given situation. The possibility was granted to us to place what was to become the Waldorf school in a city, in the very life of a city. There was no question of first insisting on the right outer conditions for the school. What mattered was to achieve what had to be achieved through the principles and methods of our education under given circumstances.

It is a characteristic feature of anthroposophic spiritual science that it can adapt itself to any outer conditions, for it wants to be able to work under all conditions of life. It has no wish to chase after utopian ideals, but wants to create something in harmony with the human potential of its members out of the immediate practical conditions and the practical needs of life in any given situation.

To repeat, no dogma is to be carried into the school. What a person standing within the anthroposophic movement does gain, however, is a way of knowing that involves our whole humanity. The educational life of our times tends to favor a certain intellectualism. Therefore there is no need to fear that the Waldorf school teaches its students that a human being consists not only of a physical body (as you can read in many anthroposophic writings) but also of an ether body, supplying the formative and organic growing forces at work in the physical body, and also of an astral body that, during earthly life, carries what was developed during pre-earthly existence—prior to physical birth or, rather, conception, and so on—into the human physical organization. None of this is taught in the school. But, if we know that human beings, when observed with scientific accuracy, consist of body, soul, and spirit, and if we grasp how this is revealed in the child as a human being in the making, we gain a deeper and truer knowledge of the human being than is possible through present-day natural science.

We do not grasp this deeper knowledge of human beings and all that anthroposophic spiritual science can learn about them only with our powers of thinking: the whole human being—thinking, feeling, and willing—is involved. This, however, is not the substance from which the training methods for work in the Waldorf school are to be drawn. Rather, anthroposophic knowledge creates in our teachers the forces of will to do all that they can for growing children in accordance with the demands of each child's organization. However odd it might sound, children are the preeminent "teachers" in the Waldorf school. Waldorf teachers are fully convinced that what they encounter in their children, week after week and year after year, is the outer manifestation of divine and spiritual beings who have come to Earth from a purely soul and spiritual existence so that they can evolve in a physical, earthly body between birth and death. They realize that each child's being unites—by means of the stream of heredity coming through the parents and their ancestors—with what is bestowed physically and etherically. Waldorf teachers have an enormously deep reverence for the young human being who, in the first days after birth, already shows how an inner soul being manifests in physiognomy, in the first limb movements, and in their first babbling that gradually grows into human speech. Anthroposophic knowledge of human beings creates a deep reverence for what the divine world has sent to Earth, and that inner attitude of reverence is characteristic of Waldorf teachers as they enter their classrooms each morning. From the daily revelations of this mysterious spirit and soul existence, they discover what they as teachers must do with their children.

This is the reason why one cannot formulate the methods of the Waldorf school in a few abstract rules. One cannot say: point one, point two, point three, and so on. Rather, one has to say that, through anthroposophic spiritual science, a teacher comes to know the growing human being and learns to observe what looks out of a child's eyes and reveals itself in a child's fidgety leg movements. Because teachers are thoroughly grounded in an understanding of the whole human being, their knowledge of Anthroposophy fills not only their intellect, with its capacity to systematize, but embraces the whole human being who also feels and wills. These teachers approach their students in such a way that their methods acquire a living existence that they can always modify and metamorphose, even in larger classes, to suit each individual child.

Anyone hearing all of this in the abstract, might well respond: These crazy anthroposophists! They believe that a human being does not only have a physical body which, as a corpse, may be carefully examined and investigated in physiology and biology. They also believe that human beings have etheric and even astral bodies. Moreover, they believe that we can come to know these if we practice certain soul exercises. They believe that, if we strengthen our thinking to the point where the whole human being is transformed into a kind of "suprasensory sense organ" (if I may use Goethe's expression), we can see more than we do in ordinary human life.

It is easy to poke fun at those "crazy anthroposophists," who speak in these terms of suprasensory beings in the sensory world. But if these convictions, based not on weird fantasies but on well-grounded knowledge, are carried into teaching, those whose task is to educate young people can observe growing children realistically, as beings of body, soul, and spirit. And this is how a child must be observed if the student's innermost being is to be revealed.

I do not wish to deride today's experimental psychology or experimental pedagogy. I appreciate and acknowledge what those scientific disciplines have achieved. Nonetheless, because of those disciplines we must deepen our pedagogy even more. Aside from their positive aspects, they show that we are not any closer to children in a direct and natural way, but just the opposite; we have become increasingly estranged from children. Conventional experiments are made with children to determine how their thinking, their memory, and even their will function. Rules and regulations are then drawn up from the ensuing statistics. Certainly, such findings are useful, especially for an anthroposophist. But, if we view them as the "be-all and end-all" foundation for education, we merely prove that we have not in any way reached the child's true being. Why do we need to engage in experiments at all? It is simply because the direct, immediate relationship between teacher and child—which was present in ancient, biblical times—has been lost under the influence of our modern materialistic culture. Conventional experiments are made because a direct feeling and understanding no longer exists for what actually happens within children. The fact of these external experiments itself proves that we have lost a direct relationship with our children and that we should try to rediscover it with all available power.

When we study contemporary experimental psychology and pedagogy, it often seems as if the experimentalist were like someone observing a person riding a horse to see how he or she does on a smooth path as compared to more difficult terrain. From such observations, the experimentalist then compiles statistics: on the smooth path, such and such a distance in fifteen minutes; on a slippery path, so many miles; on an uneven path, so many more miles; and so on. This is the way of working that we also find, more or less, in experiments made to determine whether a child will remember something for a quarter of an hour, or whether a child omits so and so many of the words to be remembered, and so on.

To return to our simile, if we were to compile statistical details about the rider, we would have to consider not only the state of the paths, but also what the horse was capable of doing on the particular paths observed and so on. However, in this way we will not succeed in discovering anything about the rider (although it would of course be perfectly possible to include the rider in statistical observations as well). It is most important not just to experiment externally on those to be educated, but that, as teachers, we have direct, natural contact with children through our understanding of their inner nature.

In anthroposophic spiritual science, one comes to understand what is given when a baby is born. We learn that a child bears within not only what we can perceive with the senses, but also a spiritual soul being that united with the physical embryo. We come to know exactly how this spiritual soul being develops, just as we learn from physical science how the physical seed develops within the flow of heredity. We learn to recognize that, independent of the inherited traits, something of a suprasensory spirit and soul nature enters. Without teaching it as a dogma (and I must emphasize this repeatedly), this perspective nevertheless becomes a means of orienting the teacher, guiding the teacher's observations of children even before they enter school.

For a child just learning to speak, the following premise is useful. We must observe not only what belongs to the stream of heredity but also what develops in the child from spiritual depths. Language is part of this. When we observe human beings in the light of anthroposophic spiritual science (discriminating between the more inner, astral body and the more outer ether body), we come to know the nature of the human will in a new way. We see the will as allied more with the astral body, while thinking is seen to be connected more closely with the ether body. We come to know how these members interact in speaking. When observing and experiencing life, we are concerned not just with outer facts, but also with placing those facts in the right light.

Now let us take a well-trained observer of life, someone trained in Anthroposophy to know human beings, and place this person beside a child who is going through the process of learning to speak. If we have really learned to look into a child's soul life, recognizing the imponderables at play between adult and child, we can learn more about children's psychology by observing real-life situations than, for example, the eminent psychologist

Wilhelm Preyer[1] did by means of statistical records.... With every vowel sound, we speak directly to a child's feelings. We address ourselves to the innermost being of the child's soul. With the help of spiritual science, we learn how to stimulate a particular soul area. In this way, we introduce a connection between adult and child that generates a close relationship between teacher and student, allowing something to flow from the teacher directly to the child's inmost feeling.

If, for example, we speak to a child about how cold it is outside, that child is taken into the realm of consonants as we work directly on the child's will. We can observe that we stimulate a child's feeling life in one instance, and in another the child's movement, which lives in will impulses. With this example, I merely wanted to indicate how to clarify everything, even the most elementary phenomena, through a comprehensive knowledge of life. Today, there is a magnificent science of language that can certainly benefit education a great deal. However, that science studies language as if it were separate from human beings. If we are trained in anthroposophic spiritual science, however, we learn to view language not as something that floats above people, who then take hold of it and bring it into life. Rather, we learn that language is connected directly to the whole human being, and we learn to use this knowledge in practical life. We learn how a child's inner relationship to the vowel aspect is connected with a warming glow in the feeling life, whereas the consonantal aspect (all that children experience through consonants) is closely linked to the movements of the will.

The point is that you learn to observe children more closely. People have gradually lost this kind of observation, this empathy with the child. Frequently today, when we try to educate young human beings, it seems as if we were actually circumventing their real being. It is as though the modern science of education has lost its direct connection with the children we wish to educate. We no longer recognize that speech is linked organically to all the processes of growth and to all that happens in a child.

---

1. Wilhelm Preyer (1841–1897), physiologist and psychologist, published *The Soul of the Child* (Leipzig, 1881).

Fundamentally, we no longer know that, in raising a child to imitate in the right way, we help that child to become inwardly warm and rich in feelings. Until the change of teeth around the seventh year, children depend entirely on imitation. Raising and educating children during those early years depend essentially upon this faculty. Unless we gain a clear understanding of this ability to imitate during the early years of life and can follow it closely from year to year, the hidden depths of a child's inner nature will not be revealed to us. We would be unable to educate our students in ways that will place them fully into life later on.

This is true not only of speech, but also of whatever we must teach our children before they enter school. As I say, until the second set of teeth, a child is fundamentally and wholly dependent on imitation. Anthroposophic spiritual science allows us to study the young child's faculty of imitation in all areas of life. Speech, too, develops entirely through imitation. However, the study of the imitation faculty enables us to look more deeply into the nature of the growing human being in other ways, too. Although contemporary psychology always thinks around the problem of how the human soul (or, as it is sometimes called, the human spirit) is connected to the human physical body, it cannot gain an exact concept of the relationship between the human soul and spirit, on one side, and the physical and bodily counterpart, on the other. Basically, psychology knows only the physical aspects of the human being, when the body, like a corpse, lacks soul and spirit. It has distanced itself from the human soul and spirit as I have described them.

This situation can be clarified best through a specific example. Contemporary science does not appreciate the importance of phenomena such as the second dentition around the seventh year. Yet the kind of observation fostered by spiritual science reveals how a child's soul forces change during that process. A child's memory and ability to think, as well as a child's faculty of feeling, change greatly during these years. In fact, one cannot see a child's soul life develop before about the seventh year. Where was the emerging soul life with which we have to deal when the child enters school before the seventh year? Where was it previously?

The method employed by scientific thinking is perfectly appropriate in the inorganic realm. When physicists today study certain substances that emit heat after undergoing a particular process, they ascribe that heat to the warmth that was formerly contained within the substance as "latent" or hidden heat. Then they study how, when subjected to a particular process, that latent heat is liberated or released from the physical substance. They would not dream of concluding that the radiating heat had somehow come into the matter from outside, but they study the condition in which the heat existed while already present there. This way of thinking, inaugurated by physics, can be applied to the more complicated reality of human beings.

If, from an anthroposophic point of view, we study how a child's memory and will assume a particular configuration in the seventh year, we will not conclude that these new faculties have suddenly "flown into the child." We will assume that they developed within the child itself. But where were they previously? They were active in the child's physical organism. In other words, what the teacher must educate was previously a latent, hidden force in the child's own being. That force has been liberated. As long as children need the forces that will culminate with the pushing out of the second teeth, those forces will be active in the child's inner realm. With the shedding of the milk teeth and the emergence of the second teeth, those forces—like the latent heat in certain substances—are released from their task and reveal themselves as new soul and spiritual capacities. These we then actively engage in our teaching.

Only by studying examples from real life can we learn to understand how soul and body work together. We can engage in endless philosophical speculation about the relationship of soul and body to each other but, when studying early childhood up to the seventh year, we must observe the actual facts. Only then will we recognize that forces that have left the organic bodily realm after the change of teeth are free to be used by the teacher in quite a new way.

The same principle applies to the whole span of human life. All of the speculative theories about the relationship of soul and body that we can find in books on philosophy and physiology are useless unless they are based on a mode of observation that is exact according to proper scientific methods.

If we observe such phenomena further, we realize that the forces in a child with which we deal as teachers are the same that were previously engaged in building up the organism. We know, too, that those forces must now assume another form and that, if we are to teach children, we must come to know those forces in their new form. But we must also get to know them in their original form—since they must be used for learning, we must be able to recognize them in their original task. Well, a lot more could be said about this. I will only point out that it is because of those forces, working in the depths of the organism, creating life, that a child imitates up to the seventh year. To understand a preschool child, we must always bear in mind this faculty of imitation.

For example, parents complain that their son has stolen money. They are looking for advice. You ask how old the child is and are told that he is four or five years old. It might sound surprising, but a child of four or five does not really steal. Such a child is still at the stage of imitation. And so, if you ask further questions, you discover, for instance, that the child has seen his mother taking money out of a cupboard every day. The child imitates this action and, consequently, he too takes money. I have even known a case in which a child took money out of a cupboard but, instead of buying sweets, bought things to give to other children. There was nothing immoral in this behavior, only perhaps something somewhat amoral, something imitative.

An incident like this makes us realize that, in educating children, we are dealing with imponderables. As teachers, we must realize that, when we stand before a child who is an imitator, we must be mindful even of our thoughts. Not only our actions but our thoughts too must be of a kind that a child can safely imitate. The entire upbringing of preschool children must be based on this principle of imitation. Even if it might sound strange, awareness of this principle must lie at the foundation of a really healthy form of early education.

The forces that cause children to imitate to such an extent that they copy even the slightest hand movement appear when they about seven and become the liberated forces with which educators and teachers must deal. Looking more closely at this development, one recognizes that, whereas a child is a compulsive imitator up to the age of seven, during the next seven years, up to puberty, the student needs to experience a natural sense of authority in the teacher as the right guide on life's path. The experience of authority becomes the main educational principle for children between the change of teeth and puberty—a principle that develops naturally to become the basic relationship between teacher and student.

It is all too easy to speak abstractly about this relationship based upon a natural sense of authority. If we wish to guide it in the right direction at every moment of our teaching life, we need anthroposophic knowledge of the human being.

Today, many people speak about the necessity and the importance of visual instruction, practical demonstration, and so forth—and they are in a certain sense quite right to do so. It is certainly right for some subjects. Anything that can be outwardly observed can be brought to the child by these methods. But we must consider, above all, the moral order of the world and human religious feelings—that is, everything pertaining to the spiritual nature of the world. The spiritual is imperceptible to outer senses and if we take the so-called visual instruction method too far, we lead children into believing in only what is sense perceptible—that is, into materialism. What really matters at this age is that through the natural relationship to the teacher, the child feels, "This adult, who is my guide, knows what is right and behaves in a way I long to emulate." If I describe such a feeling as an adult, it is naturally quite different from how a child would experience it.

During the first seven years, then, a child's activities mirror and imitate its surroundings—above all through gestures, including the subtle inner gestures that live in speech. But, during the next seven years, children develop under the influence of the words that come from the naturally accepted authority of their teacher. In order to appreciate the importance and value of this natural sense of authority, one must have a thorough foundation in true knowledge of the human being.

You would hardly expect someone like myself who, many years ago, wrote a book called *Intuitive Thinking as a Spiritual Path: A Philosophy of Freedom* to support a reactionary social belief in authority. So it is not on the basis of any authoritarian intention but solely on educational grounds that I maintain that the most essential principle, the most important force in education, between the age of seven and puberty, lies in a student's belief that the teacher, as an authority, knows what is right and does what is right. This must sink down into the child.

If students do not develop on the basis of this belief in the authority of the teacher, they will be unable, when older, to enter social life in a wholesome manner.

To understand this, we need only to know what it means for a child willingly to accept something on the basis of authority. I realize that this is for many people rather a controversial point but, actually, it is controversial only for those who, fundamentally speaking, lack the will to look at life in its entirety.

For instance, let us assume, say, that, in our second year of life nature did not dispose the form of our fingers so that they grow and develop—that nature made our fingers such that, as it were, they were cast in hard stereotyped forms. What would we do then? Insofar as we are human, then, we are growing, continuously changing beings. And as educators, likewise, this is the kind of essence that we must pour into children's souls. We must not impose on our children anything that creates sharply contoured pictures, impressions, or will impulses in them. Just as our fingers do not retain the contours that they had when we were two but rather grow on their own, so all ideas, thoughts, and feelings that we pour into children during their school years must have the essence of growth in them.

We must be quite clear: what we bring to an eight-year-old cannot be clear-cut or sharply contoured. Rather, it must have an inner capacity for growth. By the time the person is forty, it will have become something quite different. We must be able to see the *whole* human being. Anyone who does not appreciate the principle of authority during these years of childhood has never experienced what it really means when, for instance, in the course of one's thirty-fifth year, out of the dark recesses of memory, one understands some concept of history or geography—or some concept of life—that one accepted without understanding at the age of nine on the authority of a well loved teacher or parent, having taken it simply on faith. When such a concept emerges in the soul and is understood with the mature understanding of several decades later, this becomes an animating principle that calls up an indefinable feeling that need not be brought to full consciousness: something from one's earliest years lives on in one's soul. It is in this sense that we must be able to follow the forces of growth in nature.

Our educational principles and methods must not be tied up in fixed formulae. Rather, they must become a kind of refined, practical instinct for action in those who educate from a living knowledge of human beings. Teachers will then find the right way of dealing with children rather than merely artificially grafting something onto the souls in their care. This is not to deny what has been proclaimed by the great educators of the nineteenth and early twentieth centuries. On the contrary, it actually applies it correctly.

Those who wish to become Waldorf teachers know quite well that they cannot join the school as amateurs, as dilettantes. They must be moved by all that education has produced in the nineteenth and twentieth centuries. At the same time, however, they must also bring to the Waldorf school the living understanding of human beings I have discussed. Here one feels prompted to quote Goethe's dictum, "Consider well the *what*, but consider more the *how*." You will find excellent expositions of the *what*—with regard to foundations and principles—in theoretical texts on education. Even quite idealistic thoughts are sometimes expressed there, but all of this represents only the *what*. The point is not to formulate abstract principles but to be able to apply them in a living way, with inner soul warmth.

I am fully convinced that, if a group of people were to sit together (they don't even need to be very smart) to draft the blueprint for an ideal school, their schemes—prioritized by first, second, third, and so forth—would be excellent. They would be so convincing that one could not improve on them. It is even possible to invent grand ideals and turn them into slogans for great reform movements and so on. But, given life as it is, all of this has little value. The important thing is to truly observe life, bearing in mind the living human being as capable of doing what needs to be done under the given circumstances. "Consider well the *what*, but consider more the *how*." The important thing is that love of the child is at the basis of all of our educational endeavors, and that all teaching is done through inner, living experience. Against this background, the foundation of our education becomes very different from what it usually is. Keeping this in mind, then, I would like to put into words a fundamental underlying principle, once more in the form of an example.

A child is supposed to form an inner picture of a definite concept. It is capable of doing so but, in our attempts to communicate something abstract—something of an ethical and religious nature—we can proceed in different ways. For example, let us imagine that the teacher wants to convey to students—naturally in accordance with the children's age and maturity—the idea of the immortality of the human soul. We can do this with a comparison. There are two ways in which we can do this. One would be as follows. As teachers, we can believe that we are terribly clever, whereas the child is still young and terribly ignorant. On this basis, we could invent a comparison and say, "Look at the chrysalis. The butterfly comes out of the chrysalis." Then, after describing this process pictorially, we might say, "Just as the butterfly emerges from its chrysalis, so the human soul, when a person passes through the portal of death, leaves the body and flies into the spiritual world." This is one way of approaching the problem. Feeling greatly superior to the child, we think out a simile or comparison. But, if this is our underlying attitude, we will not be very successful. Indeed, this is a situation where imponderables play their part. A teacher who has been trained in anthroposophic spiritual science to understand the nature of the world and knows that spirit is present in all matter will not begin by feeling smarter than the children. Such a teacher will not invent something for the children's benefit. In other words, the teacher will believe firmly that, on a higher level, what represents the human soul leaving the body at death is represented in the natural order, on a lower level, by the emergence of the butterfly from the chrysalis. The teacher will understand the truth of this image. To such a teacher, the image represents a sacred revelation. These are two entirely different approaches. If I speak to the child out of a sacred conviction, I touch the child's innermost being in an indescribable way. I call forth in the child a living feeling, a living concept. This approach is generally true. We must not underestimate or overestimate what modern science has to say through its single-minded interest in outer reality....

This is an important consideration in establishing a living method of education, distinct from those based on mere principles and intellectual theories. This living method of education guides us to observe children from year to year. It is the *how* that matters: the individual treatment of each child, even within a larger class. It is possible to achieve this. The Waldorf school [in Stuttgart] has already demonstrated this fact during the first few years of its existence.

Here I can only give broad outlines that can be supplemented by more details. First, we receive children into our first grade, where they are supposed to learn writing and reading, as well as perhaps the beginning of arithmetic and so on. Let us first discuss reading. Reading in our present culture is really quite alien to a young child. If we go back to ancient times, we find that a kind of picture writing existed in which each letter word still retained a pictorial connection with the object it represented. In our present system of writing or printing, there is nothing to link the child's soul to what is written. For this reason, we should not begin by immediately teaching children writing when they enter primary school in their sixth or seventh year. In the Waldorf school, all teaching—and this includes writing, which we introduce before reading—appeals directly to a child's innate artistic sense. Right from the start, we give our young students the opportunity of working artistically with colors, not only with dry crayons but also with watercolors. In this simple way, we give the child something from which the forms of the letters can be developed. Such things have been done elsewhere, of course. It is, however, a matter of *how* again. The main thing is to allow children to be active without engaging the forces of the intellect, but primarily activating the will. On the basis of drawing and painting, we gradually lead a child's first will activities in writing toward a more intellectual understanding of what is written. We lead our children systematically, developing everything in harmony with their inherent nature. Even down to the arrangement of the curriculum, everything we do in school must be adapted to the child's evolving nature. To do this, anthroposophic knowledge of human beings is necessary.

I would here like to point out how one can observe the harm done to children when one does not give them concepts and feelings capable of growth, but makes them aware of the difference between the outer material world of fixed forms and their own inner mobile soul life at too early an age. Until about the ninth year, a child does not yet clearly discriminate between him- or herself and the outer world. One must be careful not to adhere to abstract concepts, as some do who say, "Well, of course, when a young child bumps into the corner of a table, the child strikes the table, thinking that the table is also alive." This is, of course, nonsense. Children do not think that a table is alive. They act toward the table as if it were a child, too, simply because a young child cannot yet distinguish the self from the table. Whether the table lives or does not is not the point. The child, as yet, has no such concept.

We must always deal with facts, not what we imagine intellectually. Until the ninth year, everything we introduce to children must be treated as if it had purely human qualities. It must be based on the assumption that children's relationship to the world is such that every thing is a part of them—as if it were a part of their own organism. One can, of course, point to certain obvious examples when children differentiate between an object in the outer world and their own being. Between the seventh and ninth years, we will not advance the finer aspects of education unless we bring life to whatever we teach, unless we make everything into a parable, not in a dead, but a truly living form. Everything must be taught in moving, colorful images, not through dead, static concepts.

Between the ninth and tenth years, a most important, significant moment occurs: it is only then that children really become conscious of the difference between their inner selves and their surroundings. This is the age when we can first intellectually introduce children to the life of plants and animals, both of whom have an existence apart from human beings. Something truly profound is taking place in a child's mind and soul at this time—a little earlier in the case of some children, a little later in others. Something is happening—fundamental changes are occurring—in the depths of their young souls. They are learning to distinguish their inner selves from the outer world in a feeling way, but not yet by means of concepts. Therefore if teachers are aware of the right moment, and can find the appropriate words, they can—acting as the situation demands—do something of lasting value and importance for the whole life of these children aged between nine and ten. On the other hand, if they miss this significant moment, they can create an inner barrenness of soul or spiritual aridity in later life, and an attitude of everlasting doubt and inner dissatisfaction. But, if teachers are sufficiently alert to catch such a significant moment and if, by immersing themselves in the child's being, they have the necessary empathy and know-how to speak the right words and how to conduct themselves rightly, they can perform an immense service for their children, who will derive benefit for the rest of their lives. In Waldorf education, the observation of such key moments in the lives of children is considered to be of utmost importance.

After this special moment in the ninth-tenth year, while all subjects had previously to be "humanized," teachers can begin to introduce simple descriptions of plants and animals in a more objective style. Then, between the eleventh and twelfth years, they can begin to introduce inorganic subjects, such as the study of minerals and physics. Certainly the lifeless world should be approached only after children have been fully immersed in the living world....

How many countless psychological and psychoanalytical discussions and arguments take place these days about puberty? We must recognize that here we are dealing with the end of a characteristic life period, just as the second dentition represents the end of an earlier period of development. Puberty in itself is only a link in an entire chain of metamorphoses embracing the whole of human life. At the second dentition in children, soul forces that had been working within the organism are liberated. Approximately between the seventh and fourteenth years, we try to guide children in the ways I have discussed. With the beginning of puberty, children enter the period of life when they can form their own judgments on matters of the larger world. Younger children draw their inner being from the depths of their organism, but as adolescents they gain the ability to understand the spiritual nature of the outer world. One of the greatest challenges to teachers is to educate children between their seventh and fourteenth years so that they are guided naturally to acquire an independent and individual relationship to the world, of which sexuality is one expression. This is one of the most important problems of a truly living education. The sexual love of one person for another is only one aspect of the whole fabric of human social life.

We must lead adolescents to develop the inner maturity needed to follow outer-world events with caring interest. Otherwise, events will pass by unnoticed. As teachers, we must try to turn young people into social beings by the time of puberty. We must also try to cultivate religious feelings in them, not in a biased or sectarian way, but in the sense that they acquire the seriousness needed to recognize that the physical world is permeated everywhere by spirit. They should not feel inwardly satisfied with merely observing the outer sensory world, but should be able to perceive the spiritual ground of the world everywhere.

During prepubescence, when students open their inner being to us, believing in our authority, we must be what amounts to the whole world for them. If they find a world in us as their teachers, then they receive the right preparation to become reverent, social people in the world. We release them from our authority, which gave them a world, into the wide world itself.

Here, in only a few words, I touch on one of the most important problems of cognition. If we train children to make their own judgments too early, we expose them to forces of death instead of giving them forces of life. Only teachers whose natural authority awakens the belief that what they say and do is the right thing, and who in the eyes of the child become representatives of the world, will prepare their students to grow into really living human beings when, later on, they enter life. Such teachers prepare their students not by controlling their intellect or their capacity to form judgments but by setting the right example as living human beings. Life can evolve only with life. We make our students into proper citizens of the world by presenting the world to them in a human being—the teacher—not through abstract intellectual concepts.

I can characterize all of this in a few sentences, but what I am suggesting presupposes an ability to follow in detail how growing children evolve from day to day. By the power of his or her example, the way in which a teacher carries something through the door into the classroom already helps a child to develop further toward finding its own way in life. If we know this, we need not make amateurish statements, such as that all learning should be fun. Many people say this today. Try to see how far you get with such an abstract principle! In many respects learning cannot bring only joy to the child. The right way is to educate children by bringing enough life into the various subjects that they retain a curiosity for knowledge, even if it does not reward them immediately with pleasure. How a teacher proceeds should be a preparation for what students must learn from them.

This leads quite naturally to cultivation of the students' sense of duty. We touch here upon a sphere that extends far beyond what belongs to the field of education. We touch on something where a method and practice of education based on spiritual foundations directly fructifies the whole of cultural life.

We all of us surely look up to Schiller and Goethe as leading spirits. To have studied and written about them for more than forty years, as I have, leaves one in no doubt as to one's full, warm appreciation of their work and gifts. There is, however, just one point that I would like to make in this context.

Schiller had distanced himself from Goethe for all kinds of personal reasons, but in the 1790s he renewed an intimate friendship with him. Schiller wrote his famous (and, sadly, too little appreciated) *Letters on the Aesthetic Education of Humanity*. Schiller's letters were influenced by the way Goethe worked, thought, and viewed the world. In those letters on aesthetic education, we find an unusual comment: "We are fully human only while playing, and we play only when we are human in the truest sense of the word." Schiller wished to point out how ordinary life essentially chains us to a kind of slavery and how the average person, forced to live under the yoke of necessity, suffers the burden of outer life. In general, people are not free to follow their impulses unless they are engaged artistically, creating and enjoying art or acting like children at play—acting in accordance only with their impulses. What Schiller describes in his aesthetic letters is a beautiful and genuine view of what it is to be human.

On the other hand, the letters show that with the advance of our modern scientific, technological civilization and for the sake of human dignity, exceptional persons like Schiller and Goethe found it necessary to demand that human beings should be allowed freedom from the daily round of duties. To become fully human, people should be relieved of the coercion of work so that they can be free to play. If we bear in mind the social conditions imposed on us by the twentieth century, we realize that we have completely changed our attitude toward life. Realizing that everyone must accept the demands of life, we feel that we carry an intolerable burden of responsibility upon our shoulders.

We must learn how to make life worthwhile again, from both the social and individual points of view, not only by introducing more play but by taking up our tasks in a more human way. This is the reason why the social question is today first of all a question of education. We must teach young people to work in the right way. The concept of duty must be brought into school, not by preaching, but in the right and natural way—which can be achieved only through a thorough, well grounded, and correct knowledge of human nature.

If we do so, we shall be founding schools for work, not schools following the attitude that teaching and learning are merely a kind of "playing about." In our school, where authority plays its proper part, students are expected not to shy away from the most demanding tasks. In Waldorf schools, students are encouraged to tackle wholeheartedly whatever is to be mastered. They are not to be allowed to do whatever they feel like doing.

The Waldorf school was begun with this in mind. Children should learn to work in the right way and be introduced to life in the world in a fully human sense. This demands work for social reasons. As human beings, students should learn to face one another and, most important, themselves in the right way. Consequently, in addition to conventional gymnastics (which evolved from human physiology and thus has its values), we introduced eurythmy into the Waldorf school. It is a new art of movement that cultivates body, soul, and spirit and a visible form of language and music.

One can learn more about eurythmy in Dornach. Just as there are speech and music that you can hear, there is also a kind of language and music that employs gestures and movements evolved from the organization of the human body, though not in the way this might be performed in dance or mime. It can be performed by groups of people who express what is generally expressed in audible speech and music. Since its introduction in the Waldorf school some two years ago, we have already been able to observe that students from the lowest to the highest grades take naturally to eurythmy lessons with the same ease with which small children take to speaking, provided the lessons are given properly and in ways suited to each age group....

"Consider well the *what*, but consider more the *how*." While reading books on educational theory and applied teaching, there are times when one feels like shouting for joy. The great educationalists have achieved the *what*. More important, however, is the right *how*. We must find ways and means of implementing the ideas into practical life in the right way. Every Waldorf teacher must seek this anew each day, for anything that is alive must be founded on life. Spiritual science eventually leads each of us to an understanding of fundamental truths that, though they are always the same, inspire us ever anew. We depend on memory for ordinary knowledge based on material phenomena. We remember what has been absorbed. We possess what we have learned; it is linked closely to us. In everyday life, of course we need our store of memory. Our intellect depends on memory, but living processes do not require memory, not even at the lower levels of human existence. Imagine believing that what you ate as a small child would suffice for the rest of your life. You have to eat again each day because eating is a part of a living process, and what has been taken up by the organism must be digested and transformed thoroughly. Similarly, spiritual substance must be taken up in a living way, and an educational method based on spiritual science must work through this living process.

This is what I wanted to describe to you in brief outline, merely indicating here what has been described in further detail in anthroposophic books, particularly those dealing with education. I wanted to draw your attention to the educational principles of the Waldorf school, a pioneering school founded by our friend Emil Molt, a school that has no desire to rebel against contemporary education. It seeks only to put into practice what has often been suggested theoretically. Anyone who surveys the kind of life which humanity, particularly in Europe, lives today will recognize the need to deepen many aspects of life. During the second decade of this twentieth century, following the terrible catastrophe that destroyed most of what was best in humanity, one must admit the importance of giving the coming generations soul-spiritual and physical-bodily qualities different from those received by our contemporaries who have had to pay so dearly in human life. Those who, as parents, must care for the well-being of their sons and daughters and who, most of all, have the right to see how education relates to life, will view our efforts without prejudice. Those among them who, as parents, have experienced the great catastrophes of our times, will doubtlessly welcome every attempt that, based on deeper social and spiritual awareness, promises the coming generations something better than what has been offered to many at the present time. The people who have most reason to hope for an improvement of conditions prevailing in contemporary education are the parents and they, above all, have the right to expect and demand something better from the teachers. This was the thinking and the ideal that inspired us when we tried to lay the educational foundations of the Waldorf school.

> *From Rudolf Steiner,* Waldorf Education and Anthroposophy I
> *(Anthroposophic Press, 1995), lecture in Aarau, Switzerland,*
> *Nov. 11, 1921 (abridged), pp. 97–127.*

10.

Psychology

The Psychological Perspective

Anyone today who observes spiritual life must see (it requires only a sufficiently unbiased eye) how soul has, on the whole, more or less been lost as far as the most important aspects of our culture are concerned. This disappearance has been increasingly evident since the second half of the nineteenth century. In a word, soul is missing in our contemporary civilization, and the individual who wants to awaken his or her soul to an inner life must do so in solitude rather than in the shared experience of the great monuments of our civilization.

Generally speaking, we have lost the ability to be awake to the fundamental drift of present-day life. Things have happened that the kind of objective observation that started in the twentieth century should have noticed. By rights, these things should have called for powerful attention to what was happening in our spiritual life. In reality, however, such phenomena are more and more allowed to pass by unnoticed. Even more, we can honestly say that they have never received any formulation in recent times that could make an impression deep enough to awaken anyone today.

To begin my observations today, I would like to present a phenomenon that, seen from the outside, will perhaps be greeted by some with a smile. Others will simply register it neutrally as one historical and philosophical error among many. Still others might angrily fight it. I will provide the simplest description of the facts that I can.

In the final two decades of the nineteenth century, I often asked myself an important question: Who is, in fact, the most intelligent person of my time? Of course, these things are always relative. So I shall ask you not to press the issue too hard and take it with a grain of salt. Having done this, I still ask you, however, to consider this question as one that can tell us something characteristic of our age, the age of intellectualism. The intellect has brought our age to its quite exceptional height. And so one must wonder: Upon what does the human intellect depend during earthly existence? Certainly, intellectual powers and activity depend on the soul. Later, we must look more closely at the soul as such. For now, however, let us say that they depend on the etheric organism (the body of formative forces), astral body, and "I" organization, which human beings bear within themselves unconsciously (at least as far as earthly consciousness is concerned).

Human beings, however, are not so far advanced in the present period of earthly evolution that they can actually manifest the activity of the intellect as it lives in these three parts of human nature. Without a physical body, our intellect would be silent during earthly existence. It would be as though we were moving toward a wall. As long as we move straight ahead without looking at our arms and hands, we see nothing of ourselves. However, if we walk toward a mirror, we would see ourselves.

Without a body, the human intellect would be like a person who is unable to see oneself. In other words, without a physical body to mirror or reflect our activity, we would be unaware of ourselves. We owe the greatness of the intellect today to the reflection of our soul's inner activity by the physical body. People do not usually confuse a mirror image with themselves. In the case of the intellect, however, this is not the case. People confuse the intellect with its reflection in the physical realm. They surrender to the reflection, with the result that the reflection, or mirror image, itself thus rules them.

To some extent, human beings today give the intellect wholly over to their physical body. When a person really succeeds in this, it produces a great perfection of the intellect. If, on the other hand, we allow our inner being to be active, we find ourselves always stumbling through various feelings and instincts, prejudices, sympathies, and antipathies. We blunder into the intellect in the same way. Then the intellect is very imperfect. However, if we allow ourselves to become dry, sober, and cold-natured and, in the process, acquire a capacity to think in a way that is determined by the parameters of the physical body, we attain a certain perfection of the intellect. We learn to think in such a way that the intellect becomes self-moving, somewhat automatic, and relatively perfected. As Hamerling describes it in his novel *Homunculus*, we unite "the billionaire's male soullessness with the mermaid's female soullessness."[1]

This is what I was thinking in the last decades of the nineteenth century, when I asked myself: Who is the most intelligent person today? Who has raised the intellect to a level of perfection as I have just described? Now, you may laugh, but I really could not come up with anyone other than Eduard von Hartmann, the philosopher of the unconscious.[2] This is not some kind of daring paradox, but rather something that came to me as the result of long—and I don't think entirely soulless—reflection on the last decades of the nineteenth century.

You can well imagine that, having declared someone the most intelligent person of the age, one gains a great deal of respect for that person. That is why I dedicated my little book *Truth and Knowledge* (my contribution to a theory of knowledge in those days) to Eduard von Hartmann.[3] What I am saying here, therefore, is said out of the deepest respect, not disrespect. The foundations of von Hartmann's philosophy are determined in the first place by the fact that he was trained as

---

1. Robert Hamerling (1830–1889) was a leading Austrian poet and philosopher during Steiner's days in Vienna.
2. Karl Robert Eduard von Hartmann (1842–1906) wrote *The Philosophy of the Unconscious*, published in 1869 in Berlin in three volumes. He also wrote works on moral consciousness (1879) and on religious consciousness and the philosophy of the spirit (1882). The object of his philosophy was to unite Hegel's "idea" with Schopenhauer's "will" in a doctrine of Absolute Spirit. He called his philosophy "spiritual monism."
3. Rudolf Steiner, *Truth and Knowledge: Introduction to Philosophy of Spiritual Activity,"* first published in 1892 (Anthroposophic Press, 1981).

a military officer. He reached the rank of first lieutenant. But then he developed knee problems. Thus it came about that he transformed the intellectualism that had been intended to serve the modern military into philosophy. It is interesting that this is precisely how von Hartmann became the cleverest man of the last third of the nineteenth century.

He saw clearly everything that a person could see clearly with the mind of the last third of the nineteenth century. He penetrated human consciousness as it is attached to the Earth. But he saw this attachment as the attachment to a human physical body. Because he was clever, he did not deny the spirit. As I said, he was very intelligent. However, he placed the spirit in the sphere of the *unconscious,* in what can never support a body or enter into intimate union with the physical world, and which therefore, because it is always metaphysical (or purely spiritual), can be only unconscious.

Von Hartmann thought we could be conscious only in the body. But if the body is not the only reality, if there is spirit, then the spirit can never be conscious, only unconscious. Therefore, von Hartmann says that when we pass through the gate of death, we should not expect to enter a different state of consciousness. Beyond earthly consciousness is only unconsciousness. When we die we pass into the sphere of the unconscious spirit. The unconscious spirit is everywhere human consciousness is not. In this sense, von Hartmann's philosophy is a philosophy of the spirit, but a philosophy of the unconscious spirit. There is no consciousness other than in a human body, but there is spirit everywhere, unconscious spirit that knows nothing of itself, or of the world, or of anything else. It is quite clear, then, is it not, that this unconscious spirit can never penetrate any reality outside itself except through a physical human body? This is clear from the outset. But saying that implies something quite remarkable. The implication is that the intellect that rises to establish the unconscious *lacks love.*

I am not saying that Eduard von Hartmann lacked love, but that his intellect, which is precisely where his importance lay, lacked love. Now a loveless intellect cannot build any bridges.

It is locked into itself. But by that token, it cannot acquire consciousness. It remains in the sphere of the unconscious. Or, one could say, it remains in the sphere of *lovelessness*.

This implies that the intellect is also a sphere of soullessness. Wherever there is no place for love, anything of a soul nature gradually disappears. Hence, we can sense an atmosphere of lovelessness in the best productions of the late nineteenth century on whose shoulders our own civilization now stands. It is astonishing to see where von Hartmann's compulsion toward the unconscious spirit, coupled with lovelessness, led him.

He observed the world of earthly life that gives humanity consciousness. But what if we were not able to live in our bodies? What if every time we woke up we were not able to submerge into our bodies and completely unite with them? What would be our prospect then?

When we awaken from sleep as earthly beings, the "I" and the astral body, separated during sleep, return into the physical and ether bodies. The "I" and astral body then unite in full inner union with the etheric and the physical bodies. These four now make one. As long as we are awake, we must speak of an inner unity of spirit and soul with the physical and bodily. But if we separate the soul-spirit from the physical body, as von Hartmann does intellectually, it would be as if, on awakening, we were to penetrate into our physical and ether bodies without melting into them, permeating but only as it were dwelling, hovering there. According to von Hartmann, the unconscious spirit dwells in the body and becomes conscious in and through physical, earthly life. Therefore he seems to think something that, were it to happen in reality, would mean that when we are awake we enter our physical and ether bodies without completely merging with them. This would be rather like living in our bodies as in a house. We could be looking around, checking everything out, but remain inwardly separated, inwardly cut off. What would happen then?

If our spirit-soul were not merged with our physical body, but instead lived cut off from it, our soul would experience unfathomable, intolerable pain. Pain arises when an organ does not function correctly and the organ becomes sick and we are excluded from a part of our physical body. If we were kept out altogether, we would, if I may put it this way, be literally metaphysical (beyond the body), and we would suffer unspeakable pain. Each morning when we awake, the threat of this suffering is to some extent present. We overcome it by submerging into our physical and ether bodies and uniting ourselves with them.

Von Hartmann was certainly no initiate. He was simply an intellectual, the best intellectual of the late nineteenth century. He grasped intellectually in his thoughts what I have just described as a reality. He imagined the world as if our astral body and "I" were not connected with our physical and ether bodies. He thought of the relationship between the person and the physical body as I have just described in the light of reality. Where did this lead him? This led him in the end to a radical pessimism. Obviously you would experience pessimism if you woke up separated from your physical body. Von Hartmann thought this, it was his invention, and what was the result? He concluded that the world is the worst imaginable. The world contains the greatest heap of evil and suffering, and the true cultural evolution of humanity can consist only in the gradual annihilation, dissolution, of the world. Accordingly, at the end of *The Philosophy of the Unconscious*, an ideal begins to emerge.

Von Hartmann lived in an age in which technology was developing rapidly. More and more machines were being invented to deal with this or that. Anyone considering everything that machines can accomplish will be fascinated by the possibilities they offer. Now if we expand the possibilities that the perfecting of the mechanical world promises for the world, a horrifying possibility suggests itself. Von Hartmann gave himself over to this horrifying thought. He thought that humanity—which, because it is reaching the intellect, is gradually becoming more and more intelligent—would increasingly come to see that the right thing for the world would be to annihilate it. He became convinced that humanity eventually would invent a new machine. With this machine, it would be possible to bore right through to the center of the Earth. Then one had only to put this machine into motion in order, with a single blow, to blast this terrible Earth, with all its physical inhabitants, into cosmic space.

We can say only that the roots of this way of thinking are actually present in everyone else, too. They may not be as smart as von Hartmann was, but they are still quite smart enough, though they lack the intellectual courage to draw the final consequences of their own logic. And one might almost say that if we seriously consider all that intellect can achieve when it is separated from the rest of the world, then this ideal that von Hartmann proposes, which is a result of one-sided intellectual development, appears as in a certain sense *necessary.*

I said earlier that people did not manage to describe correctly some phenomena of the time that were there for everyone to see. This of course would have required at least rising to the precise formulations of the philosopher of the unconscious who described this perspective in 1869. And von Hartmann was really more intelligent in this than anyone else. After he had proposed his ideal, he did something that I have described often. In the same book in which he proposed his ideal, he spoke of the spirit. Even if it was unconscious, still, it was the spirit. This was a horrible sin at the time because science had developed to the point that scientifically one was not permitted to speak of the spirit, not even in the rather harmless way of making the spirit completely unconscious.

Consequently, other intelligent people of the time saw *The Philosophy of the Unconscious,* which was successful as literature, as dilettantism. But then von Hartmann played a trick on them. An unknown author published an attack against *The Philosophy of the Unconscious,* which thoroughly refuted the philosophy of the spirit. The title of this work was *The Unconscious from the Standpoint of Physiology and the Theory of Evolution.* This anonymous work was a remarkable parody of the style of other scholars. The best natural scientists of the time, Oskar Schmidt, Ernst Haeckel, and a host of others wrote most laudatory reviews of the book, declaring that with this book, the dilettante Eduard von Hartmann had really been destroyed! What a shame, they said, that we don't know who this anonymous author was. Tell us who you are, and we shall accept you as one of us.

Not surprisingly, after this clarion call, the book by Anonymous soon sold out and a second edition became necessary. It appeared under the title "*The Unconscious from the Standpoint of Physiology and the Theory of Evolution*, second edition, by Eduard von Hartmann." As you can see, Eduard von Hartmann proved that he really was the smartest; he was not only as smart as he himself was, he was also as smart as his opponents were.

Yesterday, I said that psychoanalysis was "dilettantism squared." Today we might say, because soul qualities always multiply themselves, that von Hartmann's intelligence was "intelligence squared," intelligence multiplied by itself. Surely, we should not sleep through such phenomena as we do these days. We should be able to formulate them and hold them before souls. Then we would actually face the absurdities of our age. What was it that made Eduard von Hartmann so intelligent? He was so intelligent because his unblinking gaze had really looked at everything that it was possible to notice in his time. He was, as it were, the natural scientist of philosophy.

Approaching such a phenomenon, it is a question of being completely and empirically clear about what must be done to avoid falling into the same abyss. If we wish to find a way out of the chaos facing us in our civilization, we must take a close look at what we actually bear within us. If we really start out from the human physical body, and then move toward the spirit, we begin to approach the soul. In doing so, we meet the etheric, formative-force body. Like everyone in his time, von Hartmann had no concept of this ether body. He never rose from the observation of outer, natural, physical reality to the reality that borders the physical—that is, the ether body of formative forces.

We know that when we enter sleep, the astral body and "I" separate from the physical and ether bodies. The ether body remains with the physical body. Indeed, our earthly consciousness can never realize the constitution of the ether body. When we awake, our astral body and "I" submerge into the ether body. Then we are inside. We experience what was brought in by the astral body and "I." It would take a far more highly organized being to enter the ether body during sleep, when the "I" and astral body are outside it. A being truly able to observe objectively how the ether body actually operates would discover exactly what it is we leave behind with the physical body as ether body when we go to sleep. If we were to investigate what we leave behind, we would find that the etheric or formative-force body is, in reality, the paragon of all *wisdom* in the earthly sense and in much higher senses, too.

From the perspective of true knowledge, then, we cannot deny that we leave our physical and ether bodies behind at night. Moreover, the two that we leave behind are much more intelligent than we are when we inhabit them. After all, as far as our "I" and astral body are concerned, we are children of the more recent Earth and Moon stages of Earth's evolution.[4] On the other hand, the ether body goes back to the earlier evolutionary stage of the Sun and the physical body goes back to the first evolutionary stage of Saturn. These so-called Sun and Saturn stages, therefore, are at a much higher level of perfection. Today, we cannot, in our "I" and in astral body, measure ourselves against the sum of wisdom amassed by our ether body in the course of its Sun evolution. One might state it this way: the ether body is concentrated wisdom. However, if we wish to bring the wisdom of the "I" and astral body into the ether body, we need something to oppose it, its "counter," just as we need a mirror to see a reflection.

We need the physical body. Just as we could not stand without physical ground upon which to stand, so we could not live in our ether body if the ether body did not border the physical body and "bump into" it on all sides. If the ether body did not have a counterpart in the physical body, we could not live in our ether body. The ether body's inner life would float suspended in

---

4. According to anthroposophic cosmology based on Rudolf Steiner's spiritual research, our present Earth is the fourth stage of a seven-stage evolutionary process. These stages are both stages of consciousness and evolutionary moments in the unfolding of this "Earth-cosmos." Rudolf Steiner called these seven stages: Saturn, Sun, Moon, Earth, Jupiter, Venus, and Vulcan. Descriptions of these relationships may be found throughout Steiner's works, especially in *An Outline of Esoteric Science* and *Inner Experiences of Evolution* (see "A Guide to Further Reading").

the air. Thus we have a soul life that lives in the ether body and which, for ordinary Earth life, requires the physical body as a support. With this state of the soul, we can reach only to the mineral world. We can penetrate only what is without life. To reach the plant world, we need the ability to use the ether body *without the physical body*. How do we do that? How can we learn to use our ether body without the physical body? We can do it if gradually, by means of inner exercises, we transform ourselves from beings who, because of their physical bodies, prefer to live in the element of gravity, into beings who, by means of the light, learn to live in the element of lightness or "levity."

We must transform ourselves, through the light, into beings who no longer experience their connection with the Earth, but feel connected to the cosmic spaces. Gradually, the contemplation of the stars, the Sun, Moon, and cosmic space must become as familiar to us as plants growing in the meadow. If we are merely children of the Earth, we look down onto the plants covering the meadow. We enjoy them, but we don't understand them, for we remain earthly beings weighed down by gravity. As earthly beings bound by gravity, we have learned to stand on the Earth. But if we could transform ourselves, we could connect ourselves with the widths of cosmic space—those meadows of the heavens, seeded with stars. In our present state of consciousness, we think of the heavens as a "ceiling" rather than a floor. But once they become as familiar to us as the ground of the Earth beneath our feet, then we can begin, as we change Earth consciousness into cosmic consciousness, to learn to use our ether body as we previously learned to use our physical body. Only then will we become capable of penetrating the plant world with our understanding. For plants are not so much pushed up out of the Earth as they are pulled out of the Earth by the sky.

Goethe was filled with this yearning when he wrote his "Essay on the Metamorphosis of Plants." Many of his statements were those a person would make who felt oriented to the Sun rather than the Earth—a person who felt that the Sun pulls the force of the plant's growth out of the Earth while it is still hidden underground. He felt how the Sun's forces, interacting with the influence of the air, gradually develop the leaf, and how the Sun then slowly cooks the elements that the plant sucked out of the Earth. Read Goethe's wonderful 1790 essay, and you will find approaches to this view on every page. Goethe lived in the desire to penetrate the world of the plants. But instead of developing etheric vision to replace physical vision, Goethe only stumbled on it—repeatedly. All the same, this impulse to develop etheric vision was present in Goethe, and anyone wishing to learn from Goethe—the living Goethe, whose influence is ongoing, not the dead one—must take this impulse further.

Once we understand that human souls can develop etheric vision—for this, we need only become truly conscious of the ether body—we will be able to perceive our heavenly origins and independence from the Earth. We will be able to understand that we have been transplanted onto Earth. Then our soul will be able to say: "I am of cosmic origin. My physical body transplants me onto Earth, but my origin is cosmic. And if I can rejoice in the world of plants, what rejoices in me is a child of Heaven, who rejoices in seeing what the heavens draw out of the Earth in the plant world."

When we truly grasp our etheric, formative-force body, we rescue our souls from the Earth. If we can do that, if we are able to live in the ether body just as we usually live in the physical body—and what can bring us there is true love for the plant world—it is not only our *own* ether body that is raised into consciousness. As the physical world is raised into our consciousness by our physical body—by our senses—so the etheric world is placed in our consciousness by our ether body. And what would we sense if, just as we look out into the physical world with our physical body, we looked into the etheric world through the ether body? What would we behold then? We would see the past of all the things spread out before our physical eyes—the actual past, from which this physical world arose. We would see, in the spirit, the images of what was—of what made the present possible.

Even in most ancient times, the first initiation given to humanity was an initiation into the cosmos. The first mystery schools worked on this initiation into the cosmos. The teachers of these first mysteries initiated their students into reading in the cosmic ether, also called "reading in the chaos," "reading in the akashic chronicle"—that is to say, the reading of the past that the present conjures up before our eyes. For practical purposes, this initiation by the cosmos was the first level of initiation that humanity achieved in its earthly existence.

The second level of initiation may be attained likewise. This happens when, as we awake, we allow the astral body and the "I" to sink into the physical and the ether bodies. We "ensoul" the etheric and physical bodies; we unite ourselves with them. However, we can gain only as much of the infinite wisdom of the ether body as we ourselves carry into it. Nevertheless, it is the ether body that constantly stimulates us. Whenever we have a good intuition, it is the ether body, which is inwardly connected with the cosmos, that stimulates this intuition. We receive all the intuitions, all the genius we develop when we are awake, from the ether body by way of the universe. Whenever the ether body stimulates the astral body, our genius converses with the universe. Even if we cannot see these things, we still live within them. Our soul life always consists in our astral body and "I" sinking, in the waking state, into our physical and ether bodies.

Once the stars are as much home to us as are the meadows, to the extent that we make the cosmic space the ground of our being on high, we are able to experience the etheric world. In reality, we always experience the etheric. Without initiation, however, we cannot penetrate it *cognitively*. Nevertheless, in actuality, every human being experiences the etheric world. If we are looking for an opposing counterpart for the astral body, that counterpart, the ether body, is always there. It is just a matter of spiritual science calling our attention to what is present in every human being.

Let me give you an example. Let us say that you could not see the floor beneath you, but you were nevertheless standing on it. In fact, you would be standing on it, even though you knew nothing of it. Then let's say that someone, by scientific means, were to demonstrate that the floor is there, and were to tell you so. You would still be standing on the floor as you always were.

Likewise, someone who knows spiritual science can tell you that your astral being reaches to the upper floor, the floor of the stars. In fact, however, irrespective of what he has just said, you already do so—you already reach to the stars. In other words, as human beings with astral bodies, we already live in another world, in the world of living spiritual beings that we have described as the world of the higher hierarchies.[5]

When we are in the physical world, we look at things from this perspective. Reality, then, *is* the physical world in which there are minerals, plants, animals, and a ground to stand upon—a world from which the human being arose as the latest phenomenon in the course of evolution. By the same token, human beings, by virtue of the astral body, dwell in the world of higher hierarchies. Simply by inhabiting the world, we have the counterbalance appropriate to the astral body. We always carry within us what we learn from spiritual science. And, of course, we do so independently of its teaching. And we always bear within us the capacity to feel.

Whatever we can make our own from the world through our feelings, through this innermost life of the soul, is actually the welling up and weaving of the higher spiritual hierarchies in our astral body. Naturally, whenever we become conscious of our feelings, this experience itself is the immediate object of our perception, but the feeling itself is the weaving and working of the higher spiritual hierarchies through us. We cannot really grasp or understand soul unless we experience it immersed in the spiritual worlds of the higher hierarchies. You know that the past is unveiled to our present senses by etheric vision whenever I give a contemporary description of what was communicated in the first earthly mysteries as the initiation into the cosmos. In the same way, the soul can be deepened so that it becomes conscious of what is happening in the astral body.

This requires loving absorption in all that lived in the great mysteries as the relationship to the spiritual worlds. If we allow

---

5. Rudolf Steiner uses the term *hierarchies* to describe the nine angelic or celestial orders. See *An Outline of Esoteric Science; The Spiritual Hierarchies and the Physical World;* and *Spiritual Beings in the Heavenly Bodies and the Kingdoms of Nature* (Anthroposophic Press, 1992).

ourselves to be taught by the cosmos under the guidance of the wisdom of initiation, we reach the first level of the soul's reality. Once we penetrate what actually took place in the mysteries, we can read in the so-called akashic record not only the past of the stars, the Earth, and humanity. We can also read what lived in the very souls of the great teachers of these mysteries. We can make what I tried to describe to you in *Christianity as Mystical Fact* live within us.[6] We can bring to life what these teachers developed out of themselves in their work with the spiritual beings. In doing so, we shall approach the initiation that, in later times, was added to cosmic initiation. This I would call *the initiation of the sages.*

Thus we may speak of two levels of initiation: through the cosmos and through the sages. What the sages taught as cosmic knowledge formed the content of cosmic initiation. Looking into the souls of those who came before us in the human soul life leads to the second level of the soul's being. To enter this sphere, we can begin with outer history. We can seek to grasp and understand in an inwardly living way what still shines down to us from ancient times—for instance, the contents of the remarkable wisdom of the Vedanta or other ancient wisdom teachings. Doing so, we actually begin to grasp our own inner life and, thereby, begin to approach cosmic initiation. Moreover, if we become truly and lovingly absorbed in such things (as I did in *Christianity as Mystical Fact,* in which I explained the relationship between the contents of the old Mysteries and the Mystery of Golgotha), then we begin to approach the sages' initiation.

The present age calls for one thing and that is to look honestly into our own interiority and come to know impartially our own spirit—the spirit that illuminates the soul from inside as it were. I shall return to this later, when I describe it as the third level of the initiation required in our time: *initiation of self-knowledge.* When spiritual science speaks of the soul, it must speak out of the spirit of these three levels of initiation: by the cosmos, by the sages, by self-knowledge. In doing so, it traverses the different boundaries of soul life. *But it is impossible to begin to take even the first steps on this path without love.*

---

6. Rudolf Steiner, *Christianity as Mystical Fact* (SteinerBooks, 2006).

Here I must stress that it is precisely the present-day intellect that forgets love—loses love—when it reaches its heights. Because of this, something quite particular happens. To penetrate with love the realities described as physical body, astral body, ether body, and "I," we need to absorb something of the voice of the ruling spirit of our age. We need the goodwill to listen carefully to the voice of the genius or spirit of our time. But can human beings today really take in with the necessary seriousness what is meant by the words "the genius of our time"? For most people, is it anything more than an abstract phrase? Just try and think how remote from the understanding of true spiritual living reality people really are—and how little they know what they are really saying when they speak of the "genius of our time."

Although human beings may deny the spirit, they cannot get rid of it. The spirit is inalterably connected to humanity. When human beings fail the genius of their age, the demon of the age steps in. We can understand what happens in such cases by considering what happened in the last third of the nineteenth century. This was a time when the human intellect was able to follow the mechanism of physical life in most intimate detail. In the process, the intellect itself became automatic, mechanical. Thereby it reached its highest development—it became so clever, it reached the apogee of intelligence! But no matter how clever it became, it brought to existence only the mechanical, the materialistic, in the intellect. The intellect conducted itself as humanity does when it refuses the genius of the age. Therefore the human intellect fell prey to the demon of the age. Separated from the soul, it became mechanical, soulless, and on that foundation it built a philosophy. It had no love—it could not love wisdom. Its philosophy could only become the intellectual replica of terrestrial demonology—a demonology that can conceive the ideal of a machine boring right through to the center of the Earth and blasting the world into cosmic space.

This was the demon of the age speaking to the intellect of the age. Often when we do not wish to know the soul, it is the demon of the age that we hear. The soul then appears to the intellect as it would to us if, on awakening, we plunged into our physical and ether bodies, but did not unite with them and remained separated from them. Such an intellect is foreign to the very being of humanity, for it has freed itself from what it means to be human. An intellect united with the being of humanity grows from earthly consciousness up to other states of consciousness. An intellect that connects itself to the Earth but then cuts itself off from it is only the mirror image of the intellect. For such an intellect, all other states of consciousness are part of the unending ocean of unconsciousness. Then the human soul ceases to be conscious of its heavenly origin, and loses the awareness of its autonomy in relation to earthly life. But the human soul is characterized by the fact that in our being we oscillate between bodily and spiritual realities. Human soul life consists in this movement between the bodily and the spiritual. If we honestly believe only in the body and cannot let go of the spirit altogether, then the spirit merely becomes unconscious, and thereby we deny the soul.

Hartmann envisioned the downfall of the Earth demonically. He did so only as a person could who was asleep in his physical body and became, as it were, clairvoyant in it. At the very time that Hartmann was coming to his intellectual interpretation of earthly suffering, another man, who was his friend and exchanged many letters with him, lay on a sickbed. His body was racked with pain. Many organs of his soul-spiritual being could not gain access to his physical body. This man had the actual experience of earthly suffering; he did not just think about it. And for him the only way to deal with the soullessness of the age seemed to be satire. The man was Robert Hamerling, who in the 1880s wrote a book called *Homunculus*, in which he allowed the perspective on a soulless age to dawn. He created the image of a man who strives in all external matters, amasses more and more material goods, and eventually becomes a billionaire. Such was the frightening vista that Hamerling contemplated with the eye of his soul. The soulless billionaire—the "homunculus" who comes into the world in a purely mechanical way, without the soul's collaboration—marries the soulless elemental spirit, the mermaid Lorelei.

For Hamerling, the perspective of a soulless *Zeitgeist* came to life in the form of a man whose striving focused entirely on the material realm, a striving for spiritless intellectualism. Such spiritless intellectualism is present in nature-spirits, but its presence in human beings awakens the forces of destruction—the demonic forces of destruction whose ambition it is to blow up the entire world. For Robert Hamerling, the only way to deal with the problem of soullessness was satire. We must restore soul to modern civilization and culture. But we can do so—we can only give the world soul—when the light of spiritual knowledge illuminates human experiences on Earth. Thus, what the cleverest person of our age presented in a truly terrifying, repulsive manner and what a man who was racked in pain and saw the tragedy of this cleverness presented in satirical form—this is what humanity must transform through spiritual knowledge into the soul's perspective.

From Rudolf Steiner, What Is Anthroposophy? Three Perspectives on Self-knowledge *(Anthroposophic Press, 2002), lecture in Dornach, July 21, 1923, pp. 49–65.*

II.

HEALTH AND HEALING

MEDICINE AND ANTHROPOSOPHIC INSIGHT INTO THE HUMAN BEING

MY PERSPECTIVE DEVIATES SIGNIFICANTLY from conventional contemporary views, and much of what I have to say will necessarily sound paradoxical at best. It will be especially difficult to overcome these obstacles and move on in our two brief sessions. But as you know, ladies and gentlemen, we have learned to adjust our thinking on many questions in the course of humanity's historical development, which suggests that forbearance is in order, at least initially, when a perspective that results from truly conscientious research appears paradoxical. First of all, I would like to say by way of introduction that my purpose in presenting the medical consequences of anthroposophic research is not to introduce new ideas that will contradict the very thorough discipline of modern medicine, which is based on centuries of scientific precedent. The method of research I will describe here is not intended to overthrow modern medicine. On the contrary, it simply explores some of the recent results of the rigorous, sense-based empirical methods that medicine inherited from the natural sciences and the great scope of the questions that arise. It concludes that modern medicine is heading in a direction that it will find difficult to maintain, simply because its well-known sensory-based, empirical research methods are so very conscientious and precise. The same factors that made science great and provided such significant foundations for medicine have also made it impossible to pursue certain ways of understanding the human being and human medicine. For this reason, please allow me to first present a few general principles today. Tomorrow I will discuss the unusual qualities of a few typical anthroposophic remedies.

We anthroposophists did not choose a propagandistic approach, deciding that Anthroposophy must know something about everything and must therefore also take a position on medicine. Those of us who are firmly rooted in Anthroposophy choose to take a truly scientific approach, at least as far as our fundamental principles are concerned. The medical movement within the general anthroposophic movement came about when physicians in Germany and other countries realized that modern science and medicine raise questions that conventional methods cannot answer, at least not to the extent of providing a direct and rational connection between diagnosis and treatment. Those physicians approached me and asked whether Anthroposophy might contribute to the field of medicine by providing more penetrating insights into the human constitution than are possible using conventional methods. Thus, what I tell you today and tomorrow has been made possible by the requests of those physicians, whose individual studies and practice had left them unsatisfied or at least somewhat skeptical. From the very beginning, we certainly did not assume that we could feel free to make all kinds of amateurish contributions to a rigourous field of research and its practical applications. When the founders of *Der Kommende Tag* [The Coming Day] in Stuttgart and the *Futurum* in Switzerland advised us to support medical research, I insisted that although Anthroposophy could indeed shed light on the preparation of remedies, we should not limit ourselves to that activity and that all such efforts should be as closely associated as possible with the actual practice of medicine.

This was the origin of our institutes, which not only manufacture remedies according to the methods I will describe, but also are associated with clinics. In the course of these lectures, I will have occasion to speak about these clinics, especially the exemplary one in Arlesheim, which is headed by Dr. Ita Wegman and is directly associated with our anthroposophic facility for higher education, the Goetheanum in Switzerland. Daily interaction with patients in these clinics gives our anthroposophic medical research a vital connection to actual therapy, which we see as the most significant issue of our time. Not content with simply establishing these pharmaceutical and clinical facilities, we have also linked them to other research institutes, including an institute for biology and several institutes for physics. I will not say more about the physics institutes at this point because they are still in the very early stages of their work. The institute for biological research, however, has already produced two studies.[1] I mention them to show you that we intend to work with the same degree of precision that is demanded of other scientists. It is a matter of honest conviction rather than foolish vanity when I say—and the results themselves will convince you—that in spite of the few objections that can still be raised about details, these studies demonstrate that we aspire to the same precision that is required of other scientific foundations of medicine.

The first study published by our biological research institute is a paper on spleen function. These two lectures give me only enough time to present a few perspectives to stimulate your thinking, so please forgive me if I mention some of the issues only briefly. I became interested in spleen function in the course of my own spiritual scientific research, whose methods I will discuss shortly. Meanwhile, I will simply say that these methods allowed me to realize that spleen function—which, as you know, is a stumbling block for medical anthropology—occupies a special position among the functions of the human organs.

To put it briefly, some of the many processes that contribute to the functioning of the human body promote rhythm. These processes include not only respiration and blood circulation, but also those that take place over more extended periods of time,

---

1. The Biological Institute of the Goetheanum (Free School of Spiritual Science in Dornach), located in Stuttgart, where Dr. Lily Kolisko did her work. Her works include "Spleen Function and the Platelet Question" (1922); "Physiological and Physical Evidence of the Effects of Minute Quantities" (1923); "Physiological Evidence of the Effects of Minute Quantities of Seven Metals" (1926); "The Effects of Light and Darkness on Plant Growth" (1926).

such as the rhythm of digestion. The very nature of the human body requires that digestion be rhythmical to a degree that is not actually possible. To satisfy our bodies' demands, we would have to eat and drink with incredibly rhythmic regularity. Since we do not eat the same foods every day, even establishing very exact mealtimes would not allow us to maintain the rhythm our bodies require. We would have to approach this task with infinite knowledge of the details involved. It is easier for respiration and blood circulation to function with regularity, but we really cannot meet the body's need for rhythmical digestion, because digestion depends on interaction with the outer world.

Spleen function, however, unites with the total digestive process in the broadest sense to balance out and correct the unavoidable irregularities in our digestive rhythm. I became aware of this balancing function some time ago, and now it has been empirically verified in our biological research institute. Although it is possible to raise some objections with regard to details of the methods that were used, these methods are nonetheless as precise as any other clinical methods in use today. I believe that this study, which was carried out with tremendous devotion by Dr. Lili Kolisko, would have had great impact on medical thinking if it had been conducted in a conventional clinic. That it remains relatively unknown is due exclusively to the fact that it was conducted under the auspices of Anthroposophy. This last statement is the one I beg you not to attribute to foolish vanity on my part.

The second study transforms a scientific and medical "belief" into exact science to the greatest extent possible. Please do not assume that I am taking sides here in the debate between homeopathy and allopathy. It would not occur to me to do so, because I know how much amateurishness the ordinary homeopathic view contains. Even materialistic physics, however, cannot deny that highly diluted substances can have far-reaching effects. We can no longer assume that highly diluted substances cannot have significant effects. Just think of the effects of inhaled substances that are present in very high dilution. When we give patients therapeutic baths, we are often unaware that the substances inhaled along with the steam, substances that may be present in very high dilution, are much more important than the bath's external effects. Until now, such statements were simply a matter of scientific belief.

We attempted to confirm this belief scientifically—within its justifiable limits, of course, but the results should not be interpreted as a universal remedy. We produced dilutions of up to one in one quintillion so that we were certain that ordinary material effects were no longer present and that any effects we noted were due to qualities transferred to the medium from the original substances—that is, that we were dealing with purely qualitative effects. We were able to prove that diluted quantities of a substance develop astonishing rhythm-based effects. We tested the effect of these minute quantities on the growth of very carefully selected grain seeds. The seeds were allowed to sprout in solutions of metallic compounds in different dilutions. We proved that solutions of metallic compounds in dilutions of 1:10, 1:20, 1:50, 1:100, 1:500, and so on really do influence the growth forces of plants. We graphed interesting and very regular curves, demonstrating that when the enlivening force is influenced in a specific way at a particular dilution, the effect is reduced if the compound is diluted further and enhanced again at a still higher dilution. The result is a curve that alternately rises and falls as an exact expression and confirmation of the effects of minute quantities of matter.

These results elevate minute quantities (some of which are misused by homeopathy, and I say this advisedly) to the ranks of suitable subjects for precise research. The purpose of this last statement is not primarily to attach greater importance to our results but simply to show that at least in our initial investigations we are attempting to base our research on conventional scientific methods rather than working outside science in some amateurish way. We will then have to take conventional research methods further.

From a historical perspective, considering the tremendous successes of science in the past few centuries, especially the nineteenth century, it is quite understandable that humanity should have been hypnotized, as it were, by sensory-based observation and exact experimentation. With regard to our knowledge of the human being, however, even on a very ordinary physical level, these methods of research cannot grasp the essence of the human body's structure and functioning. Although very great advances have been made in understanding the organization of the physical human being, the otherwise fruitful precision of these methods has excluded an entire aspect of the human being that is just as real as the physical. The success of scientific research is directly proportional to the tremendous amount of energy it has spent on excluding the human soul and spirit, which even in a medical context must be considered no less real than the physical human being.

I need to explain some of the principles of anthroposophic research, especially with regard to how it leads to knowledge of the human being. It is typical of all modern research that we simply approach it as we are, with the psychological makeup (including cognitive abilities) that we acquire as a result of the conventional scientific education our culture provides. We stop short at this point. We do not consider, for example, that the attitude and soul makeup of a two- or three-year-old are very different from those of older people. We develop our psychology changes as we grow up. At age eighteen or nineteen we have abilities that we did not have as two- or three-year-olds, let alone earlier. These abilities emerge from within us.

Why, then, shouldn't adults remain relatively capable of further development? Is it really acceptable to arbitrarily cut off our psychological development? The answer to these questions depends on our inner efforts, of course. But anyone who truly attempts to surpass what is now seen as the norm of human psychological development will indeed be able to acquire different soul faculties. The details can be found in my books *How to Know Higher Worlds* and *An Outline of Esoteric Science*, among others. In principle, I simply want to point out that we can indeed learn to change and enhance the form of thinking we apply not only to ordinary life but also to experimenting and interpreting observations in conventional science.

When I say this, people usually immediately interject, "So now he's going to tell us about some kind of mystical development." However, anyone who disdains mystical development, if you want to call it that, should also reject mathematics and geometry. The essence of mathematics and geometry is to move with complete presence of mind, with no trace of the subconscious or of autosuggestion, from one idea to the next. This presence of mind, or complete consciousness, must follow our every move as we deal with a mathematical or geometric thought content, and the same inner precision can also be applied to our own soul development. The soul's ability to think continues to evolve not as a result of the vagueness we often associate with mysticism but in full clarity, not through brooding on a subject but by beginning with very specific, clearly comprehensible mental images and proceeding just as we do in mathematics, refusing to accept any thought that interferes with moving from one conscious content to another in full presence of mind. If we apply this truly exact method of soul development long enough—for some people it takes more time, for others less—we learn to take hold of our normally passive thinking as an activity. Normally, our thoughts are passively dependent on our observations, but now we begin to experience inner activity.

This inner thought activity provides our first real insight into the first level of our suprasensory existence. If we view the human body from outside and trace blood circulation in its totality, the result is a certain image or portion of the human being as viewed from outside. Similarly, by proceeding as I have just described with regard to our thinking, we begin to experience that the physical body is filled with a second, independent human being. Anyone who believes that autosuggestion is involved here is not considering the exactitude of the methods I described. The whole process takes place in full consciousness, so that the soul recognizes and rejects any hint of autosuggestion. The path resulting from these methods is the exact opposite of anything hypnosis or autosuggestion can bring to consciousness. If we follow it, we find that if we apply the exact method of observation that we have learned to the gradual process of child development, we notice a significant difference in the child's entire constitution around the time of the second dentition at age six or seven. The difference is subtle, and we generally disregard it; we must learn to notice it. We really must summon up the courage to observe the human being with the precision we have come to expect from modern research in physics. In physics, we speak of latent warmth as opposed to actual manifest warmth. We admit that certain processes release latent warmth from the substances that bound it.

With regard to the study of soul development, we must have the courage to accept what physics has already recognized. If we have the courage such research requires, we realize that we can see (and seeing is simply a question of putting our attention to it) inner soul forces appearing in a child who has undergone the second dentition. These forces were not there earlier. Even modern child psychology has not observed closely enough to say anything about this phenomenon. The peaks and valleys on the graph are not particularly high or deep; we are dealing with subtleties that require a different, spiritual type of vision. That is why this phenomenon is more or less disregarded today. To those who have acquired the vision required for spiritual research, however, it becomes clear that the faculty we call *memory* changes radically during the second dentition. Before the change of teeth, a child's memory still allows each remembered image to emerge from the organism with a certain elemental force. By contrast, the type of memory that makes us feel that we are going back to a previous experience when we remember it sets in only during the second dentition.

Many other aspects of soul experience emerge only with the change of teeth and were not evident in the child's constitution before that point. Where were they, then? They were present in the child's constitution in latent form, just as latent warmth is present in a substance. The second dentition is merely an outer symptom of the organic processes that release these faculties from the child's organism, just as physical processes release latent warmth from a substance. Modern psychology theorizes about psychophysiologic parallels and the like. It cannot understand the connection between an anatomical or physiological phenomenon and its own abstract conception of the soul. Seen abstractly, these two aspects of the human being seem so unrelated that we find no bridge from one to the other.

But human beings develop and evolve. If we look at the contents of the human soul after the second dentition, we can say that the same forces that now appear, metamorphosed into thinking in the soul, formerly existed as organic forces at work in the growth of the child's organs. Here we have an empirical connection between the life of the soul and the life of the body. We must simply look for it at the right stage of human development.

If we carry out the thought exercises I mentioned, we begin to see our own thinking as something just as strong and active, although on a soul level, as the latent thinking that is a force for growth and organization in a child's body before the second dentition. This is the "second human being" we discover in ourselves. On a higher level, it is not our ordinary, merely passive thinking, but a second part, the *ether body* (please do not be bothered by this term), that imbues and organizes us. To the anthroposophic method of research, the ether body is active within the overall human makeup as an empirical reality rather than something speculative. Naturally, I can only briefly indicate all this here. When we look at a child, we see a factor at work that we will encounter later in that person's thinking. If I want to understand the growth forces in a child, or the vitalizing element in a child's body, I must turn to imaginative cognition, which transforms the perception of those forces into conscious meaning. Any healing factors present in childhood growth forces (which are later transferred to our soul life, where they work passively) can be investigated only through inner vision and experience by applying the spiritual scientific method. Perceptions resulting from this method are not merely figments of the imagination but concrete, active forces in the human organism. Thus, inner empiricism transforms superficial anthropology into true Anthroposophy.

Once developing our thinking in a particular way has allowed us to discover the second human being, we can also discover a third entity within the physical and ether bodies. Please do not take offense at the term *astral body;* we do need a term for it, after all. There are anthroposophic reasons for the name, but at this point my purpose is only to describe the makeup of the human being.

When we learn to experience the second, etheric human being as intrinsically independent of the physical human being, it becomes a content of our consciousness. Let me assure you that it is possible to possess this consciousness, to feel the presence of this second human being, almost as securely as we possess our physical bodies during normal waking consciousness. Much harder inner work is necessary to accomplish the next step, which requires eliminating the etheric human being from our consciousness. We can take this step only by gathering sufficient strength to suggest away the existence of the etheric human being. Having entered this being, we must very consciously leave it. As a general rule, the preliminary exercises leading to this step are not especially easy. It is difficult to eliminate mental images that we have clung to for a long time, images of such immediacy that they occupy our entire consciousness—although with our full presence of mind, so that there is no question of autosuggestion. Such images are difficult to eliminate because they affect our consciousness much more strongly than the transient images of daily life and ordinary observation. But if we have practiced freeing our consciousness from anything it may contain, we will also be able to empty our consciousness and eliminate the content we ourselves created. The resulting state of consciousness is exactly like waking out of ordinary dreamless sleep, but not in the body and not in the physical world. We are outside the body and perceive a different, spiritual world around us as we awake.

You can wake up in this way by doing what I just described: emptying your consciousness again after having energized it to the greatest possible extent in order to acquire an etheric content. This empty consciousness is pure wakefulness. It contains nothing of what we otherwise experience in life or know through science. You know how difficult it is to empty your consciousness. In ordinary life (typically, when we eliminate sensory impressions), we fall asleep. The method I have described leads to empty, merely wakeful consciousness, but this consciousness does not remain empty long. It begins to receive the spiritual world or, more specifically, a third human being that is pure inner function, pure inner mobility and activity. The second, etheric human being is the enlivening element, while the third, astral human being is mobility and activity.

The fourth human being makes it possible for us to be human in the fullest sense of the word. In the course of these lectures, I may still have an opportunity to discuss this fourth being in more detail, but for the moment I simply want to say that it is the actual "I"-human. Everything I have described thus far as the physical, etheric, and astral bodies is also present in animals, but only we human beings can experience the union of these members within ourselves in a concrete rather than an abstract way. After beginning to grasp the spiritual world by emptying our consciousness, we can achieve a complete image of the "I" being by further energizing our experience of the spiritual world. These descriptions should give you an idea of the results of exact anthroposophic methods. They gradually permit us to discover the different members of the human constitution. These higher members really exist. Just as latent warmth is released and transformed into real warmth that is expressed in physical effects, the ether body, astral body, and I are expressed in the physical human being. We understand the human being only by looking at how these four members interact.

To gain an idea of this interaction, let's consider a specific detail, such as the human kidneys and their function. In every limb and organ of the human being, the four members of our human constitution work together to a greater or lesser extent. What we see when we study the kidneys by examining a corpse or making other physical observations is only the sum total of physical effects. These physical effects, however, are pervaded and energized by what I called the *ether body*—specifically, by the part of the ether body that includes the vital functions of the kidneys. The ether body, in turn, is pervaded by the astral body. Only the interaction between these members enables us to understand the makeup of the human being, even in a single organ or organ system.

Let's take a case of some sort of irregular kidney function. Since you are all experts, I do not need to go into detail. When we understand the entire issue from the perspective of anthroposophic research, we realize that the irregularity causes the kidney's physical and etheric functioning to resist the astral kidney function in some way. This is a typical case. Astral kidney function, which we can perceive only when we have emptied our consciousness, is resisted by the physical and etheric organization of the kidneys. When such resistance occurs in any living organ, its astral organization must intervene much more thoroughly and energetically than it normally would, or otherwise the organ would atrophy. The result—at least in specific cases, and the cases I describe are always concrete—is an intensification of the part of the astral organization that corresponds to the kidney and its activity. In other words, astral kidney function becomes much stronger than it ought to be, and the kidney places much greater demands on the astral body than it ought to in the overall constitution of the human being. From the perspective of anthroposophic research, the astral body performs this work in the kidney by withdrawing activity from the rest of the human body. The astral process in the kidney actually should not be there. Excessive demands are being placed on the astral kidney because of specific abnormal developments in the physical and etheric kidney.

At this point in the diagnostic process, we must know that the astral portion of the kidney is active in a way that is not necessary when the organism is functioning normally. In the kidney's present pathological condition, the physical or etheric kidney places extra demands on the astral component, which responds with activity that is not needed in a healthy kidney. Here we have the first element in understanding the nature of the patient's illness. To a thinking person, disease processes should be a great riddle, because they are actually natural processes. But normal processes are also natural processes. How do the abnormal processes of disease get mixed up with normal ones? As long as we see the human being as an arbitrary network of physical substances and functions, we have no basis for distinguishing physiological phenomena from pathological ones. We can make this distinction, however, when we know that the kidney can metamorphose when physical processes develop in it that do not occur in a normal kidney whose physical, etheric, and astral components are in harmony. This is our first insight.

Now the question is, how can we combat this disease process, which is simply due to excessive demands being placed on a suprasensory portion of the human constitution? How can we make the astral being function normally again? I want to keep my explanations concrete and detailed. I will not discuss serious kidney disease because the same principles are evident in milder illnesses. But simply in order to suggest how to treat such a kidney, I would like to take a specific example as my starting point. We know, to begin with, that we must relieve the astral body of its work in a kidney that has been "de-formed" in the broadest possible sense. In this kidney, the human astral body is doing something it should not be doing. We must remove the astral body from this abnormal kidney process.

Let's sample the results of a cognitive overview that considers the human being first and then the wider world. In the method I depicted, we shift our attention from the human being to the nonhuman natural world, where we study the particular character of *Equisetum arvense* [field horsetail]. We are more concerned with the process that is active in it than with the individual substances it contains. Because materialistically oriented thinking is now omnipresent, organic matter is usually described in terms of its content of protein, fat, carbohydrates, and so on. We focus on the individual components that superficial chemistry can tell us about. But the field of chemistry has changed in recent times, so now we focus on the so-called elements. The elements in an organic entity, however, are not very significant for what I have in mind. The most interesting thing to note about *Equisetum* is the high proportion of silica that is left behind when we analyze the plant, that is, when we separate its functions. Silica is so strongly present that it predominates and expresses its function in the *Equisetum* plant. Analysis reveals not so much the substance itself as its significance. Its significance is what we must recognize.

Equisetum is a plant, so we find no astral body in it; we do find a physical body and an ether body, however. When we study *Equisetum arvense,* we find that silica plays a major role in it—although of course there are other plants that contain silica—while certain sulfates play a supporting role. The most important components of *Equisetum,* in terms of asserting their own character in the plant, are silica—not the "substance," but the silica function—and the activity of sulfur. Then we make a very strange discovery. When we apply spiritually developed forces to understanding what is going on in the vicinity of the sulfates that are associated with silica, SiO_2, we discover a process or a nexus of functions that we can then introduce into the human organism, either internally or, if the situation requires a different method of administration, through baths or injections. I will discuss the significance of these different methods later. Actually, it is better not to use *Equisetum* as such—although the effects are visibly present in the plant itself, they are not very permanent. In our methods of preparing remedies, we first study the functional connection between silica and sulfur, for example, and then imitate it in a medicinal preparation. We convert the *Equisetum* model into a more or less inorganic preparation that has stronger effects on the human organism than if we simply used the plant itself in the form of a tea or the like. This is the essential element in the production of our remedies.

When this functional connection between sulfur and silica is incorporated into the human organism in the right way, it relieves the astral body in the kidney of the process it had to carry out during the illness. That is, when sulfur and silica as they function in *Equisetum arvense* are introduced into the kidney, the human astral body is relieved of functions it would otherwise have to perform in the deformed kidney—"de-formed" in the broadest possible sense. For the moment, the disease process is carried out by a substitute, by a remedy that has been introduced into the body.

This is the beginning of any healing process. We must be familiar with the disease process in question, and our theory of pathological conditions must be rational. We must recognize the disease process and look for places in nature where it is copied exactly. We must not simply assume that a disease process must always be combated. Instead, we need to neutralize the process, to counterbalance it with a dynamic we recognize, such as the dynamic between sulphur and silica in *Equisetum,* in order to free up the astral body, relieving it of functions it formerly had to perform in the diseased kidney. We must then take care to strengthen the patient internally, through diet and so on, so that his or her inner forces can be applied more energetically than usual to the entire astral body. Once we have substituted an external function for the astral body's excessively strong activity in the organ in question, the astral body, now fully normal and healthy, is able to eliminate the disease.

This example demonstrates how we arrive at a rational concept of healing. As a general rule, healing involves substituting a process derived from the external world for the human disease process and then energizing an internal force to overcome the disease, which cannot be overcome as long as the astral body is forced to apply its activity one-sidedly in an abnormal kidney, for example. What I have just described is or may be the case in any disease process that is due to irregularities in organs that work internally but centrifugally, if I may put it that way. Although the kidney is an organ of elimination, it initially excretes internally. If you grasp the principle I have described, you will understand that this pathological kidney process is healed by stimulating a centrifugal or outwardly radiating process in the kidney by administering *Equisetum arvense.*

Other disease processes demonstrate the polar opposite of what I have just described. Once again, I will not use the example of a serious illness to introduce the general principle, but rather one that, although it is extremely unpleasant for the patient, attracts relatively little attention compared with deeper-seated illnesses. This disease is hay fever, or allergic rhinitis. In attempting to combat hay fever, we must realize that we are dealing with a fundamental constitutional disorder based on a peripheral reduction in the forces of the third, inwardly mobile human being, the astral body. The origin of hay fever can be traced back to childhood, when generalized and generally disregarded disorders appear that then become specialized, appearing later in life as hay fever. If we know that hay fever involves a decline in certain astral functions that prevent the astral body from reaching the physical and ether bodies, our first concern must be to energize the astral body internally and redirect it to what it should be doing.

In a pathological condition such as hay fever, more externally directed centrifugal effects are apparent and must be actively counteracted. In kidney disease, we counterbalanced or offset the illness; we saw that the astral body simply needed to be freed from its abnormal work in the diseased kidney and then energized and strengthened in order to work in the direction of health. This is not true of processes such as hay fever. In such cases, we cannot begin by offsetting the disease process. Instead, it must be counteracted by a comparable process working in the opposite direction. We have found that the activity an astral body has stopped performing because it no longer has access to the physical and ether bodies can be restored by using the juices of certain fruits. The fruit must have rinds, and centripetal effects must be evident within the fruit itself. A preparation made from the juices of such fruits is administered in ointment form in milder cases or as injections in more severe cases. We have already experienced considerable success with this treatment, which drives the astral body back into the physical and ether bodies. Dr. Wegman has successfully treated many patients with our injectable remedy for hay fever. Our way of thinking does indeed yield ways of energizing a sluggish astral body. Depending on the specific fruit that is chosen, the processes these injections stimulate have an affinity for particular organs. We need to investigate which organs are affected and what tendencies reveal the affinities. The injection-induced processes demonstrate that physical symptoms due to a sluggish astral body can indeed be corrected by offsetting the astral body itself. In the previous example, we neutralized the disease process, but in this case we counterbalance a process in the area we hope to affect. In choosing a treatment, we must distinguish between centrifugal therapeutic processes, such as those I described for the kidneys, and centripetal processes, as in our hay fever remedy, for example.

On first consideration, such remedies may seem to have been dreamed up out of nothing, and in fact that is what most of our contemporaries will believe. Consequently, I have placed great emphasis not only on the need to produce such remedies but also on the need to implement our own school of medical thought in our institutes. Confirming the efficacy of our remedies, however, is not the same as testing remedies developed through empirical methods applied on the physical level. In the latter case, we depend heavily on statistics, which tell us whether the remedy is helpful in a high proportion of cases. If we begin by applying a method such as the one I have discussed here, however, our clear understanding of a specific disease process reveals the cure, so diagnosis and treatment become one and the same thing. The situation is this: if diagnosis reveals what is going on in a diseased kidney, the process that must be applied therapeutically is the same, but on a different level. For example, the disease process may be counterbalanced by giving the patient a combination of sulfur and silica as a substitute for the particular pathological process I have recognized. A cure is accomplished through a treatment, implemented by the astral body, that imitates the disease process on a different level. For example, if I introduce the *Equisetum* function into the human organism, it stays in the ether body, and the astral body is relieved of its work in the diseased kidney.

Thus diagnosis and treatment, which exist in parallel today and can come together only on a purely empirical basis, become a unity. In recognizing the nature of a disease process in this way, we discover, for example, that *Equisetum arvense* imitates a specific kidney process. If we recognize that the inner character of gall excretion in certain illnesses is the same as the process we find in *Cichorium intybus,* the plant process shows us how to relieve the astral body of the gall-excreting function it would otherwise have to perform in the liver. We make advances in healing when diagnosis is no different from treatment, while treatment becomes a truly rational science.

For instance, if we are aware of the wonderful connection between iron and certain salts and components of plant mucilage in *Anisum vulgare* [anise], we can also recognize that one of the functional elements in anise, and especially in its seed, is the same as certain hyper-inflammatory disease processes in the blood. We can relieve the blood of these disease processes by using an appropriately produced preparation that imitates the relationship between plant mucilages and iron in anise. When we treat disorders in the blood, we do not simply free up the astral body; the "I" body is also involved.

We can look at the entire natural world in this way. The beautiful natural world we see consists entirely of imitations of disease processes. Inside the human being, these processes are disease processes; outside the human being, they are the beauties of nature. We must simply understand the individual connections. We must know how to derive disease processes from the natural world and incorporate them into the human being as substitutes, freeing up the suprasensory members that have been carrying out disease processes in the body. Now we no longer depend on statistics! Inner perceptions that allow us to clearly understand and predict the effects of specific connections between the human being and the natural world are comparable to a precisely scientific and properly executed physics experiment. In physics, too, we do not proceed according to statistics, because we know (with regard to the Mariotte-Gay-Lussac Law, for example) that an experiment that is carried out precisely is conclusive. Although the situation with respect to human beings is admittedly not as simple as a physics experiment, we can nonetheless predict how a remedy will work, and then actually see *how* it works, if we have clearly understood the disease process.

Our method of developing remedies requires an attitude that has been achieved to a very great extent by Dr. Wegman at the Clinical-Therapeutic Institute in Arlesheim, Switzerland. This attitude bans all skepticism, a major obstacle to progress in medicine. The quality that Dr. Wegman possesses above all else is the all-important courage to heal. When we have the courage to heal, we will also be able to see and understand disease processes and begin to counteract them. We must not be sloppy in our work; it is especially important to note exactly how the healing process takes place and to monitor it from step to step. If we do this, we will notice when something is not as it should be, and we will be able to retrace our steps and discover what we may have overlooked. When we have the courage to heal in each single case, when our only assumption and intention is that healing will take place, we possess the strongest possible incentive, namely, a truly scientific foundation for medicine. Rational treatments are not worked out as mere consequences of exact diagnosis but are discovered in the diagnostic process itself. Treatment is available as soon as the diagnosis is made. Thus we describe a kidney ailment as very similar to what happens in *Equisetum arvense*—we transfer what we see in the kidney to an outer process in nature, and our diagnostic descriptions themselves include the therapeutic process.

From Rudolf Steiner, The Healing Process:
Spirit, Nature, and Our Bodies *(SteinerBooks, 2009),
lecture in The Hague, November 15, 1923, pp. 58–75.*

12.

GAIA AND THE FUTURE

EARTH AND THE MYSTERY OF KARMA

WE HAVE TRIED OUR BEST in a few short hours to look at the human journey through the suprasensory world, the realm in which human beings live between death and a new birth. Although we are usually unaware of it, our human forces reach into that world while we are here on the physical Earth in our physical and ether bodies. In the physical world, we sense our suprasensory existence more or less as a mystery—one that, unless we find at least a partial answer to it, leaves us without inner harmony, stability, and security. Indeed, our very life would lack energy and vitality, and true human love would remain beyond reach.

Just by observing the human being here, we can see an aspect of our suprasensory human nature, and this can help us understand why the divine spiritual realms sent us into this world of physical senses. In fact, the reason is that knowledge of the suprasensory realm must first be spoken of to people here in the physical world. We would have to approach questions of suprasensory reality in a very different way if we were to speak of them to those who have died and are passing through their existence between death and a new birth. Today, therefore, as we consider human life on Earth, it will be appropriate to conclude our study by allowing our minds to light up with what we have received so far concerning the mysteries of the suprasensory world.

Let us begin by considering human life on Earth—in other words, let us consider ourselves. First, we have our senses; they provide us with information about all that surrounds us. Our senses are the cause of our earthly joy and happiness as well as our suffering and pain. As human beings, we sometimes fail to consider how significant our sense impressions and experiences are for our lives. And studies such as we have been devoting ourselves to for the past several days take us beyond our life of the senses into spiritual realms. It might seem as though this anthroposophic spiritual science could lead us to underrate sensory life, even to the point of saying that it has little importance and that we should escape it in our own earthly life. Such an attitude, however, is not the result of a spiritual scientific study. Such feelings can never be the *ultimate* goal of spiritual science. It simply tells us that there are certain ways of living life in the senses that are incompatible with human worth and dignity, and that it is possible to give up the life of the senses in its inferior aspects and regain its deeper significance on a higher, spiritual level. We would have good reason to avoid spiritual study if it took away the meaning of all the beauty that flows into our souls when we observe the wonderful world of flowering plants and fruiting trees or any other aspect of the natural realm, such as the starry heavens and so on, and if, as a result, we were advised to abandon all this in favor of spiritual contemplation. But this is not at all how it is.

When you recall what the initiates and masters of various ages offered for the perfection and dignity of human life, you find that they never diminished the beauty, splendor, and majesty of our earthly life of the senses. Their poetry and other arts were marvelous when describing suprasensory reality. We have only to recall such images as the lotus flower to see that initiates never shied from depicting the spiritual development through images grounded in sensory experience, and that it was their belief that what we find—or at least *can* find—in the world of the senses leads to the highest.

But we human beings cannot find satisfaction in the sensory world as perceived by ordinary consciousness, because, although the impressions that enter us through our eyes and ears and other senses are connected with our "I" being and its whole life and development, it does not really give our "I" anything to support inner certainty. We gaze outward to the beauty and splendor of flowers and face a world of infinite variety. When we turn our gaze inward toward the "I," at first our ordinary consciousness feels as though the "I" has vanished. It seems like it is merely a point of spirit within us that says little more than the empty word *I*. This is also not surprising. Just consider that before the eye can see it must forget itself completely. It is the nature of our senses that they must surrender to the world so that they can mediate properly between the world and the human being. The eye has to be completely transparent to convey the glory, grandeur, and beauty of the outer world in all its brilliant color and radiance, and the same is true of the other senses.

Really, we know nothing of our senses. Is there any way we can know and understand their true nature? To do this we must again follow the path to the suprasensory world. Even knowledge of the senses is gained only by traversing the suprasensory world.

You are all familiar with my descriptions of the paths that lead into the higher worlds.[2] Try to picture vividly what *imaginative* knowledge can be. You withdraw from physical perception of the outer world and enter *imaginative* cognition. But the most interesting thing that happens on this path is something I will describe for you through an image. When you approach the world of imagination in meditation (using methods presented in some familiar book on the subject), you begin to struggle to free the ether body from your physical organism, so that this ether body (our first suprasensory aspect) becomes conscious to some degree. You can detect the point in time when you are between ordinary sensory perception and *imaginative* perception—when you have not yet attained imagination in a developed sense, but are on the way to it.

Now let us picture a person who is on the way from ordinary sensory perception to imagination and is traveling into high mountains where granite is especially abundant—granite with a high content of quartz or silica. As we work toward imagination, our soul forces can develop especially well amid an abundance of siliceous rock that is rich in quartz. We succeed in developing

---

2. See, for example, Rudolf Steiner, *A Way of Self-knowledge* and *How to Know Higher Worlds*.

certain inner soul capacities on the first attempt, because high mountain quartz rock makes a special impression on us. This quartz is initially only slightly transparent. But as soon as we have struggled through to the stage I have described, this mineral becomes completely transparent. We climb into the high mountains, and the siliceous rock appears as transparent as glass, but in such a way that one has the feeling that something flows from one's own being to unite with the siliceous rock.

Right there, at the Earth's outermost surface, through a kind of natural offering of our consciousness, we unite with the Earth's whole surface. At this moment it seems as though our very eyes are sending out streams that penetrate the quartz; at the same moment something comes to life in us that causes us to feel united with the whole Earth's existence. In this unity with the quartz—feeling one with the whole universe—we experience our first real oneness with it that is not merely the product of a dream or some abstract thought. In this way, an intimate awareness can light up within us, which perhaps I can express by saying, "Earth, you are not alone in the cosmos; you are indeed one with the great cosmos, along with me and all earthly beings." Through this experience of oneness with the siliceous rock, we no longer view the Earth as separate from the rest of the universe, but as one etheric sphere formed from the universal etheric sphere.

This is our first feeling. There are many ancient songs and ancient myths filled with wondrous revelations that sing to us across the ages in the literature from a time of inherent human clairvoyance. Today, people read such songs and myths, and like to feel that it lifts their hearts and souls. But the truth of such songs and myths eludes people of our time. We cannot even be affected by a true feeling for the Bhagavad Gita, for example, or some other Indian or Eastern literature, unless spiritual insight shows us the real possibility of our unity with the Earth, leading to oneness with the whole cosmos. In many cases, the mood of those old songs and ballads arose from such oneness. It is like a "walking in consciousness" with light, a light that penetrates the hard quartz, making it a cosmic eye through which we can look out into the vast expanses of the universe.

Indeed, we can say that when we begin from reality in our description of the suprasensory human being, we feel inherently disinclined to be abstract and theoretical. Rather, we are predisposed to present it in a way that links the feeling life of the human soul to the ideas we express. This should deeply stir our hearts whenever we study our suprasensory nature—that it is impossible to express our spiritual knowledge without uniting our thoughts and ideas with the whole human being in will and feeling. We must endure life, but one of the things most difficult to bear for those who are aware of the true human elements of suprasensory knowledge is to hear the way certain people turn spiritual understanding into fixed theories. Theoretical discussion of the spiritual world is no less painful than holding your finger in a flame.

After we have progressed a certain degree in suprasensory cognition—when we understand through imagination the suprasensory forces that are active in us between birth and death—we can continue by attaining the level of suprasensory knowledge related to inspiration. Through inspiration, we can see into the nature of what we were before birth when we descended into earthly life, and we can also see what we will become after passing through the gate of death. Everything described in these lectures can be seen—our journey through the various regions in which our countenance is formed and where we metamorphose from the previous life into a new earthly life. Through inspiration, we can view everything I have described as our journey through the various starry worlds.

Inspiration, through which we look so deeply into our own inner being, assumes a particular nuance when we consider that what can be described as our experience in the life between death and rebirth also lives in us during our life here on Earth. Indeed, all the grandeur and cosmic majesty that must be portrayed by describing the true human being as a denizen of the starry worlds—and indeed even the worlds of the higher hierarchies—is also alive in us as we stand here on the Earth, seemingly insignificant creatures from the spatial perspective within the skin of our physical bodies. Inasmuch as our knowledge can penetrate what we contain as a physical heritage of our true being between death and a new birth, we can also do something more; we can penetrate to the depths of our planet Earth, to its veins of metal ores of lead, silver, and copper, to everything that lives as the metallic elements of the rocky Earth. When observed with the ordinary senses, the metallic substances initially do little more than suggest the various kinds of earth in which they occur. But when we penetrate the Earth with the spiritually honed perception that tells us about the human spirit, something special happens to the metallic elements within the Earth. All the copper, silver, and gold in the Earth begin to speak in a rich and mysterious language. As we live on Earth, we are confronted by something that gives us a more intimate relationship with the living soul being of the Earth itself. Metal ores tell us something—they become cosmic memories for us. This is actually what happens. Consider yourselves, for example. When you nurture an active, inner stillness and allow old memories to bring many things into your soul, you feel as though you were living again in numerous past experiences. You reconnect with many who, over the course of your life, became dear and may have died long ago. You feel remote from the present and deeply involved with the joys and sorrows of previous experiences you have lived through.

Something very similar, but on a much larger scale, happens when we unite with the veins of metal in the Earth through the inner light of spiritual insight, of suprasensory cognition. This is different from the experience of quartz, in which we are transported in a kind of visual sense into the vast cosmic expanses. In this case we become one, in a certain sense, with the body of the Earth. As you perceive inwardly the metallic veins in their wonderful speech, you feel united with the innermost soul and heartbeat of the Earth itself, and you become aware of memories that are not your own. Memories echo inwardly; they are the Earth's own memories of its earlier stages, before it was our Earth; before the present animal and plant kingdoms began to dwell on it; and before the minerals that now exist in its depths. Along with the Earth, one remembers those ancient days when the Earth was united with the other planets in our solar system. One recalls ages when the Earth had not yet separated, because it had not yet condensed and become firm within as it is today. One recalls a time when the whole solar system was an ensouled, living organism, and human beings lived within it in a very different form. Thus, the metallic veins in the Earth lead us to the Earth's own memories. When we have this inner experience, we can understand very clearly why we are sent to the Earth by the divine spiritual beings who guide the universal order.

Living in the Earth's memories like this causes us to gain a real sense of our own thinking for the first time. Because we have comprehended Earth's memories, we feel how our thinking is connected with the Earth itself. And the moment we make the Earth's memories our own, we are surrounded by the beings of the second hierarchy (kyriotetes, dynamis, and exusiai). This is how, even in earthly life, we may be surrounded by the beings who surround us at a certain time between death and a new birth, as described. We fully realize that we contact beings of the second hierarchy while we are incarnated on Earth between birth and death. But these beings do more than work with us between death and rebirth to transform our being; they also play a role in forming the cosmos as a whole. Here we see how the higher cosmic order gives these beings the responsibility for everything in the Earth related to the influences of those veins of metal.

Now we can look back again. What I discussed before about the experience of quartz was probably not immediately understood, because it is not very obvious. But our marvelous experience of the Earth's memories in relation to the veins of metal *does* speak plainly. Now, however, we can return and try to understand something that perhaps was not understood at first.

Now we become aware that we are surrounded by beings of the third hierarchy (angels, archangels, and archai) as we soar into the great cosmic whole, borne by the light that permeates quartz. And we learn something very special. As we ascend into the high mountains or descend to veins of metal deep in the Earth, the reality of it is not communicated to us by our ordinary senses. We become familiar with the marvel that, in the high mountain regions of the siliceous rock, angels, archangels, and archai weave and hover over those rocky peaks. And when we descend into the Earth, we find the beings of the second hierarchy permeate the paths of metallic veins. We can also say that during earthly life we are among the spiritual beings connected with our innermost being between death and a new birth.

When a certain time has elapsed after passing through the gate of death, we arrive consciously in the realms of angels, archangels, and archai. The condition of consciousness we have developed in this disembodied state enables us to perceive the beings around us, just as we perceive the four kingdoms of the natural world during our life on Earth. But when our higher level of consciousness there enables us to behold angels, archangels, and archai, everything that the senses could perceive has disappeared, because our senses have been surrendered to the elements with our bodies. Between death and a new birth we perceive nothing of the earthly, sensory life.

Then the angels, archangels, and archai narrate for us the story of what they are doing down on Earth—this is the appropriate way to say it, since it fits the situation exactly. They recount how they are occupied with more than the life they live with us. They whisper, "We also participate in cosmic creation; we are the creative beings of the cosmos, and we look down in Earth existence upon the earthly forms shaped by the quartz rock and its relatives." Then, while among these angels, archangels, and archai between death and new birth, we realize that we must return to Earth, because during this time we come to know the beings of the third hierarchy. We also hear them speak in a wonderful way of their works on Earth. We realize that we can perceive their activities only by descending to Earth, clothed in a physical, human body, and thus partaking of sensory impressions.

Indeed, the deepest secrets of sensory perception—not just those available in high mountain country, but everything that the senses convey—are revealed to us in the wonderful words of beings we are associated with between death and rebirth. Ordinary consciousness just cannot perceive the real mystery and beauty of physical nature, which is so great that, after passing through the gate of death, our earthly memories of it are truly illumined when we hear the third hierarchy describe what we perceived with our eyes, ears, and other senses on Earth.

Thus is the connection between what is physical and supraphysical. It is also the connection between physical human life and supraphysical life.

The universe is full of splendor, and it is only proper that everything we see in physical existence delights and uplifts us. We come to know its actual mysteries once we have passed through the gate of death. The more we learn to rejoice in the physical world, the more deeply we enter into all the joy that the sense world bestows and the greater the measure of understanding that we bring to the realm of the angels. They are waiting to tell us of the mysteries here on Earth that we cannot yet understand, but that we do understand once we pass into the suprahysical realm.

And our relationship is similar in the case of the second hierarchy (kyriotetes, dynamis, and exusiai), within whom we live for a certain period between death and rebirth. We develop a special relationship with them by penetrating the Earth's memories along the path of light of its veins of metal. Here again, however, we can understand our earthly experiences of the metals only when we have crossed over into the region of the second hierarchy.

You see, one of the most beautiful experiences we can have is to be able to investigate the various relationships between metals and human health. And I have reason to hope that the anthroposophic movement will be particularly successful in uncovering the beauty to be found in this area of research. Every metal and metal compound has a specific connection to human health. As we go through life and experience health and illness, we continually form ties to the metals and their compounds that give the Earth its memories.

We must go beyond merely theorizing about the healing properties of lead and copper and their compounds and so on. These substances all constitute significant and valuable remedies if we know how to prepare them correctly. We must not be satisfied with talking in abstractions about the wonderful relationships between metals and the human being. Indeed, a feeling of reverence arises in us even now as we contemplate metallic veins in the

Earth's depths. But we must go another step and develop a deep understanding of the marvelous connection between metals and the human being—a connection first revealed to us once we have examined it from the perspective of the human being in relation to health and illness.

As I suggested, it is hoped that much can be communicated to human hearts and minds through the anthroposophic movement in connection with this knowledge, since it is extremely important. In the past it was not so important, because humankind had an inherent sense of all these relationships; they recognized that the lead process is related to this or that in the human head, and they knew the connections involved in the silver process. The ancients spoke often of such matters. People of more recent times may read about this but fail to understand a word of it, because it is approached from a modern scientific perspective as though it were merely a vague and empty set of abstractions.

Anthroposophic knowledge can deepen the mind and soul through contemplating the wonderful relationship between the metals and human health and illness. Thus, when we die we can take with us into the spiritual world something to help us understand, in a very special way, the language of the second hierarchy. As a result of such preparation here on Earth, we will take with us the necessary understanding so that the most profound mysteries of the universe can be revealed to us. This is a fact. We learn what Anthroposophy teaches us not merely out of curiosity, but for its results once we have passed through the gate of death. Spiritual science offers us exactly what we need to find the right relationship with the beings we encounter between death and rebirth. Because those beings make up the world that will then surround us, our whole being must find a connection with them.

Thus, it is possible to present a detailed image of how we find such a relationship with those beings of the higher hierarchies between death and a new birth. But there is something else related to this as we pass through those regions, for which we will be well-prepared by our understanding of what has just been described. Now we must describe another experience.

Nature will reveal her mysteries to us if we can understand the relationship between Earth's metals and human health and illness. But there is something else involved in those secrets of nature. First we hear the beings of the second hierarchy speak of the nature of one or another metallic element—gold, silver, lead, copper, and so on. On Earth, we have a certain relationship to the great spiritual world when we first learn to read. And it dawns on us that by reading we can begin to penetrate many mysteries of the world, which might otherwise remain beyond our knowledge. (Of course, I am using this metaphor for comparison only, because, as an earthly experience, there is really nothing special in this process.) Through the beings of the second hierarchy at a certain point in our passage through the life after death, we familiarize ourselves with the language describing the metals and their connection with human health and illness. This language becomes what it should only when we can raise it from the level of prose in the spiritual cosmos to that of cosmic poetry, or more accurately, when we are able to lift *ourselves* to cosmic poetry.

Initially, we are largely a tabula rasa in relation to poetry. On Earth we can come to understand the voice, the rhythm, and the whole artistic form of verse, unless we lack all feeling for poetry. Likewise, when we ascend from dry prose to the poetry of the world beyond the threshold, we rise from speech of the second hierarchy (telling us of the relationship between the metals and human health) to an understanding of the mysteries of cosmic moral existence. This moral life encompasses not only human souls, but also the divine souls of all the hierarchical beings. And the mysteries of the soul element are opened to us especially in this region.

Then we can take another step. We can experience what I described as going up into the mountains and into the Earth's depths. Everything remains still at first—we observe the quiet veins of metal and the stone along the mountain ridges. But we can go farther and try not to view things only from a dry, utilitarian perspective. Though we should not underrate that kind of observation, since we need to plant both feet firmly on the ground if we want to enter the suprasensory world, healthy in body and spirit. We can try to not stop short at what is thus far revealed to us but, instead, continue by observing metals melting in a fiercely hot fire, and how they change from a solid to a liquid. By visiting a foundry, for example, we see iron in the furnaces as it is made to flow radiantly, or witness the processes in which metal ores such as antimony are transformed not only from solid to liquid, but gradually into other states. As the metals are subjected to fire, we can allow what happens to them to affect us, and thus something quite new and different impresses the spiritual insight we have nurtured, and we develop a tremendously profound impression of the mysteries of our own existence.

I have often referred to this by saying that we should consider human beings in comparison to animals. The various kinds of anatomical comparisons made today—human and animal bones, muscles, and even blood—do reveal certain affinities. But human superiority to animals becomes evident only when we consider the fact that the spines of animals are, for the most part, parallel with the Earth's surface, whereas that of the human being is vertical. Or consider our marvelous possession of language, with which the animals are not gifted, and go on from there to our capacity to think, which is developed from speech. When we observe how speaking and thinking develop in children and how their whole orientation in life begins with attaining an upright posture, we witness the activity of the marvelous forces whereby children find their way dynamically into the world. We see how the orientation of a child's limbs expresses itself in the melody and articulation of speech. If we observe how we actually build and shape ourselves in the world of the senses, we see formative forces quietly at work. It is indeed wonderful to see a child's growth as months pass—seeing the progress from crawling to upright walking and the adjustment of the whole orientation of the child's body and limbs to the world's dynamics, and then the formation of speech and thinking from the physical being.

With the mind at rest, we can contemplate this in all its wonder, watching the quiet majesty with which it presents itself to the observer. We observe a child learning to walk and talk and think, and it seems to be the most beautiful thing one can witness in human life. We gather impressions of this beautiful element in human life, and then, on the other hand, we can also witness the melting of metals when exposed to fire. We perceive the spiritual archetype of this in children, which leads them to learn to walk and speak. The archetype of this power is revealed when flames take hold of the metal, making it flow. As the metal becomes more fluid, it becomes more volatile, and we have a clearer perception of the inner resemblance between that process—which is, in fact, metal's destiny—and the smelting and volatilizing process in cosmic fires that enable a little child to walk, speak, and think. And we realize that the beings of the first hierarchy (the seraphim, cherubim, and thrones) are involved in a twofold activity.

One aspect of this is that they speak to us from the spiritual world into which we pass midway through our life between death and a new birth, where they reveal the mysteries of planetary and other cosmic activities (as I have described during the last few days). They also work down into the visible world. Here, in the visible realm, the influences of the seraphim, cherubim, and thrones are active, on the one hand, in little children as they learn to walk, speak, and think and, on the other hand, in everything behind the Earth's process in which fire plays a role, such as when fire melts glowing metals.

Our planet Earth is indeed built up through the melting and glowing of metals in the forces of fire. As we look back to ancient times when this planet Earth was being built, we see in the metal melting through the forces of fire an aspect of the works of the seraphim, cherubim, and thrones in the earthly world—in particular, how the beings of the first hierarchy accomplish this work, supported primarily by the thrones. We can look back into the ancient times of Earth and see how metals glowed and liquefied as they were subjected to the forces of fire, and how they played a special role in the Earth's manifestation. The thrones had an especially active role in this, with the seraphim and cherubim quietly working alongside. It is the cherubim, however, who play the main role when children learn to walk, talk, and think. But it is always the beings of the first hierarchy that we see working harmoniously in both of these activities.

This kind of knowledge links earthly death with resurrection in our life beyond the threshold. Such knowledge reveals the kinship between the cosmic fires by which metals are melted and the powers that make us truly human. Thus, the whole world becomes one and we realize that our earthly life between birth and death is really no different from our life in the spiritual world beyond the threshold. Life between death and a new birth is a metamorphosis of earthly life. We know how one becomes the other, and thus how one is merely a different form of the other. When such insights lift our souls, more are added along with them.

Indeed, these other insights can also come in another way. Try to imagine what I have been describing today as the wonderful relationship between the way fire forces melt and vaporize metals and the process of children learning to walk and speak and think. If you meditate on this in such a way that it deepens you inwardly, a force will take hold of your soul that allows you to solve a great mystery of life, so that the soul is developed and enriched. I am speaking of the functioning of karma, or destiny, in the human being. We can come to a real understanding of human destiny and karma through the twofold experience of seeing a child learning to walk, talk, and think, on the one hand, and the melting and vaporizing of metals subjected to fire, on the other. Karma is revealed in the fiery smelting of metals and in the appropriate transformation of a child's animal nature into human nature while learning to walk, talk, and think. Karma is the suprasensory element that reaches into our immediate, active human life.

As we progress in our meditation, we come to understand the mysteries of destiny that weave through our life. On the one hand, we have a picture of the destiny of metals as they are subjected to fire, and on the other, the destiny of the primal human being descending to Earth and learning to walk, talk, and think. Between these images we find what we need to know of the mystery of karma for our human life.

So you see, the suprasensory human being speaks into the human world of the senses about the matter of human destiny.

This is what I wanted to speak to you about as part of our study of the suprasensory human being. We could never base such a study on abstract theories. To understand the human being, we must reach into all the mysteries involved in the being of nature as well as in the spirit of the cosmos. Ultimately, human beings are intimately connected with *all* the mysteries of nature and universal spirit. The human being is in fact a universe in miniature. But we must not imagine that whatever happens on a grand scale out in the macrocosm occurs in the same way in the microcosm. As the metals melt, majestic flames of the fire's forces flow out to the very limits of macrocosmic space—and such boundaries *do* exist.

My dear friends, try to picture these fiery forces through which metals become fluid and volatile. This vaporized substance radiates into the vast expanses of the universe, but it returns in the forces of light and its warmth. And as it returns from cosmic space, it takes hold of a child who can only crawl and helps that child to stand upright and walk. So we see the upward flow of currents in melting metals; they turn around when they have gone far enough out into the cosmos and return as the forces that lift a child into uprightness. What we see on the one hand, we find also on the other. This gives you a picture of the ascending and descending cosmic forces of metamorphosis and transformation that work in the spirit of the cosmos.

Now you will also be able to understand the true meaning of something else related to the knowledge of ancient times—the old practice of sacrifice. People sent their sacrificial flame, along with what they burned within it, out into vast cosmic space to the gods, so that it might return to work in the human world. The attitude of the priestly sage toward the sacrificial fire may be expressed in these words: "O flame, I commit to you what is mine on Earth. As the smoke ascends, may the gods accept it. May what is borne upward by flame become divine blessing, poured again upon the Earth as creative, fructifying power."

As we hear the words of those ancient, sacrificial priests, who spoke of suprasensory worlds, we realize that they, too, were speaking of the cosmic mysteries of which we are a part.

My dear friends, this is what I wanted to say to you about our suprasensory nature as human beings, as it is understood by spiritual science.

From Rudolf Steiner, At Home in the Universe:
Exploring Our Suprasensory Nature *(Anthroposophic Press, 2000),*
lecture in The Hague, November 18, 1923, pp. 88–105.

A Guide to Further Reading

Lectures and Writings by Rudolf Steiner

Agriculture Course: The Birth of the Biodynamic Method, Rudolf Steiner Press, 2005. These are the original lectures behind this dynamic agricultural method.

Anthroposophical Leading Thoughts: Anthroposophy as a Path of Knowledge: The Michael Letters, Rudolf Steiner Press, 1998. During the time that Rudolf Steiner wrote his autobiographical installments, he also wrote weekly letters (from February 1924 until December 1924) that went out to members of the Anthroposophical Society. He crystallized the path of Anthroposophy into concentrated summaries called *leading thoughts.* He hoped that they would be studied and thus support and stimulate the society. In August, 1924, Steiner introduced the Michael impulse to transform modern human consciousness. These thoughts are Rudolf Steiner's final expression of Anthroposophy and its future.

The Anthroposophic Movement, Rudolf Steiner Press, London, 1993. These lectures provide an encompassing overview of how the anthroposophic movement came into existence and what it means for today and in the future.

Anthroposophy (A Fragment), SteinerBooks, 2006. Steiner's written work (never fully completed to his satisfaction), outlining a new methodology for the study of human nature. It was written in 1910, when Steiner was working out his ideas on psychology and physiology in relation to spirit. (Those lectures are in *A Psychology of Body, Soul, & Spirit.*) These ideas, though somewhat difficult, constitute the steps he took toward a truly cognitive psychology.

Art as Spiritual Activity: Rudolf Steiner's Contribution to the Visual Arts, edited and introduced by Michael Howard, Anthroposophic Press, Great Barrington, MA, 1998. This book provides an excellent introduction to Steiner's spiritual approach to the arts, particularly architecture and sculpture. The comprehensive introduction and ten lectures include numerous illustrations.

Autobiography: Chapters in the Course of My Life, 1861–1907, SteinerBooks, 2006. Rudolf Steiner seldom spoke of himself in a personal way, but here he offers a glimpse into some of the most intimate aspects of his inner life, his personal relationships, and significant events that helped to shape the philosopher, seer, and teacher he became.

The Bhagavad Gita and the West: The Esoteric Meaning of the Bhagavad Gita and Its Relation to the Letters of St. Paul, SteinerBooks 2008. This book presents Steiner's profound engagement with Hindu thought and, above all, the Krishna in the Bhagavad Gita as they illuminate Western Christian esotericism.

Christianity as Mystical Fact, Anthroposophic Press, Great Barrington, MA, 1997, translated and introduced by Andrew Welburn with an afterword by Reverend Michael Debus of The Christian Community. This book was edited and reworked by Steiner from a series of 25 lectures given at the Theosophical Library in Berlin (October 5, 1901–March 22, 1902). Steiner describes how the ancient mysteries foresaw and led up to the Mystery of Golgotha as the turning point of world history.

The Christian Mystery, Anthroposophic Press, 1998. These early lectures from 1905 to 1908 provide a clear picture of Steiner's esoteric Christianity. He discusses many aspects of the Christian path, including prayer, the Gospels, the "Mystery of Golgotha," the esoteric meaning of the mass, and so on.

The Christmas Conference for the Foundation of the General Anthroposophical Society, 1923/1924, Anthroposophic Press, 1990. Contains the documents, lectures, and other material from the conference at which Rudolf Steiner reestablished the Anthroposophical Society.

Calendar 1912–1913: Facsimile Edition of the Original Book Containing the Calendar created by Rudolf Steiner for the Year 1912–1913, SteinerBooks, 2003. This edition contains the *Calendar of the Soul,* as well as reproductions of the esoteric seals developed by Rudolf Steiner for contemplation.

Cosmic Memory: Prehistory of Earth and Man, Garber Communications, Blauvelt, NY, 1987. Written between 1904 and 1908, this book evolved from Steiner's "reading" of the akashic chronicle, the etheric record of cosmic, historic events. It presents a unique imagination of the evolution of Earth and humanity.

Education for Special Needs: The Curative Education Course, Rudolf Steiner Press, 1998. These lectures are the culmination of Steiner's methods for educating those who are developmentally disabled.

The seed for this lecture course was in his tutoring of Richard Specht, described in part 1 of the present volume.

First Steps in Inner Development, Anthroposophic Press, 1999. This is a collection of lectures and works by Steiner that specifically describe the anthroposophic approach to spiritual practice and the requirements for its success. These are very practical and direct instructions for inner development.

The Foundations of Human Experience, Anthroposophic Press, 1996. Here Steiner laid the groundwork for the understanding of the human being from the aspects of soul, spirit, and body, the basis of Waldorf education.

Friedrich Nietzsche: Fighter for Freedom. Spiritual Science Library, Blauvelt, NY, 1985. Steiner characterizes Nietzsche as a profound truth seeker caught in the materialism of his time.

From the History and Contents of the First Section of the Esoteric School, 1904–1914, SteinerBooks, 2006. Chronicles the development of Steiner's esoteric teaching described in the final section of the *Autobiography*. It also records the events surrounding the formation of the Anthroposophic Society from the German Section of the Theosophical Society.

Goethe's Theory of Knowledge: An Outline of the Epistemology of His Worldview, SteinerBooks, 2008. Here, Steiner first outlined his understanding of Goethe's epistemology during the 1880s, which became a foundation for his future teaching of Anthroposophy.

The Gospel of St. John, Anthroposophic Press, 1984. Some of Steiner's most important lectures on Christianity and John's Gospel.

Guidance in Esoteric Training: From the Esoteric School, Rudolf Steiner Press, 1994. Contains exercises, meditations, and practices for spiritual development as given by Steiner to his students in the Esoteric School between 1904 and 1914.

The Healing Process: Spirit, Nature, and Our Bodies, Anthroposophic Press, 2000. Steiner discusses fundamental principles of anthroposophically extended medicine. Some of his most remarkable insights on medicine are contained in this volume.

How to Know Higher Worlds: A Modern Path of Initiation, Anthroposophic Press, 1994. Steiner wrote this work to lay out the conditions and methods of spiritual science, methods that, when worked with diligently, lead to a greater spiritual capacity for knowledge.

Introducing Anthroposophical Medicine, Anthroposophic Press, 1999. These lectures were given to doctors during a seminar in 1920. This book gives the essentials of the anthroposophic approach to illness and healing methods.

Intuitive Thinking as a Spiritual Path: A Philosophy of Freedom, Anthroposophic Press, 1995. Published in 1894, while Steiner was editing Goethe's natural scientific writings. As the subtitle to his *Philosophy of Freedom*, Steiner chose "Results of Soul Observation Arrived at by the Scientific Method." His basic thesis is that we need not accept the self-imposed limitation of knowledge gained through sense observation, intellectual analysis, and interpretation. Thinking, as the instrument of human cognition, can be extended through an individual's inner activity to become the primary instrument for knowledge that goes beyond the limitations of sense perception, opening the path to spiritual cognition.

The Lord's Prayer: An Esoteric Study, Rudolf Steiner Press, 2007. Steiner penetrates the esoteric significance of the Lord's Prayer by relating the seven petitions in the prayer to the seven spiritual and physical human bodies. He also discusses the difference between prayer and meditation and shows how real prayer is truly selfless.

Nature's Open Secret: Introductions to Goethe's Scientific Writings, Anthroposophic Press, 2000. This book collects the introductions that Steiner describes writing in part two of the *Autobiography*. These essays cover the full range of Steiner's spiritual views on natural science as presented in Goethe's writings.

An Outline of Esoteric Science, Anthroposophic Press, 1998. This is Steiner's essential written work on cosmology and the path to higher knowledge. It is his most comprehensive description of the events and beings of cosmic and human evolution.

A Psychology of Body, Soul, and Spirit: Anthroposophy, Psychosophy, Pneumatosophy, Anthroposophic Press, 1999. The first section of these lectures elaborates the material Steiner wrote in *Anthroposophy (A Fragment)*. In the second and third sections, Steiner further develops his approach to a complete psychology of the human soul and spirit.

Rhythms of Learning: What Waldorf Education Offers Children, Parents, and Teachers, edited and introduced by Roberto Trostli, Anthroposophic Press, 1998. This is a comprehensive introduction and overview of Waldorf education, including lectures by Steiner that cover kindergarten through high school.

Riddles of the Soul: The Case for Anthroposophy, SteinerBooks, 2009. First published in 1917, Steiner deals with the fact that contemporary humanity is at the end of a long and necessary separation of the human soul from its spiritual origins. Having gained independence, the human being can now, through inner activity, rebuild that connection. Steiner extends this to the activity of feeling and of volition and shows that they are initially experienced through the body, but may be recognized as having independent life.

Spiritual Ecology: Reading the Book of Nature and Reconnecting with the World, Rudolf Steiner Press, 2008. In these extracts, Steiner discusses human perception, the Earth, water, plants, animals, insects, agriculture, and natural catastrophes. *Spiritual Ecology* offers a wealth of original thought and spiritual insight on the future of the Earth and humanity.

The Spiritual Hierarchies and the Physical World: Zodiac, Planets, and Cosmos, SteinerBooks, 2008. This is perhaps Steiner's clearest discussion of cosmic beings and activities as they relate to human and world evolution.

The Stages of Higher Knowledge: Imagination, Inspiration, Intuition, SteinerBooks, 2009. Assembled from a series of articles intended as an elaboration and follow-up to *How to Know Higher Worlds*.

Start Now! A Book of Soul and Spiritual Exercises, SteinerBooks, 2004. This book collects most of Rudolf Steiner's practical suggestions—whether from his writings or lectures—for inner development.

Staying Connected: How to Continue Your Relationships with Those Who Have Died, Anthroposophic Press, 1999. Various lectures describe the importance of being aware of those who have died and our relationship with them. Steiner describes ways we can help our loved ones who have died and how they help us in everyday life.

Theosophy: An Introduction to the Spiritual Processes in Human Life and in the Cosmos, Anthroposophic Press, 1994. Steiner describes his own suprasensory experiences, leading to his understanding of the sevenfold human being, the laws of reincarnation and rebirth, and the spiritual path through which we may arrive at such understanding.

Towards Social Renewal: Rethinking the Basis of Society, Rudolf Steiner Press, 1994. Steiner's social thinking is not based on intellectual theory, but on a profound perception of the archetypal spiritual nature of social life. He relates the ideals of "liberty, equality, and fraternity" to modern society.

A Way of Self-knowledge: And the Threshold of the Spiritual World, SteinerBooks, 2006. Steiner's most personal statements about his own spiritual path. He speaks directly from experiences of cognitive research and explorations. Each of the meditations and aphorisms arises from his spiritual research and demonstrates how such spiritual research is to be undertaken.

A Western Approach to Reincarnation and Karma: Selected Lectures and Writings of Rudolf Steiner, introduced and edited by René Querido, Anthroposophic Press, 1997. Querido presents a historical overview of the Western perspective of karma and rebirth, which he views in relation to Steiner's spiritual-scientific research. A selection of Steiner's lectures and writings are represented, which discuss the causes and effects of karma in relation to world events, natural phenomena, illness, and so on. Steiner describes how we can come to understand our own karma in the light of past incarnations, and how we can take fuller responsibility for our own destinies.

WORKS BY OTHER AUTHORS

Almon, Joan, editor, *Meeting Rudolf Steiner: Classic Selections from "The Journal for Anthroposophy,"* Ann Arbor, MI: Anthroposophical Society in America, 2005. A collection of articles that describe life and work with Rudolf Steiner. A wide range of article are included, from intimate experiences of Steiner's dinner-table humor to descriptions of the first Goetheanum burning to the ground. Authors include: Albert Schewitzer, Bruno Walter, Arvia MacKay Ege, Andrei Belyi, Lisa Monges, and others.

Barnes, Henry, *Into the Heart's Land: A Century of Rudolf Steiner's Work in North America,* SteinerBooks, 2005. Chronicles the growth of Anthroposophy in North America since the early twentieth century.

———, *A Life for the Spirit: Rudolf Steiner in the Crosscurrents of Our Time,* Anthroposophic Press, 1997. An in-depth biography of Rudolf Steiner, his philosophy, and his work.

Bortoft, Henri, *The Wholeness of Nature: Goethe's Way toward a Science of Conscious Participation in Nature,* Anthroposophic Press, 1996. Goethean science was a key element in Rudolf Steiner's spiritual science, and this volume helps make Goethe's ideas accessible to the nonspecialist reader.

Childs, Gilbert, *Rudolf Steiner: His Life and Work: An Illustrated Biography,* Anthroposophic Press, 1995, provides a short, concise introduction to Rudolf Steiner's life and his work.

Finser, Siegfried E., *Money Can Heal: Evolving Our Consciousness: The Story of RSF and Its Innovations in Social Finance,* SteinerBooks,

2007. The author describes economic principles and practice based on Rudolf Steiner's threefold organization of society.

Hindes, James H., *Renewing Christianity: Rudolf Steiner's Ideas in Practice,* Anthroposophic Press, 1995. Reverend Hindes provides a concise introduction to Steiner's thought that led to the formation of The Christian Community and the "Consecration of Man," its essential sacrament.

Klocek, Dennis, *The Seer's Handbook: A Guide to Higher Perception,* SteinerBooks, 2005. Klocek shows how Steiner's basic exercises can be deepened and followed to gain a deep understanding and experience of spiritual beings, processes, and realities.

Lipson, Michael, Ph.D., *Stairway of Surprise: Six Steps to a Creative Life,* SteinerBooks, 2002. Dr. Lipson offers practical advice and encouragement in working with Rudolf Steiner's essential spiritual exercises.

Luxford, Michael, *Children with Special Needs: Rudolf Steiner's Ideas in Practice,* Anthroposophic Press, 1994. A small illustrated introduction to the practical application of Steiner's ideas for educating children with special needs.

Popawski, Thomas, *Eurythmy: Rhythm, Dance, and Soul: Rudolf Steiner's Ideas in Practice,* Anthroposophic Press, 1998. This is a basic, illustrated introduction to the practice of eurythmy, the art of movement inspired by Rudolf Steiner, practiced worldwide as both a performance art and a method of therapy.

Schilthuis, Willy, *Biodynamic Agriculture: Rudolf Steiner's Ideas in Practice,* Anthroposophic Press, 1994. Illustrated book that introduces the practical application of Steiner's ideas for agriculture.

Unger, Carl, *The Language of the Consciousness Soul,* St. George Publications, 1983. This book serves as a study guide for the *Anthroposophical Leading Thoughts*. In concise chapters, Unger expands the gem-like truths contained in Rudolf Steiner's aphoristic guiding thoughts and in his "Michael Letters."

Index

Abraham, 168
Act of Consecration of Man, 42
Adam, 168
agriculture, biodynamic farming, viii, 2, 28, 66, 78–79
Ahriman/ahrimanic, 40, 104–107, 109, 223
akashic record, 17–18, 265, 267
Alcoholics Anonymous, 33
angels. See hierarchies, angels
animal kingdom, 12, 45, 57, 66, 106, 112–115, 118–119, 185–186, 195, 203, 247, 266, 295, 301
  collective ego, 119
anthroposophic/Anthroposophy, vii, viii, 1–3, 7, 9–11, 13, 19, 27, 30, 32, 35–39, 41–43, 51–53, 57, 59–60, 64, 71–72, 75, 79, 92, 104, 115, 118–119, 131, 165, 175, 177, 182, 201, 209–212, 214–215, 220, 228, 230–239, 241, 244, 246, 252, 262, 265–267, 271–274, 276, 279–280, 282, 291, 299, 305
anthroposophic movement, 71, 79, 92, 174, 178, 230–232, 298–299
Anthroposophical Society, 8–9, 71–72, 76–79, 92
Anthropos, 1, 24, 63, 112
antipathies, 46, 121, 125, 140, 217, 219–220, 256
Anzengruber, Ludwig, 227–228
archangels. See Hierarchies, archangels
architecture, 48, 51, 202–205, 207–208, 211
Arendt, Hannah, 5
Aristotle, 40, 93

arts/artistic activity, 2, 7, 9–10, 16, 48–53, 72, 79, 101–103, 200–212, 245–246, 250, 291
  fine arts, 201
Assyrian, 100
astral, 17, 25, 29, 35, 44, 46–47, 105, 107, 159–160, 162, 169, 282–283, 286
astral body, 27–31, 42–45, 47–48, 50, 60–61, 105–106, 121, 130–131, 159–161, 164, 169–172, 207, 233–234, 236, 255, 258–259, 261–262, 265–266, 268, 280–286, 288
  as concentrated wisdom, 262
astral human beings, 280–281, 283, 286
atheist, 6, 228
Athena, 22
Atlantean/Atlantis, 18–19, 100–101, 105, 109, 111
Augustine, St, 12, 58
aura, human, 122, 124, 127–128, 139–140
auric membrane, 127
Aurobindo, Sri, 38, 49
authority, teachers', 241–243, 248, 251
Axial Age, first, 24

Babylonian, 18, 100–101
Baptism in the Jordan, 177
Barfield, Owen, vii, 91–94
"Barr Document," 80–90
Berlin Worker's Educational Institute, 85–86, 91
Besant, Annie, 7, 50, 74–76, 89
Bhagavad Gita, 21, 69, 293
biodynamic farming. See agriculture, biodynamic

Blavatsky, Helena P, 7, 88
  her book, *Isis Unveiled*, 88
  her book, *Secret Doctrine*, 88–90
Böhme, Jakob, 58, 75
Bolshevists, 224
brahman, 21
Bruno, Giordano, 58
Buber, 5
Buddha, Gautama, 1, 7–8, 21, 23, 35, 40, 42, 46
Buddhist, 17, 42, 66

capitalism, 52, 225
carcinoma, as related to social tumor, 222
Carson, Rachel
  her book, *Silent Spring*, 65
catharsis (purification), 43, 159–160, 162–164, 174
Chaldean, 18, 100–101
Chaldean-Babylonian, 102
change of teeth, children, 54–55, 239, 278–279
Chardin, de, Pierre T., 66
children, learning to walk, speak and think, 301–304
Chinese, 17
Christ, 1, 3–4, 7–8, 16–17, 21, 23–24, 40–43, 58, 66, 89–90, 94, 106–110, 157, 159, 166–167, 169–171, 173–175, 177, 215, 227
  Christ concept, 108
  Christ impulse, 21, 35, 108
  as Christ Sun, 158
  Christ's return, 174
  as Cosmic Christ, 66
  as Cosmic "I," 63
  as crucified Savior, 170
  as God of Light, 110
  his Incarnation, 39
  as living Christ, 89
  as the Logos (Word), viii, 21, 39, 41, 162
  as Messiah, 167, 172
  the Resurrection, 174
  as Risen Christ, 173
  as Spirit of Earth, 171
  as Spirit of Light, 104, 106
  as spiritual Sun Being, 40, 107–108
  as Sun Logos, 170–171
  as Sun Spirit, 106
Christian/Christianity, 3, 12, 16, 21, 24, 35, 40–43, 66, 68, 89, 93, 108, 111, 167, 171–172, 175–178
  esoteric Christianity, 3, 16, 35, 43, 164–167, 170
Christian Community, 9, 42, 78
  as the Movement for Religious Renewal, 42
Christmas Conference, 63, 71, 79
Christmas Foundation Meeting. See Christmas Conference
clairvoyance/clairvoyant, 2, 7, 11, 19, 28, 33, 35–36, 94, 109, 111, 166, 173–174, 293
  ancient clairvoyance, 19–21, 102
clinics, anthroposophic, 272–274
  linking with research institutes, 273–274, 287
Coleridge, 93
colors, 131, 140, 179–182, 208, 246
concentration, 159, 161
concept, 10, 16, 98–99, 103, 109, 176, 180, 182, 243–247
consciousness, 2–4, 11, 17–24, 28–29, 34, 39, 42–45, 48, 58–59, 63–65, 87, 93, 103, 106–107, 121, 123, 139, 180, 194, 200, 209, 211–212, 218, 243, 257–258, 263–264, 269, 277, 280–282, 291–293, 297
  ancient consciousness, 19–20
  emptying consciousness, 280
  consciousness periods. See post-Atlantean epochs.
consciousness soul, 30–31, 106, 121, 124–125, 128–130, 188–190
  as the soul within the soul, 121
contemplation, 37, 67, 263, 269, 291
  self-contemplation, 145
cosmic forces, ascending/descending, 304

cosmic midnight hour, 47
Courtney, Ralph, 52
criticism, 138–139

Dalai Lama, viii
Dante
    his *Purgatorio*, 44
Darwinism, 12, 91
death, 27, 30, 43–45, 192, 196–197,
    200, 204–205, 207–209,
    211–212, 249, 297, 303
demon of the ages, 268
demonic, 270
demonology, 268
dentition. See change of teeth,
    children
Descartes, René, 12, 36
destiny, 48, 55, 66, 94, 179, 192–
    199, 302–303
dharma, ix
Dionysius the Areopagite, 368
doubting Thomas, 173–174

Eckhart, Meister, 58, 87, 110
ecology movement, 65
Ecumenical Council of
    Constantinople (in 869), 27
education, 53–57, 230–253
ego. See "I"
egoist/egoistic, 104, 220
Egypt/Egyptian, 18–19, 40, 100–
    102, 104
Eiser, Kurt, 213–214, 228
elemental spirits (nature spirits), 6,
    269–270
elohim. See Hierarchies, /elohim
Emerson, Ralph W., 16, 38–39
esoteric
    knowledge, 135–136, 140–141
    teaching/training, 134–136, 142,
    165
etheric, 25, 28–29, 35, 49–50, 58,
    65, 115, 127, 159, 169, 172,
    233, 264–266, 282–283, 293
etheric body, 27–31, 43–44, 47–50,
    58, 60–61, 65, 105–106, 114–
    117, 121, 128–133, 159–162,
    164, 169–170, 172, 184,
    188, 190–191, 205, 232, 234,
    236, 255, 258–259, 261–265,
    268–269, 279–282, 284, 286,
    290, 292
    as body of formative forces, 28,
        40, 65–66, 132–133, 261–
        262, 264
    as subtle body, 25
etheric human beings, 279–281
Eunike, Anna, 8–9, 74
eurythmy, 49–50, 76, 78–79, 201,
    209–210, 251
evil, 4, 45–46, 87, 213–215, 226,
    228–229, 259
exercises, spiritual. See meditations,
    exercises
eyes, human, 115–117

fairy tales, 109
faith, 4, 10, 21, 174, 176, 215, 227,
    243
Father. See God
feeling, 10, 14, 25, 29, 31, 33–34,
    38, 100, 109–110, 112–113,
    123, 136–138, 140, 161, 171,
    177–178, 201–203, 209, 211,
    234, 237–238, 243, 245–247,
    256, 266, 293–294
Fichte, Johann G., 5, 12, 16, 80,
    224–225
    his "The Closed Commercial
        State," 224
    his concept of the "I," 5
Foundation Stone Meditation, 39,
    156–158
freedom, 4, 10, 13–17, 21, 48, 52–
    53, 55, 71, 96, 99, 137, 250,
fructified/fruits, 128, 163, 183, 189–
    191, 196, 231, 304

Gabriel, archangel, 42
Gaia, 63–71, 290
    as living Earth, 63
Gaian, 68
Galatians, book of, 16
garments (body and soul as to the
    "I"), 123–124, 130

General Anthroposophy Society,
    8–9, 63, 71–72, 77, 79, 92
  British Society, 9
  Dutch Society, 9
generic, 96–99
genius of our time, 268
geometry, 5, 277
Gervinus, 81
Gestalt (our physical form), 184–185
God (Father), 12–14, 35, 64, 109,
    141, 156, 167–169, 177, 218,
    228
  as God of the Jews, 167
  as Godhead, 168
Goethe, 5–6, 8, 16, 25–26, 66–67,
    81–82, 91–93, 188–189, 198,
    234, 243, 249–250, 263–264
  his "Essay on the Metamorphosis
    of Plants," 263–264
  his *Faust*, 78
  his "gentle empiricism," 66
  his fairy tale "The Green Snake
    and the Beautiful Lily," 58,
    74, 85
  his natural scientific writings, 5,
    66–67, 73–74
  his "spirit as divine being," 26
  his *Urpflange*, 67
Goethean/Goetheanism, 14, 66
Goetheanum,
  first, 8, 50, 71, 77–78, 273
    as Johannesbau, 77
  second, 72
Golgotha, 107, 170, 174
grace, 53, 227
Grazie, delle, Marie Eugenie, 73, 82
  her *Robespierre*, 82
  her *Shadows*, 82
Greco-Roman, 105, 109
Greece/Greek, 19–21, 41–42, 102–
    103, 107, 201–202
Greek temple, 103
  as "house of the spirit," 103
Grimm, Hermann, 74, 83, 91
Grimm, Jacob, 81
Grimm, Wilhelm, 81
Guyou, Jean-Marie, 87

Haeckel, Ernst, 74, 82, 84–85, 91,
    260
  his article, "Ethics and
    Worldview," 84
Hamerling, Robert, 256, 259–270
  his book, *Homunculus*, 256, 269
Hartmann, von, Eduard, 73, 256–
    261, 269
  his book, *The Philosophy of
    the Unconscious*, 256,
    259–260
  his book, *The Unconscious
    from the Standpoint of
    Physiology and the Theory
    of Evolution*, 261
Hauser, Kasper, 75
hay fever, anthroposophic treatment
    for, 285–287
head, 205
heart, 9–10, 53, 94, 136–137, 224,
    299
Hebrew/Hebraic, 18–19, 68, 106,
    109
Hegel, 5, 12, 16, 80, 93, 218
Helmholtz, 74
Heraclitus, 58
Hermes, 42, 101–104
Hierarchies, 23, 42, 68–70, 266,
    294, 299–300
  first (Father), 302
    seraphim (Spirits of Love), 68,
      302
    cherubim (Spirits of
      Harmony), 68, 302
    thrones (Spirits of Will), 68,
      302
  second (Son), 69, 296–300
    kyriotetes (Spirits of Wisdom),
      68–69, 296, 298
    dynamis (Spirits of Motion),
      68–69, 296, 298
    exusiai/elohim (Spirits of
      Form), 68–69, 170,
      296, 298
  third (Holy Spirit), 296–298
    archai (Spirits of Personality),
      68, 70, 296–297

archangeloi (Spirits of Fire), 21, 40, 42, 68, 70, 79, 296–297
angeloi (Spirits of Life), 12, 40, 46, 48, 68, 70, 296–298
Hindu, 17, 49, 214
Hindu Vedanta, 21
historical methodology, 86
Holy Spirit, 39, 42–43, 159, 164–165, 170–172, 177,
  as cosmic universal "I," 43, 164–165, 170
  as the dove, 170
  as illumination, 165
  united with Earth at Resurrection, 170–171
Homer, 22, 105
Hughes, Gertrude R., 15–16
humility, ix, 37–38, 137

"I," 5, 14, 16–17, 25, 27–31, 35, 38, 41, 43–45, 47–48, 50, 55, 57, 60–61, 106–107, 109, 119, 122–126, 128–131, 141–142, 156–157, 161, 165, 169–170, 180–181, 190, 193–195, 198, 207, 255, 258–259, 261–262, 265, 268, 281, 288, 291–292
  as the Absolute, 17
  collective animal ego, 119
  highest "I" (divine), 107, 157, 164
  higher "I" (self), 42, 163–164
  as holiest of holies, 123–124
"I"-being, 128, 281
"I"-human, 281
idealistic philosophy, 82
illumination, 161–165, 170, 172
imagination/imaginative, ix, 16, 20, 22, 28–29, 34–37, 93, 162, 279, 292, 294
  imaginative cognition, 279, 292
  imaginative knowledge, 28, 30, 292
  imaginative perception, 292
  imaginative thinking, 35–36, 67

imitation, by children, 56, 238, 240–241
India/Indian, 18, 100
  Indian esotericism, 89–90
individualism/individuality, 6, 15–16, 21, 31, 71, 96, 98–99, 186
initiation, 20, 42–43, 57, 59, 87, 103, 105–106, 109, 135, 154, 160–162, 164, 265–266
  Christian, seven steps of, 161
  Christian-Rosicrucian, 87–88, 161–162, 166
  Eastern, 88
  initiation by the cosmos (first), 265–267
  initiation of the sages, 267
  initiation of self-knowledge, 267
  initiates, ancient, 102
  Zeus (Jupiter), 103
inner exercises. See meditation, exercises
inspiration/inspirational, 4, 20, 28–29, 35–36, 71, 88, 93, 294
  inspirational knowledge, 28–30
  inspired thinking, 36
intellect, human, 255–256
intellectual property, 225
intellectual soul, 30–31, 106, 119, 121–122, 128–129
intuition/intuitive, 4, 11–12, 14–15, 19–20, 22–23, 29–30, 34–36, 58, 62, 67, 93, 98–99, 125–128, 265
  intuitive cognition, 30
  intuitive knowledge, 28, 30
  intuitive thinking, 17, 36
Israel, 40

Jesus of Nazareth, 7, 21, 40, 167–168, 173, 177
  his astral and ether bodies, 170
  his "I," 170
John the Baptist, 42, 177
John the Evangelist, 42, 58, 166, 171, 175
  one whom Christ loved, 177
  as writer of gospel of St John, 167

John, gospel of, 3, 21, 40–42, 162, 166–168, 170–177
Joseph, father of Jesus, 168–169
Judaism, 167
Jung, C. G., 5
Jupiter, new, 23, 262

kamaloca, 45
Kant, Emmanuel, 5, 14–15, 80, 87
  his work, *The Critique of Pure Reason*, 5–6, 13–14
Kantian, 6
karma, 1, 5–6, 9, 15, 27, 43, 45, 47–50, 77, 108, 179, 197, 290, 303
  karma and rebirth, 6, 9, 47, 49
  karmic law, 47
kidney, anthroposophic treatment, 281–287, 289
knowledge, as a concept, 162–163
Koguzski, Felix, 6, 73
Kolisko, Lily, 273
Krebel, von, Karl L., 198
Krishna, 1, 7–8, 17, 21, 33, 35, 40
Krishnamurti, 7
  as "Master Jesus," 7
Kübler-Ross, Elisabeth, 44
Kurshner, Joseph, 82
  his "German National Literature," 82, 91

Laistner, Ludwig, 83
  his book, *The Riddle of the Sphinx*, 83
Lang, Maria, 73
language, 236, 251
  of the spirits, 299–300
latent heat (warmth), 239, 278, 281
  forces in children, 239–240, 278–279
Lazarus, 42
Leadbetter, C.W., 7
Lemuria/Lemurian, 108
Lenin, 224
Lessing, 120, 191
life body. See etheric body
life force, 114

life spirit (buddhi), 31, 127, 129–131, 191
light, 39, 107
  forces, 304
  in bolt of lightning, 107
  spiritual, 164, 293, 295
Light God, 104
Locke, John, 12
Logos (Word). See Christ, as Logos (Word)
loneliness of soul, 223
Lords of Karma, 47
Lord's Prayer, 40
Lorelei, a mermaid (elemental), 269
love, 4, 16, 20–21, 24, 35, 37, 48, 53, 55–56, 68, 257–258, 267–268, 290
  love of the child, 244
  sexual love, 248
lovelessness, 258
Lucifer/Luciferic, 40, 105–107, 110
  as a god of light, 110
Luke, gospel of, 168–169
Luzifer (periodical), 75

Mahayana, 42
Mani, 87
Mariotte-Gay-Lussac Law, 288
Marriage at Cana, 175
Marx/Marxism, 52, 86
Mary, wife of Cleophas, 167
Mary Magdalene, 172–173
Master, the (M), 6, 80–81
Masters, the, 86
  as "teachers of wisdom and the harmony of human feelings," 86
materialism/materialistic, 6, 52, 82, 90–91, 168, 174, 176, 188, 200, 208, 211, 214, 218, 223–225, 227, 235, 241, 268, 274, 283
Matthew, gospel of, 167
Mauthner, 218
Maya, 14
Mayreder, Karl, 73
Mayreder, Rosa, 73

McDermott, Robert
  his book, *The Essential Steiner*,
     vii–ix
medicine, anthroposophic, viii, 2,
     59–63, 271–289
meditation/meditative, viii, 16, 25,
     27–28, 31, 35, 37, 39–40, 42,
     159, 161–162, 227, 292, 303
  exercises (practices), ix, 28–29,
     32–33, 37, 42, 48, 234, 263,
     280
memory, 180–183, 193–194, 203,
     239, 252, 278
  Earth's, 295–298
mental image, 152–153, 182–183,
     193–194, 247, 277, 280
Mendel, Gregor, 185
Merton, Thomas, viii
metals
  connection with health, 298–300
  melting of, 301–304
  metallic ores, 68–70
  veins of, 68–70, 295–298, 300
metamorphosis. See transformation
metaphysical/metaphysics, 13, 84,
     259
Michael
  as archangel, 1, 21, 40, 42
  as regent of age, 40
Michaelmas, 79
mind soul. See intellectual soul
mineral kingdom, 28, 57, 106, 113–
     115, 124, 203, 248, 263, 266,
     292–293, 295, 297–304
Molt, Emil, 53, 230, 252
Moody, Raymond, 44
Moon, old, 23, 106, 164–165, 262
moral/morality, 14–15, 32, 120, 300
  cosmic moral existence, 300
  imagination, 99
  philosophy, 15
Moses, 22, 42, 106–107
Mother of Jesus (Mary), 42, 166–
     167, 171, 173, 177
  as Virgin Sophia, 166–167
Mozart, 190

music, 50–51, 202–203, 207–208,
     251
music of the spheres, 50, 207
Mystery of Golgotha, 40–41, 59, 74,
     107–108, 170–171, 267
  as event of Palestine, 172–175
mysteries, ancient, 59, 103, 265–
     267, 304
mystery schools, 364

naturalism/naturalistic, 201
nature spirits. See elemental spirits
Nicholas of Cusa, 58
Niebuhr, Reinhold, 33
  his "Serenity Prayer," 33
Nietzsche, 58, 74, 83–84, 87

object, 25, 99, 93, 120, 125, 247
Oeser Christian (Tobias Gottfried
     Schröer), 81
Olcott, Col., 7, 88
opinions, 165, 175
oracles, 101–102, 105
  Atlantean Mercury, 101, 105, 109
  Venus, 101, 105, 109
Order of the Star, 7
Osiris, 102

painting, 208, 246
Paracelsus, 58
Patanjali
  his Yoga Sutras, 32
path of reverence, 136
Paul, St., 16, 22, 41, 58
  his Epistles, 16
Pauline, 16
percept, 98–99, 109
perception, 10, 34, 36, 55, 69, 102,
     106, 110–111, 172–173, 179–
     182, 209, 211, 223, 292, 295,
     297 266
  organs of perception, 161, 164
  spiritual perception, 111, 172–
     173
Persian, 18, 100, 104
photismos. See illumination
physical similarity, 185

pictures. See mental images
plant kingdom/plants, 12, 26, 28–29, 57, 66–67, 81, 106, 113–115, 203, 216–217, 247, 263–264, 266, 275, 284, 287, 291, 295
Plato, 18, 22, 35–36, 40, 58, 93
 his "Timaeus," 18
poetry, 50–51, 201–203, 206–207, 209, 211, 291, 300
 cosmic poetry, 300
post-Atlantean cultural, or consciousness, periods, 19, 22, 108, 161
 first, Ancient Indian, 18, 20, 31
 second, Ancient Persian, 18, 20, 31
 third, Babylonian–Chaldean–Egyptian, 18–20, 22, 31, 100–101
 fourth, Greco-Roman–Christian, 19–20, 31, 102, 109–110
 fifth, Present, 19–20, 31, 109, 160
 sixth, Slavic, 20, 23, 31, 111
 seventh, American, 20
potentization, 62
practices. See meditation, exercises
Preyer, Wilhelm, 237
 his book, *Soul of the Child*, 237
puberty, 54–57, 248
purgatorial, 45
purification. See catharsis
Pythagoras/Pythagorean, 58, 103

Raphael, archangel, 42
reading, 13
 in the chaos, 265
 by children, 245
 learning to read by children, 54
 as seeing, 17, 22
 in sensory world, 153
 in the spiritual world, 300
rebirth. See reincarnation
reincarnation, 15, 27, 43, 47–49, 77, 101, 108, 179, 188, 195–197
resurrection, 303
Revelation, book of, 42

reverence, ix, 37, 137–140, 233, 248
rhythms, effect on human body, 61–62, 273–275
Richter, Jean Paul F., 122–123
Ring, Kenneth, 44
rishis, 18
Roman, 21
Rosenkreutz, Christian, 23, 87
Rosicrucian/Rosicrucianism, 3, 87–90

sacrifice, 304
 sacrificial fire, 304
sages, 58–59
Saturn, old, 23, 106, 164–165, 262
Schelling, 5, 16, 80
Schiller, 81, 187, 249–250
 his book, *Letters on the Aesthetic Education of Mankind*, 250
Schmidt, Oscar, 260
School of Spiritual Science, 9, 63, 71–72
 medical section, 63
Schroer, Karl Julius, 5, 73, 81–82
Schure, Edouard, 6, 77, 90
 his book, *The Great Initiates*, 6
Scientific Research Laboratory, 78
scourging, 161–162
sculpture, 48, 51, 201–205, 207–208, 211
selfless, 30
sense perceptible. See materialistic
sentient soul, 30–31, 106, 116–119, 121–122, 128–130, 188–190, 193
serenity prayer, 33
sexuality, 248
Sievers, von, Marie. See Steiner, Marie
Sinnett, A.P.
 his book, *Esoteric Buddhism*, 88, 90
sleep, 27, 30, 43–44, 46–47, 65, 192, 196, 208, 258
socialization, 225
Society for Ethical Culture, 84
Socrates/Socratic, 21

Sophia, Virgin, 21, 42–43, 159,
    159, 164–165, 169, 171–172,
    174–175, 177
  as divine feminine wisdom, 1
  as purified astral body, 164–165,
    171
  as Virgin Mary, 166
soullessness, 270
Specht, Otto, 4–5
Spirit. See Holy Spirit
spirit body (atman/spirit man), 31,
    127–129, 131
Spirits of Light, 104
spiritual eye, 116–117
spiritual heredity, 186–187
spiritual (auric) membrane, 127
spiritual science. See
    Anthroposophy
spirit self (manas), 31, 47, 125, 127,
    129–131, 188–191, 195
  as Virgin Sophia, 43, 164–165,
    171–172
spleen function, 273–274
  its balancing, 274
Steiner, Franziska Blie (Rudolf
    Steiner's mother), 4, 73
Steiner, Johann (Rudolf Steiner's
    father), 4, 73
Steiner, Marie, 9, 50, 74–75, 77, 86
Steiner, Rudolf
  the "America Verse," 53
  the book, *Anthroposophical
    Leading Thoughts*, 9–10
  the book, *Anthroposophy and the
    Inner Life*, 45
  the book, *Art: An Introductory
    Reader*, 83
  the book, *Art as Spiritual
    Activity: Rudolf Steiner's
    Contribution to the Visual
    Arts*, 212
  the book, *Autobiography*, 40, 83
  "The Barr Document," 6
  the lecture, "Christian Initiation,"
    161
  the book, *Christianity as
    Mystical Fact*, 40, 59, 90,
    103, 267
  the book, *The Esoteric Aspect of
    the Social Question*, 229
  the lecture, "The Esoteric Aspect
    of the Social Question,"
    229
  the book, *The Esoteric
    Significance of the
    Bhagavad Gita*, 64
  the "esoteric empiricism," 6
  coauthor of the book, *Extending
    Practical Medicine:
    Fundamental Principles
    Based on
    the Science of the Spirit*, 9
  the lecture, "Exploring Our
    Supersensory Nature,"
    305
  the book, *Friedrich Nietzsche: A
    Fighter Against His Time*,
    5
  the book, *Friedrich Nietzsche:
    Fighter for Freedom*, 84
  the book, *Goethe as Founder of a
    New Science of Aesthetics*,
    83
  the essay, "Goethe's Secret
    Revelation," 85
  the book, *Goethe's Theory of
    Knowledge: An Outline of
    the Epistemology of His
    Worldview*, 5
  the book, *Goethe's Worldview*,
    5, 84
  the book, *The Gospel of St John*,
    43, 178
  the book, *Haeckel and His
    Opponents*, 85
  the book, *The Healing Process*,
    289
  the lecture, "The Healing Process:
    Spirit, Nature, and Our
    Bodies," 289
  his book, *How to Know Higher
    Worlds: A Modern Path of
    Initiation*, 2, 8, 11, 28–29,
    32–33, 37–39, 53, 125, 276

the book, *Inner Experiences of Evolution*, 262
his book, *Intuitive Thinking as a Spiritual Path: A Philosophy of Freedom*, 2, 5, 11–17, 83, 93, 159, 242
as a "Man of Destiny," 94
his Master (the M.), 6
his mystery dramas, 49–50, 92
as "Nietzshean Fool," 84
the book, *An Outline of Esoteric Science*, 2, 8, 11, 25, 27–29, 37, 68, 103–104, 108, 111, 119, 125, 256, 266, 276
the book, *Philosophy of Freedom*. See his book, *Intuitive Thinking as a Spiritual Path*: A Philosophy of Freedom
his book, *A Philosophy of Spiritual Activity*, 14
the book, *The Roots of Education*, 54
the book, *Spiritual Beings in the Heavenly Bodies*, 266
his book, *The Stages of Higher Knowledge*, 30
the book, *Start Now!*, 158
his book, *A Theory of Knowledge*, 82
his book, *Theosophy*, 2, 8, 25, 27, 30, 37, 43, 45, 48, 61, 75, 119, 133, 191, 197, 199, 217
his book, *Thinking in the Nineteenth Century*, 85
his book, *Truth and Knowledge*, 1, 83, 91, 93, 256
his dissertation (thesis), "Truth and Knowledge," 5, 12, 74, 91
the book, *Waldorf Education and Anthroposophy I*, 253
his book, *A Way of Self-knowledge*, 292

the book, *What is Anthroposophy?*, 57, 270
Sun, old, 23, 106, 164–165, 262
Suphan, Bernhard, 83
sympathies, 46, 121, 125, 140, 217, 219–220, 256

Tao, 17
Tauler, 87, 110
temperments, 56
 choleric, 56
 melancholic, 56
 phlegmatic, 56
 sanguine, 56
theosophical/theosophy, 3, 7–8, 75, 78, 82, 86, 89–90, 134
Theosophical Society, 7, 38, 50, 75, 88–89, 91
 German branch, 7, 8–9, 74, 91
Theosophical Congresses, 7, 75–76
thinking, 10–15, 21–22, 25, 27, 32, 34–36, 38–39, 48, 53, 63–64, 67, 69, 93, 98–100, 112–113, 115, 118–119, 125, 139, 188, 191–192, 214, 222–224, 233–237, 239, 260, 271, 273, 276, 279, 283, 286, 296, 301
 free, 15
 imaginative, 35
 intellectual, 21
 intuitive, 17
 latent, 279
 living, 10, 67
 materialistic, 214
 meditative, 10–11, 14–15, 28, 35–36, 41, 48, 66
 objective, 93
 practical, 14
 scientific–rationalistic, 13, 19
 sense-based, 13
 sensory-free, 12
 social, 222–223, 225
thinking, feeling, willing, 1, 3, 20, 22, 25, 32, 41, 64, 233
threefold social order, 25, 51–52, 78, 218, 220, 222, 225
 cultural/spiritual sphere, relates to metabolic system, 25

economic sphere, relates to
    rhythmic system, 25
movement for threefold social
    system, 78
political sphere, relates to head
    and sensory system, 25
transformation (spiritual), ix, 1-3,
    7, 11, 21, 23, 32, 39, 41-43,
    55, 64, 71, 93, 101, 130, 139,
    171-172, 204-205, 234, 248,
    252, 263, 279, 281, 283, 294,
    296, 301, 303-304
Treitschke, 83
Trotsky, 224
truths, 120

Universal laws, 135-136, 143
Upanishads, 18, 59
Upaya, ix
Uriel, archangel, 41
Urpflange, 67

vanity, 274
Vedas, 18, 59
Vedanta, 21, 35, 59
    wisdom of, 59, 267
Venus, new, 23, 262
Victor, St., 87
virgin birth, 168
Virgin Sophia. See Sophia, Virgin
Voltaire, 176-177

Vulcan, 23, 262

wakefulness, 280
Waldorf education, viii, 2, 53-57,
    72, 78, 230-234, 243, 245,
    247, 251-253
Wegman, Ida, 9, 63, 66, 272, 286,
    288-289
    coauthor of the book, *Extending
    Practical Medicine*, 9
Whitehead, Alfred North, 14
will, 15, 20, 24, 31-32, 94, 123, 126,
    174, 209-210, 234-237, 242,
    246, 294
willing, 25, 32-33, 99
wisdom, 10, 18, 88, 103, 107-108,
    178, 262, 266-268
Workers Education Movement. See
    Berlin Workers Education
    Institute

Yahweh, 22
    his "I Am Who Am," 22
yoga, 32, 35, 38, 64-65
    secret yoga, 38-39

Zeitgeist, 270
Zeus (Jupiter), temple of, 103
Zoroaster, 23, 40, 101, 103-104
Zoroasterian mysteries, 101